FIFTY YEARS OF TELEVISION

TV GUIDE

FIFTY YE

TELEV

INTRODUCTION by MARY TYLER MOORE

PREFACE BY STEVEN REDDICLIFFE

 A MELCHER MEDIA BOOK

ARS

OF

ISION

AFTERWORD by WILLIAM SHATNER

TEXT BY MARK LASSWELL

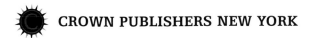 CROWN PUBLISHERS NEW YORK

LOCAL PROGRAM LISTINGS • Week of March 26-April 1

MLA

TV GUIDE

®

15¢

Gleason: TV's No. 1
Good Time Charlie

TOOTS

Imagine a perfect week of television, seven days and nights of your all-time favorite shows. Cartoons and subversive silliness on sleepy Saturday mornings, hopping dance shows on idle weekend afternoons, surprising variety on Sunday nights, indelible dramas and endlessly clever comedies—every night a celebration of creativity, every hour a treasure.

And that's what this book is all about—out of 50 years of television, one ideal week of nothing but shows America loved, the lineup of all lineups.

As Jimmie Dodd used to say on *Mickey Mouse Club*: Roll call! Bugs and Elmer. Rocky and Bullwinkle. Bart and Homer. Ed and the Beatles. Mulder and Scully. Dave and Hugh and Barbara and Tom and Jane and Bryant and Katie and Matt. Winfrey and Springer. (Together? Never!) Oscar and Felix. Andy and Opie. 86 and 99. Rob and Laura. Ralph and Alice. Tony and Carmela. Ozzie and...Ozzy(!). Johnny, then Dave.

For 50 years, the TV GUIDE week—the TV week for millions of us—has started with Saturday. And it does here: Pee-wee and Howdy Doody cut up while one Wile E. Coyote plotted against an even wilier Road Runner. Hours later, Paladin and Dillon took on the wild West, and *All in the Family* and *The Mary Tyler Moore Show* took on modern life. *Your Show of Shows* and *Saturday Night Live* took on just about everything—and won.

On Sunday, we started with the stopwatch on *60 Minutes*, and we met the Beatles. Bart Simpson reminded all of us not to have a cow (man). *The X-Files* looked for an elusive truth, and Alfred Hitchcock told us nothing was what it seemed.

And then it was off to work (but not before turning on *Today*) or school (but not before checking in with *Romper Room*) or the living room, where kids spent smart sessions on *Sesame Street* and in *Mister Rogers' Neighborhood*. The rest of us devoted stolen hours to watching the world turn in serial style (*General Hospital*, *All My Children*) or smart-person-with-a-microphone mode (*Donahue*, *Oprah*).

In times of national tragedy (the assassination of President John F. Kennedy), television explained and comforted. In times of national triumph (a man on the Moon!), television gave us a chance to see it live and celebrate. A nation saw *Roots*, and we thought about our country—and ourselves—in an entirely different way.

And on countless other occasions, in prime time, television had us laughing with Bill Cosby and Carol Burnett and Carrie Bradshaw, singing with Elvis and wanting to be a millionaire. We had to know who shot J.R., who killed Laura Palmer, who Danno was gonna book, who was gonna win Game 7. We had to see who'd be voted off the island. We had to see if Buffy survived. We had to know if anyone could survive Tony Soprano.

Here's Johnny. Here's Lucy. Here's Jerry never getting to eat in the Chinese restaurant (not that there's anything wrong with that).

And here, as Rod Serling said so memorably in a different time and a different zone, is a dimension of imagination.

—STEVEN REDDICLIFFE,
EDITOR-IN-CHIEF, TV GUIDE

TABLE
OF CONTENTS

INTRODUCTION

When Carl Reiner, the very funny creator of *The Dick Van Dyke Show*, decided to put my character, Laura Petrie, in capri pants in 1961 and give her the words for a real spat or two with her sexy husband, it was considered shocking. Today on MTV, the Osbournes go 12 rounds with gloves off every (*bleep*ing) week, and they're considered the Ozzie and Harriet of a new generation.

Things certainly have changed.

But one thing hasn't. TV still holds a very special place in our lives. Since its earliest days, television's strength has been the richness and breadth of its storytelling. Getting those stories out there hasn't always been easy, however. David Sarnoff's notion to use broadcasting for entertainment purposes was waved off; Bill Paley's concept for his broadcast network was folly; Michael Fuchs's premium pay-television channel, HBO, was sure to fail; Ted Turner's CNN was ridiculed as the "Chicken Noodle Network."

But the naysayers didn't stop these pioneers. People of vision, passion and talent, they had the confidence to face down the critics and persevere. We owe television to them and to other groundbreakers like *Sesame Street*'s Joan Ganz Cooney, MTV's Bob Pittman, Nickelodeon and Nick at Nite's Geraldine Laybourne, TV newsmen Fred Friendly and Don Hewitt, Fox's Barry Diller and, I must say, Grant Tinker, who co-founded with me MTM Enterprises as a writers' company in 1970. These risk takers were willing to go the distance in the service of their "big idea." They really thought "outside the box."

Television isn't simply about those of us in front of the camera fortunate enough to have found our way into the hearts of the viewing public. TV is about myriad contributors—engineers, businesspeople, laborers, producers, writers, directors and crews—who come together to make magic happen, at least sometimes.

The thing that is so fascinating and frustrating and wonderful about TV is that nobody really knows when that magic will strike. ABC passed on a family comedy, *The Cosby Show*, in 1984 but green-lighted a police musical called *Cop Rock* in 1990. Both were from highly regarded creators (Bill Cosby and Steven Bochco, respectively), and both were considered risky at the time. Unfortunately for ABC, the comedy made our hearts sing for eight seasons (on NBC), while the musical went silent in 12 weeks. No one recognizes the next big thing, except in hindsight.

Journalist Edward R. Murrow once said that television "will broadcast filth or inspiration with equal facility and will speak the truth as loudly as the falsehood. It is, in sum, no more or less than the people who use it." Those of us who have spent our lives making television have the responsibility of finding a balance—balance that respects our diverse sensibilities, that shows awareness of our audiences and that helps viewers find their way to truth. People often ask me why I think *The Mary Tyler Moore Show* is so evergreen. I think it's because we found that sweet spot.

TV GUIDE has walked beside us on most of TV's 50-plus-year journey of creative, business and technical exploration. Along the way, we have witnessed as viewers things that have engaged, enlightened and enraged us. Sharing our stories on that screen, we have seen our strengths, our flaws and our hopes for a better world. We have shed some tears and had some wonderful laughs. Altogether, that's not too shabby.

Over the last half century, television has been both a wake-up call and a comfort to audiences. It has challenged us to be the best we can be, and, like a certain young career woman I knew years ago, it has let us know that we just might make it after all.

—MARY TYLER MOORE

WEEK

WARNER BROS. CARTOONS

Bugs Bunny, Elmer Fudd; Wile E. Coyote, Road Runner. ABC, 1960–68, 1971–75 and 1985–2000; CBS, 1966–73 and 1975–85; NBC, 1978–82; Nickelodeon, 1988–99; Fox, 1992–94; WB, 1995–98; Cartoon Network, 2000–

Though they got their start in the 1930s as movie-matinee fodder, Warner Bros. cartoons—flying under the *Looney Tunes* and *Merrie Melodies* banners—will be forever cherished as giddy Saturday-morning TV treats for anyone who happened to be in the room when Bugs Bunny, Daffy Duck, Road Runner and Co. romped into view. The cartoons were the "world's greatest single source of animated dementia," said TV GUIDE in 1985, on the occasion of a Warner Bros. animation exhibition at the Museum of Modern Art in New York City, "fast and eternally disrespectful of authority and privilege. They are about chase, pursuit and retribution—about perennial forms of passion, in short, from the helpless romanticism of Pepé Le Pew to the voracious vainglory of the eternally thwarted Coyote." Towering over the crowd of characters, not only because of his long ears, was Bugs, whom director Chuck Jones once said he imagined as "a sort of male Dorothy Parkerish D'Artagnan." Bugs starred, along with the indefatigable Elmer Fudd, in the opera send-up "What's Opera, Doc?" (1957), considered by many to be the ultimate Warner Bros. achievement, though a strong contender for that title was Daffy's epic battle with his animators in "Duck Amuck" (1953). Jones directed both, but plenty of credit for the Warner oeuvre also went to the murderers' row of animation stalwarts who brought the creations to life: Tex Avery, Friz Freleng, Bob Clampett and Bob McKimson. And where would any of them have been without the miraculous vocal talents of Mel Blanc? Thanks to the Warner Bros. creative pool, TV GUIDE said, "these cartoons are as funny, and as enduring, as the film comedy of Chaplin and Keaton, Capra and Sturges."

HOWDY DOODY
NBC, 1947–60
COVER: PHOTOGRAPHER UNKNOWN, JUNE 25, 1954

TV journalist and pop-culture aficionado Jeff Greenfield advanced this theory in TV GUIDE in 1983: "*Howdy Doody* represents one of the most authentically subversive TV shows in American history." It sowed the seeds of '60s rebellion, he said, with kids and fanciful characters playing the insurgent heroes of Doodyville, and grown-ups either the establishment bad guys (Mayor Phineas T. Bluster) or the butts of practical jokes (host Buffalo Bob). Seltzer-spraying Clarabell the Clown, Greenfield wrote, was "the very first yippie." All this would have been news to Buffalo Bob, aka Bob Smith. During the show's prime, he was busy defending himself against charges of excessive silliness. "We're entertainers," Smith told TV GUIDE in 1954. "And have *you* ever watched a 3-year-old play?"

PEE-WEE'S PLAYHOUSE
Pee-wee Herman (Paul Reubens). CBS, 1986–91

One of the most perverse outcomes of Paul Reubens's 1991 arrest for indecent exposure was the way it tainted memories of his deliriously creative *Pee-wee's Playhouse*. In the show, which won 22 Emmys and at its peak drew almost a third of its 9.3 million viewers from adults over 18, the sweet-natured devil Pee-wee Herman manically presided over a surreal romper room populated by talking objects (Globey! Chairry!) and endearingly off-kilter characters, such as Cowboy Curtis (future movie star Laurence Fishburne). As TV Guide recalled in 1996, "Pee-wee managed to make a rare peace with the wild side of childhood."

WHY DALE ROBERTSON SCORNS TV COWBOYS
SEE PAGE 17

TV GUIDE

LOCAL LISTINGS
OCTOBER 24-30
15¢

JAY NORTH
"DENNIS THE MENACE"

DENNIS THE MENACE
Dennis Mitchell (Jay North).
CBS, 1959–63
COVER: BY RICHARD R. HEWETT,
OCTOBER 24, 1959

Jay North is "sweet, with electricity," cartoonist
Hank Ketcham told TV GUIDE in 1959, describing
the kid starring in the TV version of his comic-
strip creation. Dennis was a menace, of course,
only to grown-ups. The well-intentioned boy had
a special knack for exasperating them—
especially finicky next-door neighbor Mr. Wilson.
(Joseph Kearns, who died during the third
season's filming, was replaced by Gale Gordon.)
But kids loved Dennis, and the show became a
Sunday-night staple on CBS for four years,
making good on TV GUIDE's prediction in 1960
that children would commandeer television sets
to watch it. The magazine also had a warning for
adults: "Be prepared to like the show yourself."

LASSIE
Timmy (Jon Provost), Lassie. CBS, 1954–71; syndication, 1971–74
COVER: BY GARRETT-HOWARD, JULY 7, 1956

"With a boy and his dog," executive producer Sherman Harris told TV GUIDE in 1959, "*how* can you miss?" Indeed, the kid-plus-canine formula was such a fail-safe Sunday-night hit after its debut in 1954 that viewers weren't fazed three years later when the original boy (Jeff, played by Tommy Rettig) was jettisoned along with his whole family because Rettig got too old. Lassie found a new best friend in Timmy (Jon Provost). Audiences tuned in, after all, to see Lassie fight crime, prevent disasters and nurse the injured. The premise prospered until 1974, when *Lassie* rolled over and played dead (and she *was* only playing: *The New Lassie* premiered in 1989).

ALL IN THE FAMILY

Edith Bunker (Jean Stapleton), Archie Bunker (Carroll O'Connor). CBS, 1971–79

COVER: BY GENE TRINDL, MAY 29, 1971

Producer Norman Lear's comedy had been on the air for a month, and, struggling in the ratings, its future did not appear bright. Certainly, the show looked unexceptional: *All in the Family*'s simple set and small cast would have seemed right at home in a '50s TV lineup. It was what Archie (Carroll O'Connor), Edith (Jean Stapleton), Gloria (Sally Struthers) and Mike "Meathead" Stivic (Rob Reiner) were *saying* that blew the doors off conventional comedy. As TV GUIDE recognized in 1971, "*All in the Family* is...a complete breakthrough—one that opens up a whole new world for television and has already made the old world seem so dated that we very much doubt that any new program, from here on in, will ever be quite the same again." It wasn't just that, for the first time, racism, abortion, homosexuality, birth control and other hot-button issues were made ripe for one-liners. What established a riveting new level of reality in the format were the hilarious, often poignant struggles of four people grappling with their feelings about one another and the tumultuous world outside the Bunker living room at 704 Hauser Street in Queens, New York. The characters were types, certainly—the blue-collar bigot versus the idealistic liberal—but types never seen on TV, and never invested with the imagination that O'Connor and Reiner brought to them. Edith's foggy optimism and Gloria's caught-in-the-middle confusion were vital elements, but it was the firefighting between Archie, low on intellectual ammunition but immovable, and the implacable Meathead that permanently altered television and the way it measured creative achievement.

"WHEN I FIRST SAW THE SCRIPT FOR ALL IN THE FAMILY,

I thought, 'Well, this is certainly beyond anything that anybody's ever done in television.' I mean, not just in subject matter and how controversial and edgy it was, but in the quality of the writing, which was so far superior to anything that I had seen anywhere. But never in my wildest dreams did I think it was going to go past 13 weeks because it was, as we say in the parlance of stand-up comics, too hip for the room. And that was fine, too, because we just wanted to be part of something special and different and groundbreaking.

"There wasn't one guiding person for the show, but Norman Lear and Carroll O'Connor set a tone that allowed all of the cast members to contribute creatively. We were asked to be part of the process, and we contributed a tremendous amount to the scripts and on our feet and in rehearsal. Norman liked to stir things up and force us to dig deeper and try harder, and Carroll wanted to be as realistic and honest as possible. So you had two very, very strong-willed men fighting to make the show better, and a lot of times I was caught between them. I had respect and admiration and love for both of them, and it was tough for me at times, but it always was to make a better show—it was never a personal thing. It wasn't an easy process, but it was a great creative experience.

"I don't think *All in the Family* changed public opinion on any issues, but I think it certainly stimulated the dialogue. When you think about where we've come as a country, in terms of race relations, we've come a long, long way. Obviously, the civil-rights movement, Martin Luther King Jr., Bobby Kennedy and people like that did the heavy lifting, but we certainly played a role in shining a light on bigotry and allowing a discussion to happen.

"The last episode was my favorite. It wasn't the funniest or the best or anything like that, but it was just so emotional, and it was one of those moments where your life and your character converge. When I said goodbye to Archie, I was saying goodbye to Carroll, and I didn't have to act. It was just very, very emotional, and all the feelings were right there.... The one scene that I remember—a goofy, nutty scene that wasn't a meaningful scene in any way—was when Archie lectures me on how to put on socks and shoes. Everybody talks to me about that scene. Everybody says that they now think about how they put on their socks and shoes because of that scene."

—ROB REINER

THE MARY TYLER MOORE SHOW
Clockwise from above: Rhoda Morgenstern (Valerie Harper), Mary Richards (Moore); Ted Baxter (Ted Knight), Lou Grant (Ed Asner); Baxter, Georgette Franklin (Georgia Engel), Richards, Sue Ann Nivens (Betty White), Grant, Murray Slaughter (Gavin MacLeod). CBS, 1970–77
COVER: BY PETER KREDENSER, MARCH 19, 1977

"You know what? You've got spunk," TV news producer Lou Grant tells his beaming new associate producer, Mary Richards. "I hate spunk." It was a priceless moment—occurring in the first season of *The Mary Tyler Moore Show*—but it was hardly the last. The show was a benchmark for what could be achieved in the genre. With its two distinct comedy platforms, Mary's apartment and her office, *MTM* was an apt metaphor for the internal battle that many young women in the '70s faced as they entered the workforce. At home, where the adorably single and striving Mary's neighbors were forever dropping in (Valerie Harper and Cloris Leachman landed their own shows as a result of their work here), cooking and entertaining were sure to end badly. In one episode, Mary managed to get Johnny Carson to show up for a party only to have the power go out. Meanwhile, at work the good-hearted Mary fought to keep her innate niceness from sabotaging her ambition. Of course, that was all much harder when surrounded by male coworkers like cranky-affectionate Mr. Grant (Ed Asner), sensible yet smoldering newswriter Murray Slaughter (Gavin MacLeod) and preening fathead anchorman Ted Baxter (Ted Knight). However, like the line from the theme song, "Love Is All Around," we always knew that lovable Mary was "going to make it after all." TV GUIDE championed the show a few months into its first season, lauding the supporting actors but adding: "The show is still Miss Moore's. We admit to a slight prejudice. We think she's wonderful." So did America, and for seven years—until the whole gang shuffled off stage in its famous group hug—love was indeed all around.

TV GUIDE

Local Programs Mar. 19-25
25¢

So Long, Mary
Page 20

"MY MANAGER SAID TO ME, 'WOULD YOU LIKE TO DO TELEVISION?'"

I said, 'Yeah, I think so.' I was married and had kids and I wanted to be home, not on the road. So he put me together with a couple of writers from *The Mary Tyler Moore Show*, and we kicked around some ideas. They said, 'Bob—he's like a listener, you know? He listens to people. He reacts to people. Let's try to find a profession where somebody listens. What about a psychiatrist?'

"I had two stipulations: One was I didn't want to be a psychiatrist—I wanted to be a psychologist. I felt that psychiatrists dealt with more deeply disturbed people, and I didn't want to be making fun of schizophrenics or the John Nashes of the world. And the other one was that I didn't want to have kids. They asked, 'Why not?' And I said, 'Because I don't like those shows where Daddy is a dolt and keeps getting in trouble and the precocious kids and the wife get him out of it. "Look at the fix Daddy's gotten himself into." ' I said, 'That really isn't the kind of show I want to do.' And when I saw the first script, it felt very comfortable. I thought, 'I can play that guy because I know him.' That's the main reason, I think, that shows with former

stand-ups work. The performer knows himself better than anybody else does.

"But we weren't completely sure about whether a psychologist was a viable occupation for a comedy. There was still a kind of feeling in this country that, as Samuel Goldwyn said, 'Anybody who goes to see a psychiatrist ought to have his head examined.' There was still a sentiment that you don't go to someone and spill out all your problems. You just work them out yourself. So we didn't know if it was going to work.

"[Fans] confused the role with me. Sometimes I would come into a city, and there'd be a message from someone saying they're having a problem and would I please return their call. And I had to explain to them that it was just a role I played on television. I wasn't qualified to solve their problems. [Today when people come up to me,] the men think that they were in the service with me, and the women think I was their first husband."

—BOB NEWHART

THE BOB NEWHART SHOW
Mr. Stevens (Neil Flanagan), Bob Hartley (Newhart). CBS, 1972–78
COVERS: BY SHERMAN WEISBURD, JANUARY 20, 1973. BY BRUCE STARK, APRIL 11, 1987

A gloomy Bob Newhart told TV GUIDE in 1962, at the end of what turned out to be only one season of a variety series called *The Bob Newhart Show*, that even if he stayed in television, he'd never have the ratings of, say, a Bob Hope. But at least he'd made the attempt: "If you're a pitcher," he said, "you'd better pitch in the major leagues." A decade later, he resurfaced. The show had the same name, but this time it was an inspired comedy that had the bright idea to cast the low-key performer as a psychologist. Bob Hartley did a fine job counseling his wacko clientele (though real progress was tough with that epic paranoid Elliot Carlin, memorably played by Jack Riley). But back home in his Chicago high-rise apartment, it was his wife, Emily (Suzanne Pleshette), who held the tighter grip on reality and sometimes seemed to think Bob was certifiable. The show was a hit throughout much of the '70s. Then the comedian amazed the television industry by launching *Newhart*, about an inn owner in Vermont, which became a hit of the '80s. Two series, two home runs: Those are big-league, hall-of-fame numbers anyone can appreciate.

Incredible Tempo: A Weekend With Welk

LOCAL LISTINGS APRIL 6-12

TV GUIDE

15¢

LAWRENCE WELK

THE LAWRENCE WELK SHOW
ABC, 1955–71; syndication, 1971–82
COVER: BY AL HIRSCHFELD, APRIL 6, 1957

Could you blame TV GUIDE for missing the boat on *The Lawrence Welk Show*? When the program surfaced as a summer replacement series in 1955, the magazine called the accordion-playing bandleader with the heavy German accent "rather stiff and ill at ease"—which was true. It also said the show lacked "sparkle and verve"—true again. Finally, the magazine declared that it was nothing more than "a pleasant and relaxed hour of viewing"—right again, and more than enough, apparently, for America, or at least rockphobic America, who adored Welk's "champagne music." For nearly three decades, you could find Welk and his well-scrubbed musicians performing traditional popular fare, to the accompaniment of a gently puffing bubble machine. A-one, and a-two...

AMERICAN BANDSTAND
Dick Clark. ABC, 1957–87; syndication, 1987–88
COVER: BY ROBERT GIUSTI, DECEMBER 30, 1978

The World's Oldest Living Teenager, Dick Clark, explained the secret of the world's longest-running sock hop, *American Bandstand*, to TV GUIDE in 1970: "People-watching! You just can't beat it! It's been going on since folks just sat in the railroad station. All it needs is a personality to head it up who will subjugate himself to the audience, and that's me." Certainly, one attraction was the astonishing array of music stars lip-synching their latest hit—everyone from the Doors, Buddy Holly and Stevie Wonder to Public Image Ltd., Blondie and the Beastie Boys performed on the show. But it was teenagers' insatiable urge to study one another's personal style with an anthropological intensity—while the benign chaperon Clark looked on—that made *Bandstand* classic viewing for more than 30 years.

THE LORETTA YOUNG SHOW
NBC, 1953–61
COVER: **BY ELMER HOLLOWAY, NOVEMBER 10, 1956**

In the early 1950s, actress Loretta Young broke ranks with the movie industry and plunged right in to the nascent medium of television, producing and starring in her own dramatic anthology series. Rather than committing the career suicide predicted for her, Young flourished. She swept in to introduce each show dressed in a sumptuous designer dress (available in stores the following week for a not-inexpensive $200 to $600) and starred in more than half of the show's 300 inspiring stories, portraying a housewife one night, perhaps, and a queen the next. A devout Catholic, Young concluded the evening by summing up the episode's message with a poem or Bible passage. "I don't miss movies one bit," she said in a 1958 TV GUIDE cover story (one of 11 featuring her). Having grown up in the Hollywood studio system, she was delighted to be in charge of her own show, reaping its profits, supervising the scripts and exercising the sort of career control that her movie peers could only dream of.

THE JACK BENNY SHOW
CBS, 1950–64; NBC, 1964–65
COVER: PHOTOGRAPHER UNKNOWN, FEBRUARY 5, 1954

Jack Benny was such a familiar and popular comedian after 18 years on the radio that when he moved to the new medium of television in 1950, he didn't need a specific format—or even a regular weekly schedule—to immediately claim a prominent place in the ratings. All that was required was his well-loved persona as a violin-mangling, perennial 39-year-old with easily bruised feelings ("Well!") and a less easily opened wallet. Airing sporadically, and later biweekly, on Sundays throughout the '50s, The Jack Benny Show was a bona fide variety show on some nights (the remarkable guest list included Frank Sinatra, Marilyn Monroe and Humphrey Bogart) and a single-sketch, quasi-situation comedy on others. That sort of flexibility "could cement his career in TV another 20 years," TV GUIDE said in 1954, "so long as the old master of the double take and perfect comedy timing retains that 39-year-old youthfulness." As it happened, he would stay on the air another 11 years, finally going weekly in 1960. Benny was in reality an adept violinist, but he didn't need to reveal that as a performer—his music was in his comedy.

YOUR SHOW OF SHOWS

Sid Caesar, Imogene Coca. NBC, 1950–54

COVERS: BY PHILIPPE HALSMAN, JANUARY 25, 1958, AND FEBRUARY 19, 1955

Of all the ambitious endeavors undertaken when television was broadcast live with no margin for error, *Your Show of Shows* was perhaps the most breathtaking of all. For 90 minutes every Saturday night, extravagantly gifted comedians Sid Caesar and Imogene Coca led a small army of actors, singers, dancers and guest stars into action—supported by such comedy writers as Woody Allen, Mel Brooks, Larry Gelbart and Neil Simon. The array of entertainment offered was daunting. In a nod to highbrow culture, *Your Show of Shows* would feature grand opera, ballet and Broadway-worthy production numbers. But the centerpiece, and what *Your Show of Shows* would be remembered for, was its comedy—particularly Caesar's staggering repertoire of double-talking foreigners, bogus authorities on any subject, henpecked husbands and almost any other characters the writers dreamed up. Caesar was perhaps the only entertainer in the world who could perform mime without making you want to strangle him. *Your Show* burned brightly for four years, but the frenetic pace was brutal. The strain began to show, and viewership sagged. "By its very nature...the show is beginning to pall," TV GUIDE said in 1954 as the ratings declined. "But even as it stands, it is well worth the effort to catch Caesar and Coca in one of their frequent flights into sheer comic greatness." Even though the two could hilariously, effortlessly send up the famous roll-in-the-surf scene in *From Here to Eternity*, the show couldn't go on forever. Caesar and Coca would later return to television, but they never quite recaptured the magic of those madcap early years.

"THE NETWORKS HATED LIVE COMEDY, BECAUSE THEY COULDN'T CONTROL IT.

For all intents and purposes, there was nobody editing me. There was nobody saying, 'Cut this out, cut that out.' You were your own editor, and it was much more personal because it was from you to the audience. You couldn't depend on tricks and technology.

"I allowed no cue cards, and there wasn't anything such as a Tele-PrompTer. If something happened, you just kept on going, and a lot of times a laugh came where you didn't expect it. A lot of times you'd expect a laugh and it didn't come, and you still had to make your timing. You had to think fast because you couldn't stop and say, 'Hold it, hold it, hold it. Let's back it up.' And the audience knew it.

"I didn't do anything political because you couldn't. We could do a generic politician, but you couldn't zero in on one guy. The comedy was 'Look at me, look how crazy I am!' But I never went with jokes. I never said, 'Where's the joke?' I said, 'What's the situation?' And we always played up the situation because that's what made it funny, not the joke."

—SID CAESAR

FANTASY ISLAND
Top left: Mr. Roarke (Ricardo Montalban), Tattoo (Herve Villechaize). ABC, 1978–84
COVER: BY AL HIRSCHFELD, MARCH 1, 1980

THE LOVE BOAT
Top right: Julie McCoy (Lauren Tewes), Burl "Gopher" Smith (Fred Grandy), Capt. Merrill Stubing (Gavin MacLeod), Isaac Washington (Ted Lange), Dr. Adam Bricker (Bernie Kopell). ABC, 1977–86
COVER: BY BRUCE STARK, DECEMBER 24, 1983

Talk about offshore assets: From the late '70s to the mid-'80s, ABC owned Saturday night with its back-to-back escapist hours, *The Love Boat* and *Fantasy Island* (both produced by mass-appeal wizard Aaron Spelling). *Fantasy Island* posited a tropical outpost where regular Joes could live out their dreams. "All the elements were there," Ricardo Montalban, who played the island's suave host, told TV GUIDE in 1980. "*Fantasy Island* is every book ever written." It was also, as the magazine noted in '78, every moral ever mouthed: "Ordinary folks shouldn't yearn for wealth, glamour and power because the best things in life are free and there's no place like home and so forth." The unspoken proverb aboard *The Love Boat*, meanwhile, was "love conquers all." Each episode introduced three romantic story lines (strangers meet, a quarreling couple reunites, etc.) that were enacted, over the years, by a battalion of old-time movie stars and B-grade TV personalities, all under the command of Gavin MacLeod as Capt. Merrill Stubing. Viewers got to see characters whose lives "change for the better," MacLeod told TV GUIDE in '82, plus "opulent surroundings, sumptuous food and beautiful, scantily dressed bodies." Bon voyage!

Clockwise from below, right: Patrick Swayze (guest host), Chris Farley; Mike Myers, Dana Carvey; Will Ferrell, Cheri Oteri; Joe Piscopo, Eddie Murphy; John Belushi. NBC, 1975–

COVER: BY JACK DAVIS, JULY 29, 1978

"It's so *weird*," John Belushi told TV GUIDE in the spring of 1976, "to go on TV and do what you want." That exhilarating sense of freedom was palpable both to the performers of *Saturday Night Live* and to its almost disbelieving audience during the show's first season. Television in the mid-'70s wasn't that far removed from its censorious roots, and here was a gang of smart, funny young players with a rock and roll sensibility who were wantonly making barely disguised references to sex, drugs and unholy acts. "The traditional variety show needed to be redefined," Lorne Michaels, *SNL*'s creator and longtime producer, told the magazine in 1999 for its 25th-anniversary tribute. Over the course of that quarter century, *SNL* was declared dead many times, but no matter how stale certain seasons seemed, something fresh and funny always emerged as the show continued to reinvent itself with new ideas and cast members. It was a lesson Michaels learned early, after the first season, when breakout star Chevy Chase left and Belushi and Gilda Radner stepped in to pick up the slack. In subsequent years, an amazing roster of comics and their characters rose to the occasion: Bill Murray's lounge singer, Eddie Murphy's Gumby, Mike Myers and Dana Carvey's suburban basement rockers Wayne and Garth. The list goes on (and *on*: Is there any other show in history with a longer all-star reel?). In 2002, the series' drive to innovate even achieved the impossible: Tina Fey and Jimmy Fallon's "Weekend Update" segments acquired a buzz they hadn't had since the days of Chevy Chase. There is no rational explanation for *SNL*'s amazing, never-ending rebirth. Could it be...Satan?

"SATURDAY NIGHT LIVE CHANGED THE FACE OF COMEDY-VARIETY ON TELEVISION.

Everything that came before it had been taped and sweetened. The *Sonny and Cher* show. The *Smothers Brothers* show, which I had worked for. These shows were too pat. There were no surprises. *SNL* has always had surprises.

"The first year of the show was the only year that I was there, and I became very famous very fast. But the ratings really only started coming up in the second year, after I left. Most of the time that first year, we thought, 'We're just this late-night, top-of-the-minors show, so this is a chance to do what we love to do,' which was heavy satire, political stuff and parody. I thought we might be kicked off the air for that matter. I didn't know.

"At the time, there was another show called *Saturday Night Live with Howard Cosell*—which meant we couldn't name the show *Saturday Night Live*. This is the whole reason—and the only reason—I came out and started the show by saying, 'Live from New York, it's *Saturday Night*!' We couldn't use the word 'live.' But when Cosell's show went

off the air, we got the rights to call it *Saturday Night Live*.

"We were able to do political satire that could actually affect the nation. Gerald Ford wrote in a book that my imitation of him—I made no attempt to do an actual impression of him, but instead just this clumsy guy—really did influence the 1976 election. And we were also doing things nobody had done before us, like parodies of TV commercials. I wanted the show to be about television. I wanted to puncture the traditions of TV and do some taboo things. That was my concept as a head writer back then. I think it changed the way we look at commercials and made commercials themselves become more self-conscious and aware of how to be funny. The 'Weekend Update' news segment became the precursor for things like *The Daily Show*. But it wasn't the first of its kind. There had been shows like *That Was the Week That Was* even earlier.

"There used to be this idea that if people can see you for free on television, they're not going to pay to see you in a theater. But

I obviously broke through to film. It took me about 20 movies to learn how to act. And 60 to learn how to behave. For guys who had talent—like Eddie Murphy and Mike Myers—the show became a kind of show-case, a launching pad. John Belushi was kind of upset that I became the star; he rightfully thought he should have been the big star. But I told John, 'I say my name every week—I say, "I'm Chevy Chase and you're not"—and nobody can even pro-nounce your name, much less sell it.' These are just empirical things that have nothing to do with talent. And eventually John did become a big movie star.

"If there is any reason that the first cast of *SNL* was the best cast, it's because we had nothing on the line. None of us expected we were going to go anywhere. I was recently watching one of the first-year shows with my daughter, and I started laughing out loud. Dan Aykroyd and John and I were up there doing something, and I saw a real looseness there, a complete devil-may-care attitude. 'Who cares if we get the lines right? Let's just be as funny as we can, because we don't know if we'll be on next week.'

"I always take offense when I hear people say, 'No one can compare to the first cast,' because it's not fair to the casts that came after us. But I must admit, we were damn good. We were very funny."

—CHEVY CHASE

SUPER
BOWL
XIII

NFL AND THE SUPER BOWL
Joe Namath, January 12, 1969
COVERS (CLOCKWISE FROM ABOVE): BY GEORGE GIUSTI, JANUARY 20, 1979. BY NICK FASCIANO, JANUARY 19, 1980.
BY BRAD HOLLAND, JANUARY 24, 1981. BY JEFFREY LOWE, JANUARY 24, 1998

In 1989, author David Halberstam chose six momentous events for an article in TV GUIDE called "TV That Changed Our Lives." One of them was the 1958 National Football League championship between the New York Giants and the Baltimore Colts, won by Johnny Unitas and the Colts in overtime. "The game marked many things," Halberstam wrote. "The ascent of pro football to a level enjoyed in the past only by baseball; the explosion of sports as a crucial ingredient in...a new television-driven, entertainment-oriented society; and, perhaps most importantly, it marked the ability of television to find an event that it favored (that is, something it could cover well) and virtually reinvent it, taking it from something ordinary to something that was part of the national fabric." If TV favored football, then it was positively smitten with the Super Bowl. Joe Namath making good on his boast that the underdog New York Jets would beat the Colts in 1969's Super Bowl III helped turn the affair into an unprecedented summit of social, athletic and corporate interests. After all, the games themselves were often less than memorable: Only because of a last-minute Joe Montana-engineered comeback victory for the San Francisco 49ers over the Cincinnati Bengals in '89 did the game make it into TV GUIDE's "50 Greatest TV Sports Moments of All Time" (1998). Yet thanks to Apple Computer's bravura Orwell-inspired commercial in 1984, advertisers turned the TV showcase into their own Super Bowl of creativity; even if the game was a lemon, viewers knew the day wasn't a total loss if the *ads* were good. That's the thing about the Super Bowl—and, on a lesser scale, the NFL's regular-season games—as a national gathering: Just like any family get-together, what happens at the event isn't as important as the fact of the gathering itself.

NASCAR
Final practice for EA Sports 500, Talladega Superspeedway, Talladega, Alabama, October 20, 2001; Tony Stewart at Sharpie 500, Bristol Motor Speedway, Bristol, Tennessee, August 25, 2001

COVER: BY CIA STOCK PHOTOGRAPHY, FEBRUARY 16, 2002

Until the advent of cable television, stock-car racing was a TV afterthought: The Daytona 500—the sport's Super Bowl—didn't even air live until 1979. But with cable's embrace, the National Association for Stock Car Auto Racing flourished, and by '96 it could even make a credible case as "the hottest sport of the '90s," as TV Guide put it. The year 2001 was momentous: NASCAR drew more TV viewers than ever, an impressive start to its six-year, $2.4 billion contract with Fox, FX, NBC and Turner Sports. But the sport also tragically lost elite driver Dale Earnhardt in a crash at Daytona. The overwhelming outpouring of grief that erupted across the nation demonstrated not only the sport's triumphant popularity, but also the special kinship between NASCAR's fearless competitors and their millions of fans.

Cliff diver in Acapulco (1968). ABC, 1961–97

ABC's Wide World of Sports reveled in the "thrill of victory and the agony of defeat," as the famous opening line from longtime host Jim McKay goes, for 36 years. "Our original idea," Roone Arledge, executive producer for four years and later vice president of ABC Sports, told TV GUIDE in 1966, "was to give viewers the kind of human picture story they couldn't find in their sports sections." An early, misbegotten attempt to depict the "soul" of the Le Mans Grand Prix road race cured Arledge of that vision: "Today, we leave the art to Fellini and Kazan. We stick to action. This is what our viewers want." The action might come from anywhere: figure skating; Irish hurling; the Tour de France; rattlesnake hunting; the Olympics; the '72 Fischer–Spassky chess match in Reykjavik, Iceland; the Indy 500; Evel Knievel's abortive Snake River Canyon motorcycle jump; the Kentucky Derby; or Howard Cosell verbally sparring with Muhammad Ali. It should have been enough to make even sports junkies sprint into rehab, but instead ABC proved that America's fascination with the baseball-football-basketball trinity could easily be expanded to accommodate virtually any form of athletic drama. (That was Yugoslavian ski jumper Vinko Bogataj epitomizing the agony of you-know-what when he turned himself into a human yard sale at the 1970 International Ski Flying Championships in Oberstdorf, Germany.) In an era of X Games and multiple ESPN channels, the concept hardly seems groundbreaking, but in the 1960s and '70s there was something utterly exotic about watching, say, Acapulco cliff divers plummet 87 feet into the perilous waters of the Pacific. As early as 1969, however, TV GUIDE was feeling sated—if you've "seen too many sports you don't like, move over. We're with you"—but nonetheless acknowledged the show as "a truly staggering undertaking—easily the most remarkable program in its field."

THE THRILL OF VICTORY…

"I CAN REMEMBER WATCHING CRONKITE AND REALIZING THAT WALTER WAS NOT AN ANCHOR WHO WAS CHAINED TO THE DESK.

He went out and did other things. When Walter was covering the space program, he would go through some of that training, and you would see him in a space suit dealing with gravity issues. And I would just say, 'Man, that's a great job.' I didn't know anyone else who was doing anything like that.

"60 Minutes has succeeded because we do good work. And I think that we don't talk down to our audience. We go out every week, and we say, 'Hey, here are three stories we think you should be interested in. You might not like it, you might not agree with the points of view expressed by the people in those stories, but we think you should know about this.'

"Unfortunately, I would say that people who live in other countries, in many European countries, know more about us than we know about them. I think the biggest change in network news is probably the dramatic decrease in the amount of foreign coverage. When I'm overseas on assignment and I look at a local program in London or in Paris, there's always something on it about the United States. But there's not always something about Paris or London on our broadcasts. We are the economic giant of the world, the only military superpower. We are the most important country in the world. But we are a stronger country when we know more about what's going on in the rest of the world. We are a better, more informed population when we know and understand the concerns of other people."

—ED BRADLEY

60 MINUTES
CBS, 1968–

Tick-tick-tick-tick-tick... For decades, that sound has set the Sunday-night rhythm in millions of households as football- and dinner-sated Americans settled in to root for a show that turned investigative journalism into dramatic entertainment. *60 Minutes* has offered many pleasures over the years—Morley Safer's intriguing exploration of the paradisiacal Maldive Islands, Harry Reasoner's tribute to the movie *Casablanca*—but the real draw is watching correspondents such as Mike Wallace knock some ne'er-do-well heads together. When it first went on the air in 1968, the show seemed an unlikely candidate to become not only a TV institution but also a staggering network profit center and inspiration for a legion of imitators (including its own legitimate offspring, *60 Minutes II*). At the time, documentary-style television was considered a prestige operation, not a lure for viewers or advertisers. In fact, it wasn't until the mid-'70s that a few adjustments to the show—adding correspondent Dan Rather to the team and moving to its now-customary Sunday-night slot—turned it into the news and ratings juggernaut it became. Over the years, executive producer Don Hewitt's crew covered thousands of stories, from Rather's trek into Afghanistan during the Soviet invasion to Ed Bradley's interview with Oklahoma City bomber Timothy McVeigh. One of the great joys of watching the show is seeing "something that does not appear often in nonfiction television," TV GUIDE said in 1984: "the process of watching the correspondents discover the story at the same time that we do." Or, as Wallace described it to the magazine: "What we were able to do is bring the technique of live reportage to the documentary." Although some things on *60 Minutes* have changed over the years—remember the righty-lefty "Point-Counterpoint" spats of James Kilpatrick and Shana Alexander?—the show now feels like an American landmark. It is hard to imagine that these 60 minutes won't go on...forever. *Tick-tick-tick-tick-tick...*

COVERS (CLOCKWISE FROM ABOVE):
BY CHARLES SANTORE, APRIL 23, 1977
BY DARRYL ESTRINE, APRIL 27, 1996
BY ROBERT PHILLIPS, FEBRUARY 25, 1984

TV GUIDE
WHICH TV COWBOYS CAN REALLY RIDE?

Local Listings
February
14-20

15¢

BACKSTAGE
WITH
GINGER
ROGERS

SEE
PAGE 8

Alfred Hitchcock

ALFRED HITCHCOCK PRESENTS
CBS, 1955–60; NBC, 1960–62
COVER: BY MAX YAVNO,
FEBRUARY 14, 1959

"The more outrageous a subject can get, the better I like it," Hitchcock told TV GUIDE in 1959. "I am no different from a child who gloats over the horrific." The master filmmaker found plenty to gloat over during his decade as the host and occasional director of *Alfred Hitchcock Presents*, an anthology of "situation tragedies," as he once described these tales of murder, mystery and surprise. The show's "best feature," TV GUIDE said, was Hitch himself, "a sly grin on his cherubic face" as he introduced the ultimate horror: the next commercial break.

THE X-FILES
Fox, 1993–2002
COVERS: BY DAVID LAVY, DECEMBER 21, 1996

Though there is only one *X* in *The X-Files*, for fans this show was a sexy triple-*X* feature: sci-fi action, nefarious plots and horror-story creatures—all wrapped in a lushly produced package. When the series debuted in 1993, it tapped into the conspiracy-theorist gene lurking in millions of otherwise rational viewers, transfixing them with tales of FBI cases considered too bizarre for the bureau to solve—until it put agents Fox Mulder and Dana Scully on the job. David Duchovny played the romantic dreamer with an Oliver Stone-like paranoia to Gillian Anderson's rational pragmatist. The matchup provided the ingredients for a classic romantic pas de deux, except the couple stubbornly remained nothing more than coworkers and friends. The sexual tension between Mulder and Scully crackled for an amazing seven years without consummation (frustrated fans should have demanded an FBI investigation into *that*) before Duchovny left in 2000, announcing that he was tired of the grind. Creator Chris Carter's brainchild continued for two more years, still looking ravishing at $4 million per episode but unable to make up for Duchovny's departure. And perhaps the X-files themselves had become exhausted. After all, over the years Mulder and Scully tracked down everything from evil clones and a human-size parasite feasting in a New Jersey sewer system to a cocooning monster that emerged every 30 years to kill. Bidding goodbye to the show as its end in spring 2002 approached, TV GUIDE said: "Nothing on TV lasts forever, not even a landmark like Fox's marvelously inventive *X-Files*, with its dense and dark explorations of paranoia, government conspiracy and otherworldly menace—and the resilient humanity of its charismatic leads."

"SCIENCE-FICTION SHOWS
CAN BE HOKEY BUT GRITTY AT THE SAME TIME.

They lend themselves to a certain kind of moralizing. You can be moralistic and allegorical and get away with it. You can tell a poignant story, teach lessons and still make it fun. This is a harder thing to do when you're dealing with a show that takes place in the real, everyday world.

"When I was a kid, I liked the message of *Star Trek*—you know, the hokey moral of the day. The same thing with *The Twilight Zone*.

The cool thing about these shows was picking up on these messages, these little ironic tags—whether it was 'be kind to strangers' or 'don't prejudge people.' You kind of felt smart when you got what they were talking about.

"Incidentally, my mom loved Captain Kirk. She thought he had a good build. She liked the way he filled out his Starfleet uniform."

—DAVID DUCHOVNY

THE SIMPSONS

Santa's Little Helper, Marge Simpson, Homer Simpson, Bart Simpson, Lisa Simpson, Maggie Simpson, Snowball. Fox, 1989–
COVERS: OCTOBER 21, 2000 (THE SIMPSONS™ AND ©2000 TWENTIETH CENTURY FOX FILM CORP. ALL RIGHTS RESERVED)

It was the Christmas season, 1989, a time when TV is blanketed with counterfeit sentiment and saccharine fables. Then the pilot episode of *The Simpsons* elbowed its way onto the air: "Simpsons Roasting on an Open Fire" introduced viewers—those who had missed creator Matt Groening's short segments of the cartoon family on *The Tracey Ullman Show*—to what would become the most exhilaratingly subversive, reliably hilarious series on television. In fact, the popularity of *The Simpsons* burned so hot at first that the show seemed destined for the life span of a fad—in the early '90s, every other person you saw seemed to be wearing a Bart Simpson T-shirt emblazoned with one of the lovable, underachieving fourth-grader's catchphrases ("Ay caramba," "Don't have a cow, man"). It soon became apparent that the show wasn't just a brilliant cartoon; it was one of the best comedies on television, period, with enough complexity and emotional nuance to last a very long time. Nine years

later, TV GUIDE would declare that "America's funniest family is more irreverent—and irresistible—than ever," praising the show's "textual density" and characters that had more "heft than the flesh-and-blood characters of other sitcoms." The Simpson family itself—led by Homer, the tenderly negligent dad, and Marge, the practical mom with the impractical hair—was captivating, but so was the supporting cast of Springfield residents ("Worthy of a Preston Sturges movie," said TV GUIDE, which also found them worthy of 24 covers in one week). Celebrities gladly lent their voices to the show, and over the years we heard everyone from Buzz Aldrin and Johnny Carson to Hugh Hefner and Barry White. But the voice that will always conjure *The Simpsons*, the spoken *syllable* that instantly evokes the show's appreciation for life's unexpected turns and our futile attempts to anticipate them, is Homer's utterly eloquent *d'oh!*

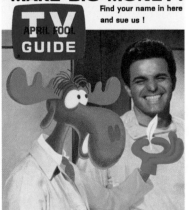

THE BULLWINKLE SHOW

Bullwinkle Moose, Rocket J. Squirrel. ABC, 1959–61; NBC, 1961–64; ABC, 1964–73
SPECIAL INSERT COVER: PHOTOGRAPHER UNKNOWN, MARCH 30, 1963

Jay Ward might have been a graduate of the Harvard School of Business Administration and a real-estate dealer in Berkeley, California, but he loved cartooning a lot more than calculating square footage. And it didn't pay too badly, either. In 1959, after his success with *Crusader Rabbit*—a series of five-minute animated TV segments for kids—Ward dreamed up Rocket J. Squirrel (aka Rocky the Flying Squirrel) and a moose called Bullwinkle. They first appeared on ABC in *Rocky and His Friends*, then moved to NBC, where—in recognition of the dim-witted moose's popularity—the billing changed to *The Bullwinkle Show*. As it jumped around from evening to afternoon to morning slots on two networks over the course of 12 years, *The Bullwinkle Show* became a classic that was fun for kids, who loved the goofy characters, and irresistible to adults, who dug the sophisticated puns and clever satire. The "irreverent, outrageous humor...made Bullwinkle the best-known moose in television," TV GUIDE said in '62. Rocky and Bullwinkle, natives of Frostbite Falls, Minnesota, were forever fending off the hapless spies Boris and Natasha. There were also plenty of other deeply amusing segments, including the "Fractured Fairy Tales" parodies (wonderfully narrated by Edward Everett Horton), "Peabody's Improbable History" (the wealthy dog-genius Mister Peabody and his adopted boy, Sherman, tramped through history using the Way-Back Machine) and, of course, the gripping adventures of Dudley Do-Right, the Canadian Mountie who felt almost as tenderly toward the beautiful Nell as he did toward his horse. Anyone who doesn't have a tender spot of his own for the *Bullwinkle* gang—seen in omnipresent reruns over the years—must be a descendant of Snidely Whiplash.

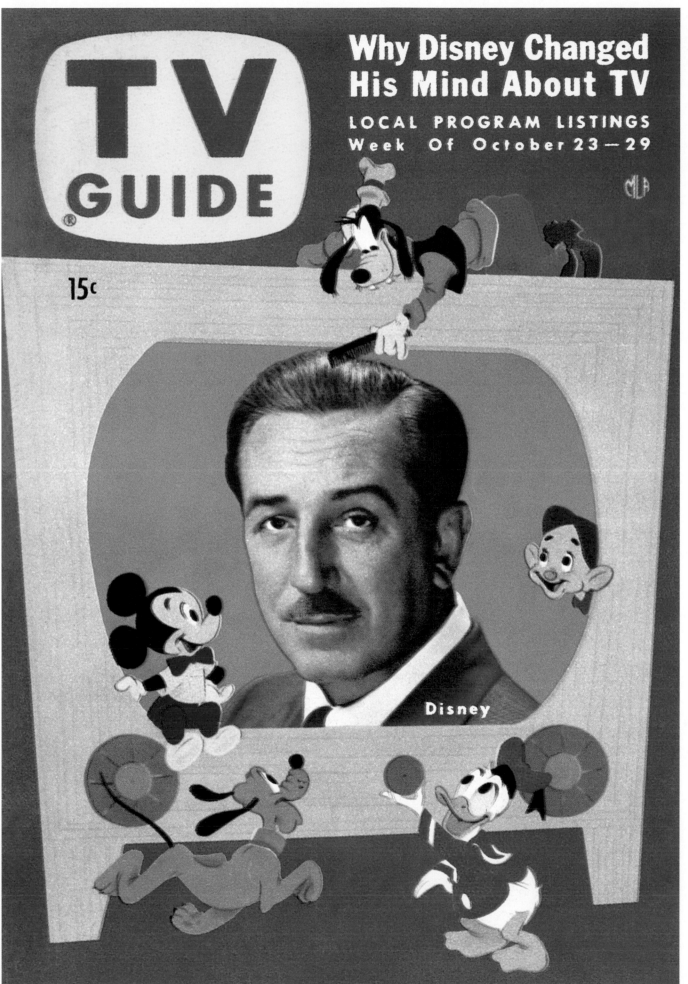

TV GUIDE

®

15c

Why Disney Changed His Mind About TV

LOCAL PROGRAM LISTINGS
Week Of October 23 — 29

Disney

WALT DISNEY
**ABC, 1954–61, 1986–89
and 1997–; NBC, 1961–81
and 1989–90; CBS, 1981–83**
COVER: BY WALT DISNEY PRODS.,
OCTOBER 23, 1954

In its early days, television was anathema to Hollywood movie studios, which generally shunned it for siphoning off filmgoers and turning out inferior entertainment. "Of all the moguls, only Walt Disney sensed opportunity rather than disaster in the new medium," TV GUIDE said in 1978, in anticipation of the 25th anniversary of Disney's historic 1954 leap onto the airwaves. His immediate success with *Disneyland* (it went through eight different names, including *Walt Disney's Wonderful World of Color* and *The Wonderful World of Disney*) opened the floodgates for Hollywood's rush into television production. But the show, divided into segments called "Adventureland," "Frontierland," "Fantasyland" and "Tomorrowland," also instigated a change in the way the TV industry thought about programming. For one thing, it provided a fresh outlet for Disney's animated movies, and it popularized the nature documentary, sending flocks of imitators into the field. The art of cross promotion, meanwhile, was practically invented by the show, which featured insider looks at the building of the Disneyland theme park and previews of forthcoming Disney theatrical releases. Finally, the continuing saga of *Davy Crockett*, starring Fess Parker, presaged the TV miniseries. (It also touched off one of the great fads of the 1950s, making the coonskin cap a must-have childhood accessory.) "I'm really having fun with television," Disney told TV GUIDE in 1957. "I haven't had so much fun since my early days in the business when I had the latitude to experiment. With TV, it's like a cage has been opened—and I can fly again." And again and again: *Disney*'s status as a beloved TV institution has prompted repeated reinventions—most recently on ABC, the show's original home and a network now owned by—who else?—the Walt Disney Company.

"**I, Claudius** was just an incredible production for television. The level of writing, the production values, the acting— it was really TV at its best. There wasn't one false note in it. We always think the British do everything better, and maybe it's just empire envy. But if you think about it, the acting of Derek Jacobi as Claudius and Siân Phillips as Livia—in a way, she was really the paradigm for Tony Soprano's mother, Livia."

—Larry Gelbart, creator of M*A*S*H

MASTERPIECE THEATRE
Alistair Cooke; Livia (Siân Phillips), Augustus (Brian Blessed) of *I, Claudius* (1977–78); Queen Elizabeth I (Glenda Jackson), Davison (John Graham) of *Elizabeth R* (1972); Rose (Jean Marsh), Mrs. Bridges (Angela Baddeley) of *Upstairs, Downstairs* (1974–77). PBS, 1971–

In more than 30 years, not much has changed about *Masterpiece Theatre*. Sure, host Alistair Cooke, the British journalist who struck just the right note of informed hospitality with his introductions, retired in 1993 and gave way to American journalist Russell Baker. And the original sponsor, Mobil Oil, merged with Exxon in 1999, so that viewers now settle in to watch the ungainly *ExxonMobil Masterpiece Theatre*. But the stately signature music by Jean-Joseph Mouret remains, as does the anthology series' mission: to make a home for original works and adaptations—usually British, usually multipart—that are too classy for American commercial networks. Of course, that doesn't preclude their being hugely entertaining: *Upstairs, Downstairs* was itself a masterpiece of storytelling, about the sea change in British culture after World War I, as seen through the lives of the moneyed Bellamy family upstairs and the servants quartered downstairs. The year *Upstairs* ended, *I, Claudius* began, with Derek Jacobi as the Roman emperor brilliantly stuttering and stumbling his way through poet Robert Graves's comic horror tale of Rome's decline. Not every *Masterpiece* offering lived up to its billing, but as TV GUIDE noted in 1978, "that's the price paid for excellence." What was admirable about British TV, the magazine said, was its "chanciness—the occasional attempt to bring off something difficult and hazardous," reminding American audiences that "we could do with fewer mediocre successes and more grand failures." On the series' 15th anniversary, Cooke wrote a piece for TV GUIDE downplaying his role in its success. The producers, he said, chose the menu, while "I was, at this end, simply the headwaiter."

HAVE GUN, WILL TRAVEL
Paladin (Richard Boone). CBS, 1957–63
COVER: BY PHILIPPE HALSMAN, MAY 10, 1958

When Westerns ruled television, the triumvirate atop the ratings for three consecutive years (1958-61) was *Gunsmoke, Wagon Train* and *Have Gun, Will Travel,* in that order. Of the three, *Have Gun* was the most intriguing: A dandified hired gun named Paladin lived in vaguely decadent opulence at a San Francisco hotel, but observed a code of honor so strict that he'd turn on his employer if that's where the ethical needle pointed. In an unusual twist, this Western hero dressed in black when he was on the job, and star Richard Boone was hardly a rock-jawed cowboy prototype–he looked, TV GUIDE said in a three-part profile in 1961, like he had been "recently stung by hunting wasps, for the face is pocked and puffy and, in Boone's words, more 'interesting' than handsome." Paladin solicited work with a wonderful marketing tool (and one of the coolest talismans of that television era), a business card that bore the image of a chess-piece knight. Alas, Paladin didn't survive the endgame: The popularity of Westerns waned, and *Have Gun* traveled off the air in '63.

GUNSMOKE
Kitty Russell (Amanda Blake), Marshal Matt Dillon (James Arness). CBS, 1955–75
COVER: BY GARRETT-HOWARD, MAY 11, 1957

"Good evening. My name's Wayne"—as in *John* Wayne, who was dressed in full cowboy gear as he introduced the first episode of *Gunsmoke* on September 10, 1955. "Some of you may have seen me before," Wayne said. "I hope so. I've been kicking around Hollywood a long time. I've made a lot of pictures out here. All kinds. Some of them have been Westerns. That's what I'm here to tell you about tonight—a Western. A new television show called *Gunsmoke*. No, I'm not in it. I wish I were, though, because I think it's the best thing of its kind to come along. And I hope you'll agree with me. It's honest, it's adult, it's realistic." Wayne was right: *Gunsmoke* was like no other TV Western before it. And with the oater icon's imprimatur—and his friend James Arness as Matt Dillon—it began what turned out to be a historic run. Twenty years later, when the doors of the Long Branch Saloon

finally quit swinging, *Gunsmoke* owned the record—and still does—as the longest-running prime-time series featuring continuing characters. Audiences accustomed to the impossibly courageous leading men on kid-oriented Westerns like *The Lone Ranger* loved the bracing stories of a hero who wasn't particularly popular with anyone but his immediate friends, such as saloon owner Miss Kitty (Amanda Blake) and Doc Adams (Milburn Stone). Dillon was a hero who could be wounded in gunfights and beaten up by bad guys, a hero who didn't talk to his horse. Arness also rarely spoke to the press, but in 1987 he talked to TV GUIDE about the success of the series. "What made the difference was they didn't try to do an entertainment fiction-alized Western," Arness said. "They really tried like hell to make it hot and dry and dusty, and people were ready for it."

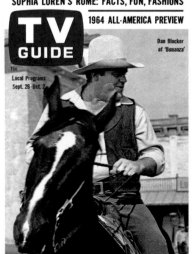
BONANZA

Eric "Hoss" Cartwright (Dan Blocker), Ben Cartwright (Lorne Greene), Adam Cartwright (Pernell Roberts), Little Joe Cartwright (Michael Landon). NBC, 1959–73

COVER: BY CARL FRITH, SEPTEMBER 26, 1964

Bonanza occupies such a familiar place in TV history that it's easy to overlook how atypical it seemed when it first began airing. In an era of *Shane*-inspired heroes who were rootless loners, here was a TV Western—the first in color—that still featured gunplay and pounding hooves, but centered on a family. Even in that respect, though, it broke the mold: This family consisted of four men—thrice-widowed Ben Cartwright and the grown sons he had from each marriage. Although watching *Bonanza* became a Sunday-night tradition for millions of households throughout the 1960s, creator David Dortort was just as averse to TV-family conventions as he was to Old West clichés. "We do not have any moms built into our show.... We don't have any little brats who talk like Leonard Bernstein," Dortort told TV GUIDE in 1960. "We deal with a love affair between four strong men and, even more importantly, with the land and with roots." The strongest of the quartet working the sprawling Ponderosa ranch near Virginia City, Nevada, was the 300-pound "Hoss," memorably played by Dan Blocker as not the brightest bull in the herd, but the biggest-hearted one. He was a gentle foil to Michael Landon's hotheaded Little Joe, and a humorous counterweight to the reserved, cerebral eldest brother, Adam, who was written out of the series in 1965 when actor Pernell Roberts tired of the role. "I think the show is popular basically because of the four characters, not because of the stories—which are sometimes terrible," Blocker told TV GUIDE. *Bonanza* easily coped with Roberts's departure, but Blocker's death in 1972, coupled with a switch to Tuesday nights after 11 years in its Sunday slot, was more than the remaining two strong men could handle.

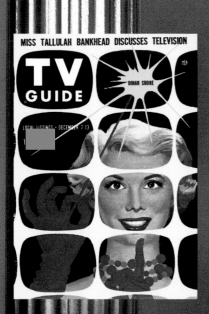

THE DINAH SHORE CHEVY SHOW
NBC, 1956–63
COVER: BY AL PARKER,
DECEMBER 7, 1957

Singer Dinah Shore's gracious, friendly style helped turn *The Dinah Shore Chevy Show* into a TV fixture. The variety series had plenty of guest stars (Ginger Rogers, Jimmy Durante, Ella Fitzgerald), but Shore—singing "See the U.S.A. in your Chevrolet" and giving a big show-ending kiss to the audience—was the real draw. "The show is like a party," Shore told TV GUIDE in 1959. "I like people to have a good time at my parties." Cowboy star Roy Rogers told the magazine in '57 that he liked being a guest because "you just don't have the tension" of other programs. The reason? "That girl knows what she's doin', that's why."

COMING:
CUR-MERCIALS
TO
BRAINWASH
YOUR
DOG see page 8

THE ED SULLIVAN SHOW
Clockwise from above: Elvis Presley; Sullivan with the Beatles; Diana Ross; plate spinner; Liza Minnelli and Judy Garland. CBS, 1948–71
COVER: BY PHILIPPE HALSMAN, JUNE 17, 1967

From our vantage point more than a half century later, it's easy to blame the infancy of television for the fact that someone like Ed Sullivan could get on the air as the host of his own variety show. After all, the guy looked like the runner-up in a Bogart-imitates-Nixon contest. But even back then, Sullivan's mug raised eyebrows. "In 1948, television writers laughed at his appearance," TV GUIDE recalled 20 years later. He didn't just look stiff; the introducer also suffered from the chronic inability to actually make introductions. Sullivan heralded Massachusetts-born singer Robert Goulet as a Canadian. He turned clarinetist Benny Goodman into a "trumpeter," columnist Walter Winchell into a "sports star" and a visiting group of New Zealand natives into "the fierce Maori tribe from New England." That list of blunders, though, also provides a glimpse of the tremendous range of guests who appeared on *The Ed Sullivan*

Show (it was called *Toast of the Town* from 1948 to '55). What Sullivan lacked in on-air skills he made up for with his reporter's instincts to jump on timely subjects and a willingness to fly anywhere in the world to check out an act. The list of stars who made their first television appearance on his show includes the Beatles, Dinah Shore, Lena Horne, Eddie Fisher and the comedy team of Dean Martin and Jerry Lewis. Despite all these high-octane acts, Sullivan singled out the unplanned speech of a less well-known guest as his most memorable moment: In 1953, playwright, producer and director Josh Logan (*South Pacific*) touchingly addressed the country about his own experience with mental illness and the need to de-stigmatize it. "As far as I'm concerned," Sullivan told TV GUIDE in 1968, three years before his epic run ended, "it was the all-time big moment on the show."

"Although it's somewhat politically incorrect, The Sopranos
seems to mirror more closely the
world we really live in, the world
my friends and I know. It's
shocking and upsetting, but so is
what really happens in our lives."
—Edie Falco

THE SOPRANOS

A.J. Soprano (Robert Iler), Carmela Soprano (Edie Falco), Tony Soprano (James Gandolfini), Meadow Soprano (Jamie-Lynn Sigler); Paulie Walnuts (Tony Sirico), Silvio Dante (Steven Van Zandt), Tony Soprano, Christopher Moltisanti (Michael Imperioli). HBO, 1999—
COVER: BY FRANK W. OCKENFELS 3, JANUARY 8, 2000

In 1999, the broadcast networks, already bloodied by a long turf war with the cable channels, were kneecapped by a deadly new foe: *The Sopranos*. The HBO series, unfettered by network censors or squeamish advertisers, capitalized on America's abiding fascination with the Italian Mafia, asking the question: What would happen if a shrewd but depressed mobster, struggling to operate a RICO-diminished business while living the wealthy suburban life, suffered an is-that-all-there-is midlife crisis? The answer proved to be one of the most riveting, funny and appalling series ever on television. Suffering panic attacks, Tony Soprano (James Gandolfini) sought the help of therapist Dr. Jennifer Melfi (Lorraine Bracco) and started to plumb his relationship with his poisonous mother, Livia (the brilliant Nancy Marchand, who died after the second season). Shuttling between his meat-market Mafia clubhouse, the Bada Bing! strip club and his Jersey Luxe house, Tony managed to avoid prison, kill his rivals, deal with his children's problems at school and almost convince his wife, Carmela (Edie Falco), that despite his incorrigible cheating, he really loved her. But while this tale of a mobster on Prozac might easily have been played just for laughs—the feature film *Analyze This* was released the same year—instead creator David Chase and the superlative cast managed to achieve a moral and artistic complexity that went far beyond the usual sex, violence and *braciole*. As TV GUIDE critic Matt Roush observed: "Carmela once told her husband, 'You're like an alien life force among us,' and she's partly right. James Gandolfini as Tony Soprano truly is out of this world."

DAY

On TV covers:

TV's One-Sided View of SOVIET RUSSIA See page 6
Local Programs • August 5–11
15¢
HUGH DOWNS AND BARBARA WALTERS OF 'TODAY'

How TV Can Improve Americans' Health Page 4
Local Programs May 14–20
25¢
Tom Brokaw of 'Today'

TODAY

Clockwise from top: Al Roker; Willard Scott, Jane Pauley; Matt Lauer, Katie Couric, Jenny Larou, Jeff Scott; J. Fred Muggs, Dave Garroway; Rudolph Giuliani, Couric, Bryant Gumbel, Mario Cuomo. NBC, 1952–
COVERS: BY SHELDON SECUNDA, AUGUST 5, 1967. BY DANIEL KRAMER, MAY 14, 1977

"Good morning to you," said bow-tied host Dave Garroway, announcing the debut broadcast of Today on January 14, 1952, "the very first good morning of what I hope and suspect will be a great many good mornings between you and I." Critics weren't so sure—they panned the experiment in morning news, information and entertainment that viewers were supposed to dip in and out of as they got ready for their day. Ratings stayed as soft as a soggy Cheerio for the first year. But then someone had the inspiration to bring in the loose cannon J. Fred Muggs, a chimpanzee that had kids begging their parents to tune in. The ratings soared, and soon Today became a habit for millions. "As television and society changed and matured," TV GUIDE said in January 2002, marking the show's 50th anniversary, "so did Today—never more noticeably than in its presentation of women." The program that for years had featured a comely new "Today Girl" every day shook up the industry in 1974 by anointing Barbara Walters as a bona fide cohost. Almost 30 years later, the show set another record, signing cohost Katie Couric to a five-year deal reportedly worth $65 million, making her the highest-paid television journalist in history. Couric and cohost Matt Lauer were just the latest in a long line of stars who made Today so memorable: Hugh Downs, John Chancellor, Tom Brokaw, Jane Pauley, Bryant Gumbel, Al Roker, Ann Curry and many others. "It's been on all these years without me and Hugh, and it will go on after Katie and Matt," Walters told TV GUIDE in 2001. "Our grandchildren will probably still be watching it." Watching it, and waiting to hear the weather report from someone who might be sending birthday greetings to Willard Scott on *his* 100th.

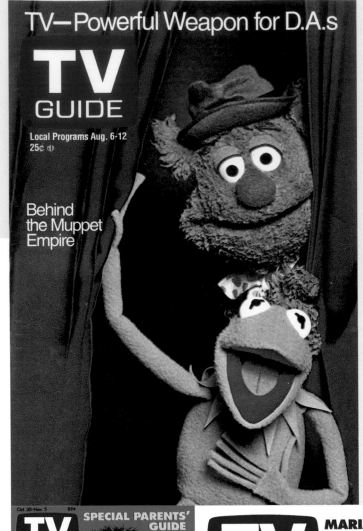

TV—Powerful Weapon for D.A.s

TV GUIDE

Local Programs Aug. 6-12
25¢

Behind
the Muppet
Empire

15¢ Local Programs July 10-16

TV GUIDE

'SESAME STREET':
How well has it
worked? What
have they learned?
What next?
Page 20

The Cookie Monster

Oct 30–Nov 5   89¢

TV GUIDE

SPECIAL PARENTS'
GUIDE

TV THAT'S
GOOD
FOR
YOUR
KIDS
SURPRISE!
THERE ARE
SMART
SITCOMS,
TOONS, AND
GAME SHOWS

Ernie (top) and Bert
of PBS's Sesame Street

TV GUIDE

MARIAH CAREY
Up close with the
sweet-voiced
singer in
her first
TV special

Nov. 13–19
89¢

**First
Lady
Meets
First
Bird!**
Sesame Street's
Birthday Bash
By Judy Blume

PLUS:
Video Game Guide
**Return to
Lonesome Dove**

Hillary Rodham
Clinton and Friend

SESAME STREET
PBS, 1969–

COVERS (CLOCKWISE FROM ABOVE): BY JACK DAVIS, JULY 10, 1971. BY KEN REGAN, AUGUST 6, 1977.
BY MARC BRYAN-BROWN, NOVEMBER 13, 1993, AND OCTOBER 30, 1993

In 1967, documentary producer Joan Ganz Cooney launched a company called the Children's Television Workshop. CTW was formed with the backing of federal and foundation dollars, and its intention was to create educational programming to help inner-city children do better in school. What Cooney and her crew came up with, as TV GUIDE raved in 1970, was "far and away the greatest children's program that has ever been on the air." Three decades later, it's easy to forget just how startling the world of Bert, Ernie, Cookie Monster and Kermit the Frog really was. The quick-cut stream of cartoons, savvy Muppets, grown-up characters and catchy songs were by themselves a groundbreaking approach to children's programming, but then to marshal all those forces for the purpose of teaching preschoolers the alphabet and numbers—well, that was simply astonishing. *Sesame Street* never lost its city-street setting or multicultural mind-set, yet right from the start, children of every social and economic background clustered around the TV to watch it. By the mid-'70s, some critics had begun to doubt its value, but TV GUIDE concluded that the show "has kept its basic promise—to be imaginative, to use television to teach as well as amuse young children." Besides, what's not to love about a program that, in its early days, showed Burt Lancaster doing push-ups while counting to 10, and much later morphed the Fine Young Cannibals' "She Drives Me Crazy" into "C Drives Me Crazy"?

MISTER ROGERS' NEIGHBORHOOD
**Fred Rogers. PBS, 1968–75
and 1979–2001**

After a staggering 33 years, Mister Rogers finally
hung up his cardigan and put away his comfy
shoes for the last time in 2001. Although children's television had evolved radically over the
course of his three decades in residence, the
changes never seemed to touch Fred Rogers's
neighborhood, where he reigned as a gentle,
avuncular presence for countless millions of
preschoolers. Using songs, puppets and simple
chats directed to the camera, he helped kids
understand their feelings while showing them a
good time. What was the appeal? "It is, simply,
that he doesn't either play up to children or talk
down to them," said TV GUIDE in 1970. "And above
all, he doesn't put them down."

ROMPER ROOM
Miss Connie with students. Syndication, 1954–94

"The world's largest kindergarten," as TV Guide described *Romper Room* in 1956, had gotten its start in Baltimore two years earlier but spread faster than chicken pox through a playground via syndication and locally produced versions. The format: A pleasant woman (often a teacher) tried gamely to organize preschoolers into finger painting, sing-alongs and other toddler-targeted activities. Highlights dimly recalled by nearly every baby boomer alive included the Do Bee report card ("Prayer sayer," "Truth teller," "Turn taker," etc.) and the Magic Mirror, when "Miss" whoever gazed through an empty mirror frame and named all the children she could see in TV land—while millions of kids listened raptly each day to find out if they would be called.

COME ON DOWN!

THE PRICE IS RIGHT
From top: Bill Cullen with contestants; Bob Barker. NBC, 1956–63; ABC, 1963–65; syndication, 1972–74, 1985 and 1994; CBS, 1972–
COVER: BY CURT GUNTHER, JULY 28, 1962

Whether hosted by Bill Cullen, Dennis James or Bob Barker, everything always seemed to ultimately go right for *The Price is Right*. In 1976, two decades after the debut of the guess-the-cost-of-the-merchandise game show, TV GUIDE said that four-year host Barker "looks as if he will be around a lot longer." A whopping 26 years later, there he was—on CBS, as the only host of a daytime network game show.

JEOPARDY!
Alex Trebek. NBC, 1964–75 and 1978–79; syndication, 1974 and 1984–
COVER: BY ULI ROSE, JANUARY 27, 2001

Back in 2000, when *Who Wants to Be a Millionaire* was bigfooting the ratings, the usually unruffled Alex Trebek was feeling decidedly perturbed when he spoke to journalism students at the University of Georgia. As TV GUIDE reported, the *Jeopardy!* host dissed the competition for asking no-brainer questions like "What's the usual color of Post-Its?" Trebek's irritation was understandable. For nearly 40 years, *Jeopardy!* had been TV's fortress of knowledge. Outside the gates, in the game-show wilderness, you might find contestants wearing funny hats, models caressing dining-room sets and hosts doubling as cheerleaders. But once you were inside the *Jeopardy!* compound with your thumb poised over the button, the rule was strictly "May the smartest person win." The show has moved around from networks to syndication since its launch in 1964, but the format has always remained the same: Contestants, after selecting from a category, are given an "answer" (e.g., "The Greek god of shepherds") and must supply the correct "question" ("Who is Pan?"). Created by Merv Griffin, who also hit the jackpot with *Wheel of Fortune, Jeopardy!* was originally hosted by the genial Art Fleming, who remained the face of the show for 15 years in daytime. After a few years off the air, *Jeopardy!* returned in 1984 with bigger dollar amounts and Trebek as host. That's when the show entered what has to be regarded as its classic era. Trebek seemed perfectly suited to the job: polite, efficient, commiserating, but ever so slightly condescending toward losers and winners alike. He always gave the faint impression that he could run the table if someone would just give him the chance. TV GUIDE in 1987 called *Jeopardy!* "the truest, purest test of general knowledge on the air today"—and that remained true well after the ratings reign of Regis Philbin's *Millionaire* began to wane.

"I THINK GAME SHOWS HAVE LASTED SO LONG BECAUSE THEY ARE BASICALLY FEEL-GOOD TELEVISION.

You're not dealing with the problems of the world. The viewers are watching ordinary people having, in some cases, spectacularly rewarding moments on national television. They're watching their peers do well. I used to liken game shows to the Great American Dream. Anybody can be president, anybody can do well, anybody can be rich. And game shows provide people with that opportunity. They make America feel better. A lot of the talk shows in recent years have gone into confrontational situations. They deal with problems, emotional distress, physical abuse, but game shows are just the opposite. You say, 'Well, isn't this nice, look at that. This little girl here lost her job, and now she just won $32,000 and a brand-new car.' We've got a lot of stories like that. One of our contestants had come to California and was on his last legs—he had no money and couldn't pay the rent. All of a sudden, he made it on *Jeopardy!* and won a lot of dough, and that enabled him to stay in California. His appearance on our show got him noticed, and he wound up being a radio commentator.

"On game shows, people have a chance to win big and demonstrate some measure of skill, whether it's coming up with a correct estimate of how much something costs in a supermarket or, as in the case on *Jeopardy!* and some of the other quiz shows in the past, coming up with very esoteric correct responses to difficult questions.

"But game shows have changed dramatically in terms of presentation. If you look at *Jeopardy!* today and compare it to the 1964 edition that aired on NBC, it's night and day. We have electronics; we have our clue crew of four young people who travel around the country and videotape clues to insert into the program; we even have celebrities doing clues for us. If you look at *Who Wants to Be a Millionaire* and *Weakest Link*, the presentation is very slick. They've almost got a rock-concert feel with the bank of lights above that switch and move. And there are sound effects and heightened drama. The presentation is head and shoulders above what used to be the case. If you think back, the early television game and quiz shows evolved from radio quiz shows. They were very static and not particularly eye-pleasing. But then again, in the 1950s a lot of television was like that. Television has evolved in the past 50 years by leaps and bounds."

—ALEX TREBEK

THE '50s

May 29, 1953
Photographer unknown
Queen Elizabeth II

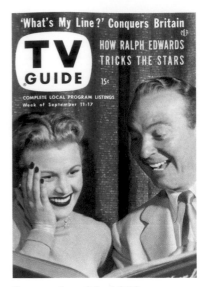

September 11, 1953
Photographer unknown
Joan Caulfield and Ralph Edwards
of *This Is Your Life*

January 1, 1954
Photographer unknown
Bing Crosby

January 1, 1955
By Elmer Holloway
Loretta Young of *The Loretta
Young Show*

July 2, 1955
By Graphic House
Tommy Rettig of *Lassie* and Aaker Lee of
The Adventures of Rin Tin Tin

September 3, 1955
By Gaby Rona
Jody Carson and Johnny Carson of
The Johnny Carson Show

November 26, 1955
By Phillipe Halsman
Martha Raye of *The Martha Raye Show*

August 17, 1957
By Al Hirschfeld
Phil Silvers of *The Phil Silvers Show*

August 31, 1957
By Warner Bros.
Clint Walker of *Cheyenne*

September 14, 1957
By Arthur Williams
Fall Preview

November 2, 1957
By Al Hirschfeld
Lucille Ball of *I Love Lucy*

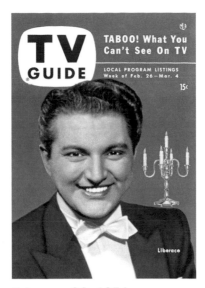

February 26, 1954
Photographer unknown
Liberace of *The Liberace Show*

May 14, 1954
Photographer unknown
Frank Sinatra

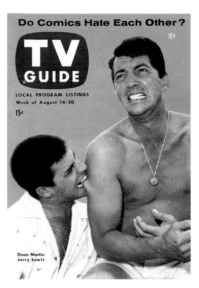

August 14, 1954
Photographer unknown
Jerry Lewis and Dean Martin

October 16, 1954
Photographer unknown
Red Buttons of *The Red Buttons Show*

December 24, 1955
By Larry Fritz
Christmas

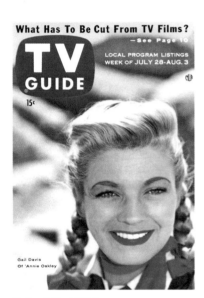

July 28, 1956
By Garrett-Howard
Gail Davis of *Annie Oakley*

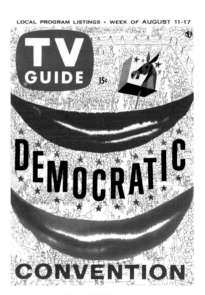

August 11, 1956
By KMLG-Barron
Democratic Convention

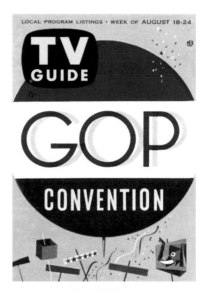

August 18, 1956
By Kramer, Miller, Lomden, Glassman
GOP Convention

December 28, 1957
By John Engstead
Ricky Nelson of *The Adventures of Ozzie & Harriet*

March 22, 1958
By Al Hirschfeld
Perry Como of *The Perry Como Show*

April 26, 1958
By Dave Preston
Guy Williams of *Zorro*

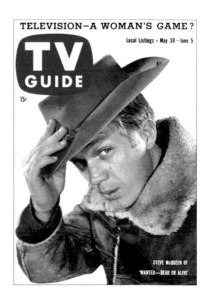

May 30, 1959
By Gene Trindl
Steve McQueen of *Wanted—Dead or Alive*

THE FRENCH CHEF
Julia Child. NET and PBS, 1963–73

"Part of cooking," Julia Child told her TV audience in 1964, "is in recovering one's mistakes. A cook's motto should be 'Never Despair.'" It was a message that millions of American cooks—so intimidated by French cuisine that they despaired of even attempting it—needed desperately to hear. And Child, a cooking instructor and author, was the perfect person to deliver it: With a fascinating blend of absolute focus and a *c'est la vie* offhandedness, she delightfully demystified Cordon Bleu cooking for a country stuck in a swamp of meat loaf, ketchup and SpaghettiOs. "Julia Child is not just a natural, she is without doubt the most natural performer television has yet uncovered," TV GUIDE said in '68. "She is so completely oblivious to the camera that she seems to come right through to us without any camera at all." Throughout her long public-TV career, Child was famous for slamming pots around and slopping mixtures onto the countertop ("Oh, bother!") in her enthusiasm for the task at hand. "It's an absolute *tragedy* if you don't have something that's really your life's purpose," she told the magazine in 1970. Never has missionary zeal provided such a tasty TV dinner.

IT'S A GOOD ING

MARTHA STEWART LIVING
Syndication, 1993–

Martha Stewart's empire of domestic perfection wouldn't be complete without conquering the republic of television. So she launched a typically surgical strike: the syndicated *Martha Stewart Living*, which invited viewers to assiduously take notes on activities like cooking elaborate chocolate-filled puff pastries—or to daydream about living a life where such an undertaking was even conceivable. "I hope it's an interlude for people," Stewart said in TV GUIDE, "and a place to turn to get a sense of the lovely, the delicious and the elegant."

TABLOID TV
Security guard and guests on *The Jerry Springer Show*, **1998**
COVER: BY GARY HANNABARGER (2), MARC BRYAN-BROWN AND STEVE HILL, APRIL 1, 1995

Alan Burke and Joe Pyne pioneered what the latter called "fist-in-the-mouth" television in the 1960s. But they, and Morton Downey Jr. in the late '80s, largely relied on vitriol spewing back and forth between a repellent guest and a disgusted host. It took the trash TV, tabloid talk-show epidemic of the 1990s to discover the ratings gold mine of pitting guest against guest under the sleaziest possible pretext—and rabid studio audiences roared in delight at the obscenity-bleeped, hair-pulling punchfests that resulted. Jenny Jones, Ricki Lake, Geraldo Rivera and Jerry Springer ("the emcee of our darker side," TV GUIDE called him in '98) flourished by turning afternoons into an exploitation circus. When guests of Jones and Springer were later murdered in what seemed to be emotional fallout from the shows, both hosts claimed only a remote connection to the actual content of the productions and their guests. "I show up and I do the show. I have no idea who they are," he told TV GUIDE in 2000. But Springer had a pretty good idea of who he was. When he was beating *The Oprah Winfrey Show* consistently in the ratings in 1998, he told the magazine: "It's not fair to Oprah to put me in the same conversation as her. She's made a positive imprint on the medium."

THE GONG SHOW
Chuck Barris. NBC, 1976–78; syndication, 1976–80

The dislocated, post-'60s pop culture of the mid-'70s never looked more merrily bizarre than during *The Gong Show*'s day and night half hours. Here, an endless stream of the talentless but indefatigable—a dentist playing "Stars and Stripes Forever" with his drill, for instance—was rated by a panel of B-list celebrities. (Jaye P. Morgan, Jamie Farr and Phyllis Diller were regulars.) The truly bad got gonged, the winners pelted with confetti by a midget. "People always like to see other people fed to the lions," frenetic host and producer Chuck Barris told TV GUIDE in 1978. "To get out there and be tormented, that takes guts." Guts: required. Talent: optional.

DONAHUE
Syndication, 1970–96
COVER: **BY ARNOLD ZANN, MAY 27, 1978**

Before Oprah Winfrey, Sally Jessy Raphaël and all the rest of the microphone-clutching, guest-prodding, audience-challenging daytime talk-show hosts, there was Phil Donahue. Those TV heirs "are all my illegitimate children, and I love them all equally," Donahue told TV GUIDE in 1992, 25 years after the daddy of all audience-participation talk shows started out in Dayton, Ohio, with *The Phil Donahue Show*. Though he certainly did his share of non-sensational shows—presidential candidate Bill Clinton was a guest in '92—Donahue cheerfully admitted that "sometimes you have to tap-dance a little faster to draw a crowd.... We got here by being outrageous. We've televised an abortion and the birth of a baby. I've wrestled women, belly danced and was thrown out of a Roller Derby ring. I've been body wrapped, acupunctured. We are tabloid—I'm happy to wear the label." He was also happy to wear a skirt for a transvestite fashion show in 1988, though Donahue told the magazine that his wife, actress Marlo Thomas—whom he met as a guest on his show—wasn't so thrilled. She "felt that this would give critics a big opportunity to take potshots." But the only potential critics Donahue himself worried about were his millions of largely female fans, who were represented by his studio audience ("Wait a minute," he'd say, interrupting guests and looking out into the crowd, "there's a lot of wisdom out here"). "The secret of it all," TV GUIDE said in 1978, "is that Donahue has one quality that is almost nonexistent" among TV interviewers: "He still cares. He still thinks that somehow, some way, it all matters." *Donahue* closed down in 1996, and its silver-haired host seemed to retire from television. But he apparently got bored being on the other side of the TV screen: In 2002, at age 66, he signed up to host a new talk show on cable-news channel MSNBC.

THE OPRAH WINFREY SHOW

Clockwise from left: Winfrey with Toni Morrison; Nelson Mandela; Tina Turner. Syndication, 1986–

COVERS (FROM TOP): BY PAUL ELLEDGE, JANUARY 7, 1995, AND MAY 16, 1992

There was a specific moment when it became clear that Oprah Winfrey was going to become an unprecedented hit on television. Early in 1984, the Baltimore talk-show cohost took on the thankless task of turning around a bottom-dwelling morning chat show in Chicago, home base of Phil Donahue. Two months later, Winfrey was beating Donahue on his own turf. If she could do that, she obviously could do anything—as Winfrey quickly demonstrated, becoming within a few years the unrivaled ruler of the daytime television landscape. Witness the power of "Oprah's Book Club," which turned unknown authors into household names. Appraising the Oprah phenomenon on a more personal level, TV GUIDE said, "She is a one-woman mission hell-bent on lifting other women out of their self-image as helpless victims." One advantage was that her own life had been an *Oprah*-worthy nightmare: a childhood spent shuttling from one caregiver to another, troubled teenage years, an adulthood with an emotionally traumatic romance and a lifelong struggle with her weight. The drama on her show came from guests and audience members, who spoke unguardedly in her presence knowing that if they cried, she would be there to cry with them, offer a hug and, in one case, confess that she, too, had been sexually abused as a child. "People like me because they see themselves in me," Winfrey told TV GUIDE. "That's how it is on TV. It's either, 'I want to be like that,' or 'I *am* like that.'" Winfrey offered both options: She had struggled and suffered, but at the same time she was now a daily advertisement for the power of personal responsibility. She had become, after all, one of the richest entertainers—one of the richest *people*—in America. "My feet are still planted firmly on the ground," she told the magazine in '88, after syndication of *The Oprah Winfrey Show* had made her a millionaire. "They're just wearing more expensive shoes."

WHAT WE ALL CAN DO TO CHANGE TV

It was a night that changed my life forever. Sunday night, December 27, 1964. The Supremes were on *The Ed Sullivan Show*. It was the first time I had seen a black woman on television with such beauty and grace. I was a 10-year-old girl sitting on a cold linoleum floor in Milwaukee. I was inspired by the possibilities of what I would be. That, to me, is one of television's greatest functions: to inspire us, to give us hope and to help us improve our lives.

I always felt better after watching *The Andy Griffith Show*. Life was so simple—the characters all really cared for one another, and the biggest scandal was whether those were really Aunt Bee's pickles in the pickle contest. Even though I never saw a black person in Mayberry, I always thought that if one of us dropped in, Andy and Aunt Bee would give us a slice of pie and make us feel right at home.

Another one of my favorites was *The Mary Tyler Moore Show*. Mar' showed every young woman that independence was worth obtaining—she showed us the possibilities. Watching the show made me feel good about being a single woman with a career in the '70s. I wanted an *O* on my wall, because Mar' had an *M* on hers. I mourned the day *The Mary Tyler Moore Show* went off the air. It left a void. Television was never the same for me.

Since then, I rarely watch TV—not even my own show.... And for years, I made it a point never to watch other talk shows—I didn't want to be accused of imitation. But because there's been so much criticism of the genre, I began

looking around recently to see what all the fuss was about.

Picture me at home, flipping through the channels to see what I can find.

Aha—here's a talk show. The host is telling us that not even he knows which of his guests is telling the truth. We can call a 900 number and decide if a guy who looks like a Barry White wannabe is really the father of this teenager's baby. Is he lying? Is she? The call will cost 75 cents. *Click!*

Another talk show, this one with a kissing contest. I imagine there is an audience for this, judging by the reaction of the kiss-cheering supporters. *Click!*

The next day, I catch another talk show, and the issue is "Men Who Are Dogs." I can't believe it. The men are discussing the number of babies they have fathered and the number of women they have had—and they have the audacity to boast about it.

All this is in my mind a few weeks later when I am deciding whether to keep my own show going—or quit. I wonder, is this a sign that my time in TV has come and gone? I believe life gives you subtle and sometimes not-so-subtle messages that can guide you to the right answers. Should I just get out of the business and let the "Kissing Contest," "Men Who Are Dogs" and "Big-Butt Contest" rule? Another host did that show, with Nipsey Russell as one of the judges. Yes, Nipsey Russell of *To Tell the*

Truth is now rating the size of women's behinds on national television. Why?

I understand that the push for ratings causes programmers to air what's popular, and that's not going to change. I am embarrassed by how far over the line the topics have gone, but I also recognize my own contribution to this phenomenon.

Ten years ago, when my show was first syndicated, we started doing what we called "confrontational TV"—adult incest survivors confronting their abusers, children of alcoholics confronting their parents and victims of crime confronting the people who attacked them.

I believe it was important to introduce these issues and face the truth of who we were. We grew up in a society that for years denied dysfunction. TV brought some of that to the surface, but the problem, as I see it now, is that it didn't evolve from there. We needed to be solving these problems. Instead, TV got stuck *thriving* on them, and for the worst possible reasons— exploitation, voyeurism and entertainment.

This became very clear during my most humiliating moment on television. A man came on the show with his wife and mistress. Both women had given birth to children—his children—in the same time period. Neither woman knew it, and they found out on my show. The audience gasped. I was speechless. It's irrelevant that neither I nor the producers knew this bombshell was coming—because the pain on their faces remains a memory seared in my brain. People should not be surprised and humiliated on national television for the purpose of entertainment. I was ashamed of myself for creating the opportunity that allowed it to happen.

For many days afterward, I thought about them. What happened in the grocery store? Did the checkout clerk say, "Aren't you the woman whose husband was cheating?" How did their coworkers react? Were their mothers embarrassed?

Well, that was five years ago. As my friend and mentor Maya Angelou always says, "You did then what you knew how to do. When you knew better, you did better."

Since then, I've done a thousand more shows, shook 200,000 more hands and come to understand the power of this great medium a lot more. When I began my talk show, I was so thrilled to have the opportunity that I never thought much about the tremendous influence TV could have. Now I feel both the power and the enormous responsibility that come with it.

Thirty-seven years ago, Edward R. Murrow said of television, "This instrument can teach, it can illuminate—yes, and it can even inspire. But it can do so only to the extent that humans are determined to use it to those ends. Otherwise, it is merely wires and lights in a box." He continued, "There is a great and decisive battle to be fought against ignorance, intolerance and indifference. This weapon of television could be useful."

I believe we can use television for incredible changes, but only to the extent that people demand it. We all must ask for more shows that are positive and uplifting, that give messages of hope and possibility. I think of the 10-year-old girls sitting on the floor watching TV today, and wonder if there are shows on the air that will inspire them as I was inspired. We need shows with images of life as we would like it to be. We need to ask programmers for positive role models for ourselves and our children, for television that will strengthen the human spirit.

Television, like life, provides choices. By controlling the choices you make, you change what TV offers. It's only when viewers decide that they've had enough of violence, sensationalism and trash that it will end. Television is a reflection of who we are and who we say we want to be. It's time to offer new choices, new possibilities. It's time to elevate our potential.

—OPRAH WINFREY, EXCERPT FROM TV GUIDE, NOVEMBER 11, 1995

MTV

Carson Daly of *Total Request Live* **with fans**
COVER: BY LORRAINE DAY, AUGUST 3, 1991

As every trivia buff knows, the cable music-video network MTV launched in 1981 with the Buggles' "Video Killed the Radio Star," and as the rest of the world knows, almost nothing involving visual art has ever been the same. The music business was transformed by the network's star-making ability, of course (hello, Cyndi Lauper, Madonna, Duran Duran, et al.), but television, movies, advertising, fashion...you name the creative endeavor, and MTV's DNA is probably in there somewhere. Over time, the network began playing fewer and fewer videos as their visual-shorthand novelty wore off (even Michael Jackson's innovative "Thriller" video got old after the 73rd viewing) and found new success in other areas of programming, from the diabolical genius of the *Beavis and Butt-head* cartoon and *Celebrity Deathmatch* claymation to the trendsetting inspiration of *The Real World* (a reality-TV forerunner) and the network's biggest hit yet, *The Osbournes*. But MTV hasn't totally abandoned its music-video roots—just listen to the fan frenzy surrounding the countdown show *Total Request Live*. As Aerosmith lead singer Steven Tyler told TV GUIDE on the network's 20 anniversary, "MTV is like a stake in the tent of the rock and roll circus. It's really that integral." Thanks to the onetime upstart cable channel, the tent is now pitched daily in 350 million households worldwide, in 140 countries.

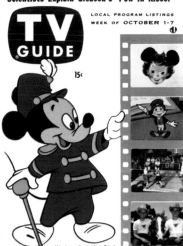

MICKEY MOUSE CLUB
Walt Disney with Mouseketeers. ABC, 1955–59
COVER: BY WALT DISNEY PRODS., OCTOBER 1, 1955

A year after the show's 1955 debut, *Mickey Mouse Club* director Sidney Miller—himself a former child actor—told TV GUIDE what a relief it was to be working with "normal kids," most of whom just "happened to take dancing or singing lessons when they were younger," compared with the showbiz brats he'd grown up beside. The normalcy of the Mouseketeers, along with a five-times-a-week afterschool time slot, might help explain the show's devoted following and, decades later, the warm memories many have of the M-I-C-K-E-Y theme song. The two dozen Mouseketeers introduced cartoons, acted in filmed serials, danced, sang and formed the audience for visitors (Tuesday was "Guest Star Day" and Friday was "Talent Roundup Day," when young performers were made honorary Mouseketeers). Oddly, only one breakout star emerged during the show's four years on the air. It was the girl, said a perplexed TV GUIDE, whose "singing is just adequate and whose dancing is only fair...neither brilliant nor dull, neither stagestruck, lazy nor ambitious." Still, those limitations didn't stop Annette Funicello from going on to beach-blanket immortality in the 1960s—helped along, no doubt, by legions of adolescent former *Mickey Mouse Club* fans.

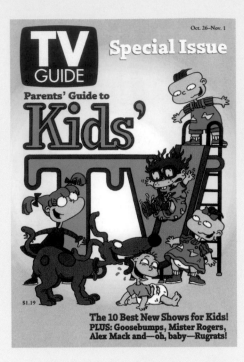

Oct. 26–Nov. 1

TV GUIDE

Special Issue

Parents' Guide to

Kids' TV

$1.19

The 10 Best New Shows for Kids!
PLUS: Goosebumps, Mister Rogers,
Alex Mack and—oh, baby—Rugrats!

RUGRATS
Nickelodeon, 1991–
COVER: BY NICKELODEON, OCTOBER 26, 1996

"Animated" was the last word you'd apply to the kids' cartoon genre in the 1980s—the moribund format hadn't seen a spark of invention since Bullwinkle last tried to pull a rabbit out of his hat in the 1960s. But then, in 1991, *Rugrats* toddled onto the Nickelodeon schedule, helping to ignite a new era of creativity fostered by kid-oriented cable channels hungry for programming. Even a decade later, with the airwaves brimming with fresh cartoons like *The Powerpuff Girls* and *SpongeBob SquarePants*, *Rugrats* remains a major player,

presenting its tyke's-eye view of the world long after good-hearted Tommy and his best pal, the fearful Chuckie, should have been in junior high. Instead, they carry on in a universe where the fridge can be scary and potty training a nightmare. Gabor Csupo, cocreator of the show, told TV GUIDE in 1998: "You have to watch it to realize it's not just for babies. We write on two levels: for kids and adults." Which helps explain why parents, instead of groaning when the *Rugrats* theme song sounds, often sink into the sofa to watch, too.

"WHEN YOU'RE MAKING ANIMATED TELEVISION FOR CHILDREN,

you should never talk down to them and you should give them a lot of credit. They're smart, and they want to see something new or fresh or funny so they can talk about it. You can't hit them over the head with educational stuff because they can smell that from a mile away. And kids want to be entertained. If you can entertain and sneak in some cool information, that's the best way to do it. And if the cartoons are funny and they're telling a good story with great characters, it doesn't matter if they're stick figures or beautifully rendered three-dimensional computer animation. If it holds your attention and it's engaging, then it can be anything."

—GABOR CSUPO, COCREATOR OF *RUGRATS*, *THE WILD THORNBERRYS* AND *ROCKET POWER*

ABC AFTERSCHOOL SPECIALS
Sharon Lee (Jodie Foster) of "Rookie of the Year" (1973).
ABC, 1972–96

ABC Afterschool Specials didn't have a unifying theme, other than trying to put something more substantial than *Brady Bunch* reruns in front of school-age kids. The specials ran the programming gamut and included documentaries, interviews, cartoons (like Hanna-Barbera's eco-minded "Last of the Curlews," 1972), dramas (such as 1980's "Schoolboy Father," starring Rob Lowe) and discussions (the Oprah Winfrey–moderated program "Shades of a Single Protein," 1993, about race). The shows themselves were not always as memorable as some of their amusingly direct titles—"Me and My Hormones," "Can a Guy Say No?" and "Please Don't Hit Me, Mom." Nevertheless, the term "afterschool special" lives on—as a loose synonym for any mild entertainment with a worthy message.

GENERAL HOSPITAL
Laura Spencer (Genie Francis), Luke Spencer (Anthony Geary). ABC, 1963–
COVERS (FROM TOP): BY PETER KREDENSER, AUGUST 23, 1980. BY MARIO CASILLI, JULY 17, 1982

General Hospital premiered on April Fools' Day in 1963, and more than once over the course of the next four decades, the soap opera appeared to be pulling the audience's leg—a villain's diabolical plot to freeze the entire city of Port Charles, the hospital's hometown, comes to mind. But as TV GUIDE said in 1972, "if you'll promise not to breathe a word of it to a living soul, we just love this show. It's really so awful that it is, in its awful way, wonderful." The wonderful awfulness reached a sort of peak in 1981 when the wedding of Luke and Laura drew the biggest audience ever for a daytime drama. Your heart had to go out to the bride after all she'd been through: While still a teen, Laura had killed a boyfriend who was sleeping with her mother, joined a commune and married her childhood sweetheart before falling for a shady character who, despite raping her in a deserted disco, still held a claim on her affection. Oh, the troubles Laura had known! Not that her fellow characters couldn't empathize: Life in Port Charles often seemed to be just one long string of car wrecks, murders, disappearances, amnesia attacks, nervous breakdowns and Byzantine romantic entanglements. It was the top-rated soap for much of the 1980s, with much of the credit going to producer Gloria Monty, who kept those story lines rattling. (Having pop star Rick Springfield in the cast didn't hurt, either.) In 1996, the death of actor John Beradino, who played *General Hospital*'s director of medicine, Steve Hardy, marked the passing of the show's last original cast member. But *General Hospital* itself would not die. It finished the decade with respectable ratings, steaming toward 2003 and its 40th anniversary as one of TV's greatest successes.

WEDDING OF PRINCE CHARLES AND LADY DIANA
July 29, 1981
COVER: BY RICHARD AMSEL, JULY 25, 1981

Regardless of all that would later transpire, the wedding of Prince Charles and Lady Diana Spencer was a truly enchanting moment. It was a celebration of "the consummation of love and the hope of a posterity," as author Anthony Burgess wrote in TV GUIDE in anticipation of the event, which was seen by a worldwide television audience of 750 million (including many Americans who had to get up as early as 5 A.M. Eastern Time to catch the festivities). "The common man has had too complete a triumph and has dressed us all in gray," Burgess wrote. "It will be a shot in the arm to see gold and scarlet and purple again, and to hear the silver trumpets."

ALL MY CHILDREN

Bianca Montgomery (Eden Riegel), Erica Kane (Susan Lucci),
Jack Montgomery (Walt Willey). ABC, 1970–
COVER: BY ROGER PRIGENT, NOVEMBER 10, 1990

Launched during the social tumult of 1970, *All My Children* immediately distinguished itself from the competition by grappling with hot-button topics of the day. Not that the denizens of the fictional New York City suburb of Pine Valley neglected to pursue more customary concerns—many of which revolved around the evil queen of all bitches, Erica Kane, a role that Susan Lucci made "the most famous soap-opera character in the history of daytime TV," as TV GUIDE declared in 1989. *AMC* fans are particularly devoted, even by soap standards: Carol Burnett had already been a three-time guest star when she told the magazine in '89, "I can't get through the day without it."

"I THINK DAYTIME TELEVISION HAS BEEN QUITE GROUNDBREAKING.

And I feel so lucky to have been part of it. This is really [creator] Agnes Nixon's doing. Before I ever came onto the *All My Children* canvas, she was known for addressing important social issues. That's a hallmark of Agnes's work. My character, Erica, had the first legal abortion on daytime television, and recently we did a really innovative and beautifully written two-year story line about the relationship between Erica and her 16-year-old daughter, Bianca, who was coming out about being gay.

"Also, we have the luxury of time. That's what daytime drama has that other mediums don't. Because it's five days a week with no hiatus, you can explore things very realistically and with continuity. There doesn't have to be a cliff-hanger at the end of 13 or 22 weeks. You can continue exploring issues and do so in a lot of detail—which allows someone like Agnes, who has a social conscience as well as a tremendous ability to entertain, to do groundbreaking work. It gives her the perfect forum. This luxury of time also allows you to have better character development and lets the viewers get to know the characters. They grow very attached. Erica has really been naughty over the years, but viewers have also seen all the underpinnings, so they understand her better. She's a complicated character, and they get to love her *and* hate her."

—SUSAN LUCCI

THE ASSASSINATION AND FUNERAL OF PRESIDENT JOHN F. KENNEDY

Clockwise from far left: John F. Kennedy Jr.; Lee Harvey Oswald, Jack Ruby; Lyndon B. Johnson, Jacqueline Kennedy. November 22–25, 1963

COVER: BY ARTHUR WILLIAMS, JANUARY 25, 1964

It was 1:40 P.M. Eastern Time on Friday, November 22, 1963, when the words CBS BULLETIN blacked out the live production of *As the World Turns.* "In Dallas, Texas, three shots were fired at President Kennedy's motorcade," intoned the voice of Walter Cronkite. "The first reports say the president was seriously wounded...." Over the next four convulsive days, television was transformed. It would no longer be just the most dominant form of national entertainment. Instead, it found that it could also bear witness for an entire country, if not the world, and make an "historic contribution," as President Lyndon B. Johnson wrote in a special section of TV GUIDE two months later.

The section was the magazine's attempt to combat the fleeting nature of the medium and provide "a permanent reminder" of what the nation had experienced in those four days of nonstop news coverage. Indeed, the magazine pointed out, certain TV images remain indelible parts of the national memory: distraught news anchors struggling to maintain their composure as they confirm Kennedy's death; Jacqueline Kennedy, still in her blood-spattered pink suit, arriving with the casket and a new president in Washington; the still unbelievable live coverage of Lee Harvey Oswald being shot by Jack Ruby; John-John's heartbreaking salute to his father's casket.

But there were many smaller moments, too. Among the anchors who hurried on to the air and stayed for hours, the magazine said, "it was Cronkite who agonized the most and controlled it best." NBC took its cameras outside in New York City, capturing grief-stricken reactions of people gathered on the sidewalk who were hearing the news from car radios. ABC replayed tape taken earlier that day of the president and first lady, smiling and bathed in sunlight, arriving at the Dallas airport. Condolence statements were broadcast from former president Dwight D. Eisenhower, Gen. Douglas MacArthur and former Illinois governor Adlai Stevenson. That night, viewers saw Oswald led through the Dallas police station, a scene of bedlam that foretold Sunday's disaster. It was also on Sunday that about a quarter of a million citizens began filing past Kennedy's body, lying in state in the Capitol rotunda. Viewing that scene, Edward P. Morgan on ABC said to his colleague, Howard K. Smith: "You keep thinking, Howard, that this is a dream from which you will awake—but you won't."

On Monday, the entire nation witnessed the stately funeral. "This was," said Charles Collingwood at CBS, "the day we were restored to sanity." It was also a time of beginning, TV GUIDE noted, for a new government and a new era in television. The medium had "gained a new sense of what it could do," a sense that it was "capable of encompassing not just life's trivia, but the deepest of human experience."

WE, THE TV JURY

How and why we watched the true-crime story of the century

PLUS: Top TV trials

O.J. SIMPSON BRONCO CHASE
June 17, 1994
COVER: BY MARK MALABRIGO,
JULY 30, 1994

TV GUIDE simply called it "O.J.: The News as Miniseries." And that was in July 1994, when the country had only been through the slo-mo Bronco chase (seen by 95 million TV viewers) and pretrial hearings. The bloody glove, DNA evidence and LAPD officer Mark Fuhrman all lay ahead, in the gripping, tedious and appalling criminal trial of O.J. Simpson for the stabbing deaths of his ex-wife, Nicole Brown Simpson, and her visitor, waiter Ronald Goldman. Author Neal Gabler, writing in that issue of the magazine, called the story "the news equivalent of a great beach read"—with a football hero, a gorgeous blond, tempestuous romance, etc.—but he also pondered the overwhelming news coverage of the case. "The media are no longer primarily purveyors of information," Gabler wrote, "they are purveyors of drama." They are also great ones, he said, for turning a trashy melodrama into "a festival of national reflection and self-criticism." Whatever the meaning of Simpson's eventual acquittal on criminal charges and his loss in a subsequent civil trial, Gabler recognized that it all would play out in a "theater called America," where the nation would find "a common subject, if not exactly common ground."

CHALLENGER
January 28, 1986
COVER: BY NASA, FEBRUARY 24, 1990

Throughout the 1960s, space exploration was the repository of the nation's dreams, with families clustering around TV sets to share in the communal pursuit. But by the mid-'80s, rocket launches from Cape Canaveral were barely even noteworthy—that is, until one devastating day in 1986. There was the usual thunderous liftoff, the slow, powerful climb into the Florida sky. Then came the horrible explosion, the smoking debris plummeting for what seemed like an eternity down into the Atlantic. Once again, Americans huddled around their TV sets, only this time it was not to celebrate, but to mourn the stunning loss of seven lives.

"SEPTEMBER 11 WAS SUCH A HUGE TRAGEDY,

but in a terrible way, it brought the television news business back. We'd been doing half-hour news programs, with 10 minutes of news and then [the rest] like a magazine piece: 'You and Your Money.' 'You and Your Health.' 'You and Your Diet.' TV newsmagazines were doing celebrities. We were doing movie stars in trouble. The week before 9/11, I had a 30-minute interview with Anne Heche.

"It was horrific, but for the industry it made a big difference. After 9/11, all of us were mobilized. We were doing reports and special interviews. We were on all the time. On *20/20*, we did almost every program live. One of my colleagues sent me an e-mail: 'What a terrible tragedy. But isn't it amazing that we're now back in the news business?'"

—BARBARA WALTERS

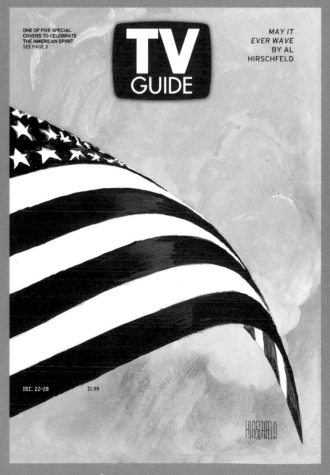

ONE OF FIVE SPECIAL COVERS TO CELEBRATE THE AMERICAN SPIRIT SEE PAGE 3

TV GUIDE

MAY IT EVER WAVE BY AL HIRSCHFELD

DEC. 22–28 $1.99

HIRSCHFELD

SEPTEMBER 11, 2001
Police officers at the World Trade Center, New York City, September 12, 2001
COVER: BY AL HIRSCHFELD, DECEMBER 22, 2001

Television has never seemed more pitiless as an unblinking witness to history than it was on September 11, 2001. The still unbelievable images of jetliners smashing into the World Trade Center towers, and of the buildings' dumbfounding, terrible collapse, will stay with viewers for the rest of their lives. But as TV GUIDE said later that month, the medium's coverage of the aftermath of the terror attacks—in New York City; Washington, D.C.; and Pennsylvania, where United Airlines Flight 93 crashed—also "provided a reassuring reminder that we were all in this together. Our enemies hadn't destroyed our ability to communicate: to share grief, express hope and investigate the truth."

EDWARD R. MURROW
From top: 1959; 1951
COVER: BY AL HIRSCHFELD,
NOVEMBER 3, 1956

"For courage, intelligence and dignity," TV GUIDE said in 1958 of Edward R. Murrow's *See It Now* documentary series, "it has demonstrated an excellence rare in any form of journalism." Murrow tackled civil rights, the smoking/cancer link and, most memorably, Sen. Joseph McCarthy's anti-Communist witch-hunt, setting a standard that reporters have aspired to for generations. As author Theodore H. White wrote in TV GUIDE in '86: "His exploration of television's new range was so powerful in its impact on our dreams and lives that in American journalism only Horace Greeley and Walter Lippmann matched him in shaping our history."

How To Pick The Election Winner Early
See Page 8

TV GUIDE
LOCAL PROGRAM
LISTINGS · WEEK OF
NOVEMBER 3—9
15¢

Edward R. Murrow

and THAT'S the WAY IT IS

THE MAN WHO HAS THE LAST LAUGH ON TV *see page 3*

TV GUIDE
15¢ • Local Programs • July 2-8

WALTER CRONKITE
From top: 1960; Cronkite
with John F. Kennedy, 1960
COVER: BY PHILIPPE HALSMAN,
JULY 2, 1966

"I never did have any desire to be a pundit," Walter Cronkite told TV GUIDE in 1966, recalling his days as a reporter before being installed as the *CBS Evening News* anchor in '62, "though I do like to think I have always brought a certain compassion to my coverage." That instinctive sensitivity, along with a comfortable but authoritative manner, helped make Cronkite the definitive network-news anchor for 19 years. Every major event of the '60s and '70s—John F. Kennedy's assassination, the *Apollo* rocket launches, Vietnam, political conventions, Watergate—seemed to have the same narrator: the voice most trusted by America.

CNN AND THE GULF WAR
Antiaircraft fire over
Baghdad, Iraq,
January 18, 1991

"There has never been anything like the way that television has colored, shadowed, illuminated and distorted the war in the Persian Gulf," veteran media analyst Jeff Greenfield wrote in TV GUIDE in 1991, as Operation Desert Storm unfolded. During those riveting days, CNN for a time became our only window into bomb-rocked Baghdad, Iraq, thanks to a special phone line that enabled the cable channel to keep reporting long after the major news networks were knocked off the air. The networks had no choice but to broadcast their rival's coverage, and officials of countless governments tuned in to stay informed. Although CNN had been around for a decade, it was the Gulf War that finally vindicated the concept of a 24-hour news channel.

"Nothing changed news coverage like the advent of CNN. Its impact has enormously affected every aspect of broadcasting. Twenty-four-hour news changed the world."
—Larry King

BROADCAST NEWS
COVERS: BY PHILIPPE HALSMAN, JULY 9, 1960. BY RICHARD AMSEL, OCTOBER 26, 1985

In May 2002, when Tom Brokaw announced his intention to retire as *NBC Nightly News* anchor in two years and the network said it planned to install Brian Williams in his chair, it was only fitting. Brokaw's retirement would mark the end of nearly a half century when network anchors incontestably ruled TV news; Williams would be coming over from MSNBC, one of the 24-hour cable-news operations that had helped make it unlikely we would ever again see network anchors accorded the status they enjoyed for decades. Though television had offered news reports since its infancy, it wasn't until NBC teamed sober, seasoned correspondent Chet Huntley with a young and wryly detached David Brinkley in 1956 that the modern network-news era got under way. *The Huntley-Brinkley Report*'s brisk pace and wide range (for starters, Huntley reported from New York City, Brinkley from Washington, D.C.) made it the dominant news show for most of its 14 years. Meanwhile, a tradition of granite stability developed at CBS, with Douglas Edwards in the 1950s, Walter Cronkite and his fabled tenure in the '60s and '70s, and Dan Rather ("equal parts Will Rogers and Edward R. Murrow," TV GUIDE said in 2002), who took over as anchor in 1981 and began a run of more than two decades. That time included a 1993-95 session of coanchoring with Connie Chung—a chemistry-free arrangement spurred by the rise of the longtime underachiever, ABC's *World News Tonight*, which began thriving after Peter Jennings's arrival in '83. Jennings built a reputation as the "go-to anchor in times of crisis," TV GUIDE said in 2001, an assessment that was prompted by September 11, 2001, and its aftermath. Though the age of the network anchor might be waning, or maybe just changing, that emergency reminded us why the need for a reliable, calm and clear source of news will always remain.

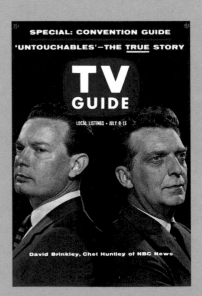

TV GUIDE

Oct. 26–Nov. 1
60¢

Network News Today:
Which Counts More—
Journalism or Profits?
Page 6

·AMSEL·

Advice to
<u>Tom Selleck</u>
Why
Magnum
Must Get
Tougher,
More
Passionate
By Romance Novelist
Janet Dailey
Page 16

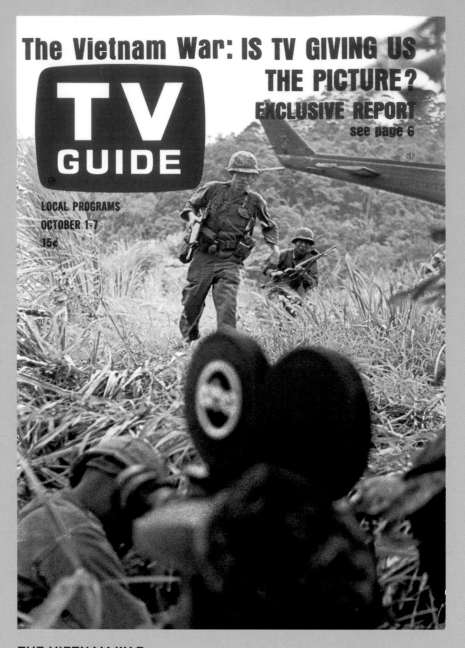

THE VIETNAM WAR

COVER: BY NEIL HICKEY, OCTOBER 1, 1966

In September 1973, eight months after the United States and North Vietnam signed a cease-fire agreement and the Vietnam War started to come to its ragged conclusion, TV GUIDE began publishing a three-part investigation of television's role in reporting more than 10 years of conflict and in shaping public opinion. Even then, the conventional wisdom that prevails three decades later had already begun to form: It was the sight of bloody American soldiers and body bags on the nightly news that turned public opinion against the war. But that assumption was "not warranted," said TV GUIDE, after reviewing a decade's worth of network newscasts. "Television was neither monolithic nor consistent in its coverage and commentaries." Indeed, as the Vietnam War progressed, so did the nature of the televised war—and public opinion with it. In the period between 1962 and 1968, the magazine reported, a time when TV reporters were shuttled around the war zone by military press officers in helicopters, coverage focused on the overwhelming technological advantage of the growing U.S. force. In 1967, a *Newsweek* magazine poll found that 64 percent of Americans said that TV news broadcasts made them *more* supportive of American involvement in Vietnam. Then came the Tet Offensive in 1968, when "the televised picture of gradual progress in the war was abruptly shattered." With Saigon under assault, TV GUIDE reported, "merely by stepping outside their hotels, correspondents found themselves willy-nilly in the midst of bloody fighting." Reporters scrambled to get footage of the chaos and violence, and networks paid for expensive satellite transmissions to rush those dispatches to the air. Even though the Tet Offensive was successfully repulsed and the Vietcong grievously damaged by their losses, they "paradoxically won a decisive psychological victory in America," TV GUIDE said. "The American public was unable to digest the unprecedented violence and gore they saw during Tet." CBS newsman Walter Cronkite was equally stunned; he flew to Vietnam to gauge the situation himself and, upon returning, told his viewers the war was a "bloody stalemate." That appeared to be an assessment almost universal in network newsrooms, and post-Tet coverage reflected it, until peace negotiations began in late '68 and "television gradually changed its focus to the story of the American withdrawal," TV GUIDE said. The magazine's series ended with these words: "It is no doubt true that television was to a large extent responsible for the disillusionment with the war, as those in the media take relish in pointing out. But it is also true that television must take the responsibility for creating—or at least reinforcing—the illusion of American military omnipotence on which much of the early support of the war was based."

KENNEDY-NIXON PRESIDENTIAL DEBATES
Below: Sen. John F. Kennedy, Frank McGee, Vice President Richard M. Nixon. September 26, October 7, October 13, October 21, 1960

The prevailing opinion is that the 1960 presidential election just may have hinged on these unprecedented TV debates, when a sweaty, ill-at-ease Vice President Richard M. Nixon, who had disdained wearing makeup, wilted under Sen. John F. Kennedy's charismatic gleam. While experts are still debating the ultimate impact of "The Great Debates," as they were billed, one point is inarguable: The face-offs revealed television's tremendous power to shape public perceptions of a candidate.

A FORCE
THAT HAS CHANGED
THE POLITICAL SCENE

The wonders of science and technology have revolutionized the modern American political campaign. Giant electronic brains project results on the basis of carefully conducted polls. Automatic typewriters prepare thousands of personally addressed letters, individually signed by automatic pens. Jet planes make possible a coast-to-coast speaking schedule no observation-car back platform could ever meet. Even wash-and-wear fabrics permit the wilted nonstop candidate to travel lighter, farther and faster.

But nothing compares with the revolutionary impact of television. TV has altered drastically the nature of our political campaigns, conventions, constituents, candidates and costs. Some politicians regard it with suspicion, others with pleasure. Some candidates have been advised to avoid it. To the voter and vote getter alike, TV offers new opportunities, new challenges and new problems.

But for better or worse—and I side with those who feel its net effect can definitely be for the better—the impact of TV on politics is tremendous. Just 40 years ago, Woodrow Wilson exhausted his body and mind in an intensive cross–country tour to plead the cause of the League of Nations. Three weeks of hard travel and 40 speeches brought on a stroke before he had finished "taking his case to the people" in the only way then available. Today, President Dwight D. Eisenhower, taking his case to the people on the labor situation, is able to reach several million in one 15-minute period without ever leaving his office.

Many new political reputations have been made on TV—and many old ones have been broken. The searching eye of the television camera scrutinizes the candidates—and the way they are picked. Party leaders are less willing to run roughshod over the voters' wishes and handpick an unknown, unappealing or unpopular candidate in the traditional "smoke-filled room" when millions of voters are watching, comparing and remembering.

The slick or bombastic orator, pounding the table and ringing the rafters, is not as welcome in the family living room as he was in the town square or party hall. In the old days, many a seasoned politician counted among his most highly developed and useful talents his ability to dodge a reporter's question, evade a "hot" issue and avoid a definite stand. But today a vast viewing public is able to detect such deception and, in my opinion, willing to respect political honesty.

Honesty, vigor, compassion, intelligence—the presence or lack of these and other qualities make up what is called the candidate's "image." While some intellectuals and politicians may scoff at these images—and while they may in fact be based only on a candidate's TV impression, ignoring his record, views and other appearances—my own conviction is that these images or impressions are likely to be uncannily correct. I think, no matter what their defenders or detractors may say, that the television public has a fairly good idea of what Eisenhower is really like—or Jimmy Hoffa or John McClellan or Vice President Nixon or countless others.

This is why a new breed of candidates has sprung up on both the state and national levels. Most of these men are comparatively young. Their youth may still be a handicap in the eyes of older politicians—but it is definitely an asset in creating a television image people like and (most difficult of all) remember.

This is not to say that all the politicians of yesteryear would have been failures in the Age of Television. The rugged vigor of Teddy Roosevelt, the determined sincerity of Woodrow Wilson, the quiet dignity of Abraham Lincoln and the confidence-inspiring calm of Franklin D. Roosevelt—all would have been tremendously effective on television.

Can you imagine the effect of televising FDR's "fireside chats"?

But political success on television is not, unfortunately, limited only to those who deserve it. It is a medium that lends itself to manipulation, exploitation and gimmicks. It can be abused by demagogues, by appeals to emotion and prejudice and ignorance.

Political campaigns can actually be taken over by the public relations experts, who tell the candidate not only how to use TV but what to say, what to stand for and what "kind of person" to be. Political shows, like quiz shows, can be fixed—and sometimes are.

The other great problem TV presents for politics is the item of financial cost. It is no small item. In the 1956 campaign, the Republican National Committee, according to the Gore report, spent over $3 million for television—and the Democratic National Committee, just under $2.8 million on television broadcasting.

If all candidates and parties are to have equal access to this essential and decisive campaign medium, without becoming deeply obligated to the big financial contributors from the worlds of business, labor or other major lobbies, then the time has come when a solution must be found to this problem of TV costs.

This is not the place to discuss alternative remedies. But the basic point is this: Whether TV improves or worsens our political system, whether it serves the purpose of political education or deception, whether it gives us better or poorer candidates, more intelligent or more prejudiced campaigns—the answers to all these questions are up to you, the viewing public.

It is your power to perceive deception, to shut off gimmickry, to reward honesty, to demand legislation where needed. Without your approval, no TV show is worthwhile and no politician can exist.

That is the way it always has been and will continue to be—and that is the way it should be.

—SEN. JOHN F. KENNEDY,
EXCERPT FROM TV GUIDE, NOVEMBER 14, 1959

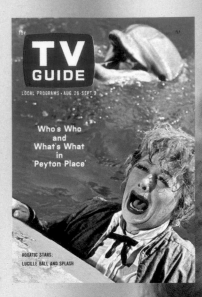

Who's Who
and
What's What
in
'Peyton Place'

AQUATIC STARS:
LUCILLE BALL AND SPLASH

LUCILLE BALL
1957. Opposite page, top:
Ethel Mertz (Vivian Vance),
Lucy Ricardo (Ball), Ricky
Ricardo (Desi Arnaz), Fred
Mertz (William Frawley)
of *I Love Lucy*
COVER: BY SHEEDY-LONG,
AUGUST 28, 1965

Hollywood studio heads took one look at the luminous beauty of Lucille Ball and thought, "Glamour girl." It required the fledgling medium of television—and the roll-the-dice attitude of its pioneers—to see the former model's genius for physical comedy and rescue her from B-movie limbo. *I Love Lucy* made its debut in 1951, a perhaps unlikely candidate for becoming one of the defining shows of TV's classic era—for one thing, Ball insisted on working with her husband, Desi Arnaz, a Cuban bandleader who spoke English with an accent thicker than the Havana phone book. Nevertheless, this domestic comedy about a young couple setting up house instantly hit home with millions of postwar Americans who were doing the same and launching the baby boom. Yes, the carrot-topped, blue-eyed actress made an uncommonly attractive homemaker, but she never put on airs, stuffing her face full of production-line chocolates or pretending to get blotto as the spokeswoman for an alcohol-laced health tonic called Vitameatavegamin ("Do you pop out at parties? Are you un-poop-ular?"). A 1953 episode heralding the arrival of Little Ricky—and mirroring the real-life birth of Desi Jr.—drew a prodigious 72 percent of the TV audience. In 1960, Ball divorced the carousing Arnaz ("I've been humiliated," she told TV GUIDE 10 days later) but continued to be a power in Hollywood as president of Desilu Productions and star of *The Lucy Show* and *Here's Lucy.* Those series had different casts and premises, but one constant remained: an indomitable comedian who enjoyed a "poop-ularity" achieved by few performers before or since.

VITAMEATAVEGAMIN
FOR HEALTH

HAPPY DAYS
Arthur Fonzarelli (Henry Winkler), Richie Cunningham (Ron Howard), Ralph Malph (Donny Most), Warren "Potsie" Weber (Anson Williams). ABC, 1974–84
COVER: BY GENE TRINDL, DECEMBER 15, 1979

Roiled by the cultural upheaval of the '60s, America started in the early '70s to look back fondly to a simpler era of hot rods, drive-in movies, poodle skirts and teens in search of fun. This nostalgia made hits out of the stage musical *Grease* (1972) and the movie *American Graffiti* (1973), the latter featuring Ronny Howard, ex-Opie of Mayberry, as a nice-guy adolescent. TV producer Garry Marshall, who had been trying unsuccessfully to interest the networks in a '50s-themed show starring Howard, suddenly found himself very popular. But not as popular as *Happy Days* itself would become. Howard starred as Richie Cunningham in the comedy, which was saved from predictability—high school kid from nice family in Milwaukee comes of age—by the presence of a leather-jacketed greaser named Arthur Fonzarelli. "This is a very *little* part," Marshall recalled warning Henry Winkler before he took the role as the Fonz. "Don't start up if you want a bigger part." But Winkler's ability to show a tough guy's vulnerability, especially when he counseled Richie about life, turned him into such a star that audiences soon overruled Marshall. A classic episode that became a holiday tradition found the Fonz, alone on Christmas with just his motorcycle and a shabby sprig of a tree, agreeing to join the Cunningham celebration at their home. *Happy Days* ran until 1984, but the Smithsonian couldn't wait: It enshrined Fonzie's leather jacket in 1980.

"WHEN I WENT TO PARAMOUNT STUDIOS TO AUDITION FOR HAPPY DAYS,

I only had enough money to stay in California for another month. And at the end of that month, I got the call: Would I like to play Fonzie? I told them that if I could show the other side of him when he takes off his leather jacket, it would be my pleasure. The first time I knew that the role had really taken off was when I went to make a personal appearance in Little Rock, Arkansas, and there were thousands of people waiting for me at the airport at 11:30 at night. It was an unbelievable time. [It was around then] that my wife and I had our first date. When you take a girl out, you're already nervous, and at that particular moment, if you walked into a 7-Eleven, I was on every cover on the newsstand. The entire time we were driving around, I was waving to people. Stacey kept saying to me, 'So, who is that?' and I said, 'I don't have the slightest idea. If they're waving at me, I'm waving back.'

"In this cast, there was a feeling of family—we still have that feeling. And I'm very, very proud that I was a part of *Happy Days*, and proud that the show somehow connected with so many people around the world. [Even today] I'm invited into people's homes for dinner wherever I go. There hasn't been a place that my wife and I have traveled to where people haven't been so warm that they've treated us like a part of their family."

—HENRY WINKLER

THE ANDY GRIFFITH SHOW

Andy Taylor (Griffith), Opie Taylor (Ronny Howard). CBS, 1960–68
COVER: BY RICHARD R. HEWETT, MAY 11, 1963

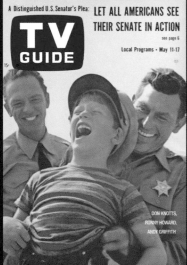

From the first moments of *The Andy Griffith Show*, you knew there was something different about it: The chipper, carefree tune whistled over the opening credits stood out amid the noise and clutter of TV. Griffith, who had used his North Carolina accent to make his name as a comedian in the 1950s, slipped easily into the role of Andy Taylor, sheriff of the mythical small town of Mayberry, North Carolina. At a time when Marshal Matt Dillon was facing down six-shooters on *Gunsmoke* and Eliot Ness was gangbusting on *The Untouchables*, Sheriff Taylor had almost no law enforcing to do—other than letting Otis, the town drunk, occasionally crash for the night in a jail cell. Instead, Andy helped Floyd the barber, gas-pump jockey Gomer Pyle and the rest of Mayberry's denizens sort out their entirely noncriminal troubles—often in spite of the "assistance" from the sheriff's tightly wound,

pop-eyed deputy, Barney Fife, played to jittery perfection by Don Knotts. "It won't be all comedy," Griffith told TV GUIDE a few days before the show's debut in 1960. "We'll be usin' lots of fine character actors. It's sort of easy to get too much of me. I'm stoic. I mean, I just sort of sit there and nothin' much happens." Stoic or not, Sheriff Taylor used his good sense and ingenuity to carry the day on most occasions, whether he was settling a long-standing feud between two mountain families or teaching a life lesson to his son, Opie (little "Ronny" Howard). The formidable Aunt Bee, of course, was also a stalwart presence, always prepared to help out her widower nephew in between pie-making sessions. In 1968, Griffith left the show, which was rechristened *Mayberry R.F.D.*, but the original series continued to run in syndication like a long, lazy river.

THE BRADY BUNCH

Marcia Brady (Maureen McCormick), Peter Brady (Christopher Knight), Cindy Brady (Susan Olsen), Bobby Brady (Mike Lookinland), Jan Brady (Eve Plumb), Greg Brady (Barry Williams). ABC, 1969–74
COVER: BY GENE TRINDL, APRIL 4, 1970

In its 1970 review of *The Brady Bunch*, TV GUIDE virtuously pleaded that the "millions of stepchildren nowadays" deserved "something more than this mish-mush." Perhaps they deserved more, but many of them also apparently yearned for just such an idealized portrait of two partial families blissfully living as one. In the five years of its original run and, perhaps most important to the development of a devoted cult following, in its seemingly permanent status as an after-school TV baby-sitter, the comedy presented a vision of family life where nothing—not even the deaths of mom's first husband and dad's first wife—could dim the happiness of the six children. As married widow and widower Carol and Mike Brady, Florence Henderson and Robert Reed handled the half-dozen kids (she had three girls, he had three boys!) with the help of Alice, the housekeeper-counselor played by Ann B. Davis.

Not that the children presented too many challenges: Plots tended to revolve around such white-knuckle issues as why Jan tied up the phone for so long, what possessed Marcia to enter her stepdad in a Father of the Year contest and whether Peter's class-project volcano would function. "There's nothing really wrong with *The Brady Bunch*," said the magazine. "But nothing is really right, either. Everything is so contrived that you don't believe what goes on any more than you believe sketches in a variety show." Funny that should come up: The cultural power of the show was so strong that *The Brady Bunch* did inspire a variety show, *The Brady Bunch Hour*, in 1977—not to mention a Saturday-morning cartoon, a TV-movie, two prime-time specials, two satirical feature films, a stage production and several books. Just try to find someone who *hasn't* heard this story of a lovely lady and a man named Brady.

THE TRIBE HAS SPOKEN

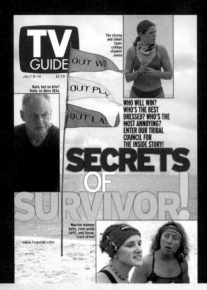

SURVIVOR
Rudy Boesch, Kelly Wiglesworth, Richard Hatch. CBS, 2000–
COVER: BY DENNIS MARSICO, JULY 8, 2000

"Remember those innocent days," TV GUIDE asked in 2001, "before we took it for granted that people will eat pretty much anything for money, no matter how much it squirms?" The reality-television phenomenon, from *Fear Factor* to *Big Brother*, taught us plenty about the way humans behave under TV's glare, but no series was more instructive than the trendsetting *Survivor*. The debut series in late spring of 2000 was like nothing else on television, a "prime-time cocktail of *Who Wants to Be a Millionaire*, *Gilligan's Island* and *Lord of the Flies*," as TV GUIDE described it at the time. That first season on the tropical island of Pulau Tiga, contestant Richard Hatch ("the naked fat guy," David Letterman liked to call him) proved to the world that secret alliances and greed were a winning combination. With sequels in Australia, Africa and the Marquesas, the show's white-hot popularity began to wane—the genre became more familiar, word spread that the "reality" was rather contrived and contestants seemed all too aware of their possible stardom. But for a while, watching regular folks plot and scheme against one another in an exotic place was a nationwide guilty pleasure.

GILLIGAN'S ISLAND
**Skipper (Alan Hale Jr.), Ginger Grant (Tina Louise),
Gilligan (Bob Denver): CBS, 1964–67**
COVER: BY IVAN NAGY, MAY 8, 1965

The storms that tossed the S.S. *Minnow* were nothing compared to the critical tsunami that greeted this improbable comedy about a charter-boat crew and passengers marooned on what looked more like the site of a Burbank luau than a tropical isle. TV GUIDE was more tolerant than most: Yes, "it's the viewer's intelligence that sometimes gets slapped" by the show's slapstick, the magazine said in 1965, but "the fact remains there are bright touches, too." Viewers made it a hit and a long-running syndication champ, with the kitschy appeal of Gilligan and his fellow castaways even winning a special place in the pantheon of Gen-X heroes.

MR. VAN DOREN

ON THE AIR

YOU BET YOUR LIFE
NBC, 1950–61
COVER: ILLUSTRATOR UNKNOWN, JULY 24, 1953

You Bet Your Life wasn't so much a quiz show as a Groucho Marx performance with a few questions tacked on. The host teased contestants; a decrepit duck dropped from the ceiling with $100 as a reward for saying the secret word; and if players somehow failed to win anything, they'd get one last chance with a softball final question ("Who's buried in Grant's Tomb?" was a favorite). But the essence of *You Bet Your Life* was just Groucho being Groucho. "I don't insult the people on my show. I spoof them," he told TV GUIDE in 1953. "There's a big difference between kidding and ridicule." Viewers loved it—here was a comedy genius in their living room every week, after all—and made the show one of the great hits of the 1950s.

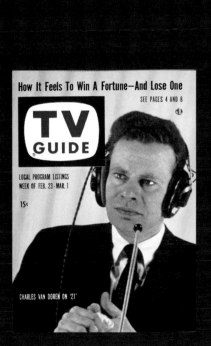

TWENTY ONE
Charles Van Doren. NBC, 1956–58
COVER: BY AL WERTHHEIMER, FEBRUARY 23, 1957

The quiz-show scandals of the 1950s started with revelations about an NBC game called *Dotto*, but the most spectacular disgrace resulted from the network's rigging of *Twenty One*—and the stunning downfall of its most celebrated champion, Charles Van Doren. The affable college professor was so popular after winning a grand total of $129,000 (grand indeed, at the time) that he was rewarded with a job as a cultural commentator on NBC's *Today*. As *Twenty One* host Jack Barry gushed to TV GUIDE a year before the scandals broke, the Van Doren phenomenon basically ensured the game show's success: Before him, when the less appealing Herb Stempel reigned, producers were unable to even get enough audience members to fill the studio seats. With Van Doren, however, they had to "turn on the fire hose to get them all out of there," Barry told the magazine. "Charlie was just right for our show. No freak with a sponge memory, but a genuinely charming young guy." Of course, as Robert Redford's 1994 movie *Quiz Show* depicted, a fantastic memory wasn't required: Van Doren had already been fed the answers, which made his isolation booth a tad superfluous. In 1958, *Twenty One* was deep-sixed.

What Folks Back Home Say About Presley

TV GUIDE
LOCAL PROGRAM LISTINGS
WEEK OF SEPT. 22–28

is The '$64,000 Question'
Entirely On The Level?

Hal March

THE $64,000 QUESTION
Bertha Key, Gloria
Lockerman, Hal March.
CBS, 1955–58
COVER: BY AL HIRSCHFELD,
SEPTEMBER 22, 1956

The unanticipated popularity of
The $64,000 Question in the
summer of 1955 touched off an
explosion of game-show mania
that swept the country. The Hal
March–hosted show was a smash
almost instantly, making walking
celebrities out of its regular-folk
contestants as they answered
increasingly arcane trivia questions and the jackpot swelled.
(One winner, psychologist Joyce
Brothers, even parlayed her fame
into a long media career.) Soon,
the airwaves were teeming with
copycats, all hoping to cash in on
the phenomenon. It didn't take
long, however, for the craze to
collapse: Revelations that shows
like *Twenty One* were fixed put
an end to all the fun and games
by 1958. As early as 1956,
TV GUIDE was reporting "nasty
whispers" about *The $64,000
Question*'s being rigged and gave
producer Steve Carlin space to
reply (his answer: "Absolutely
not"). No evidence of cheating
was ever proved against it, but it
was canceled nonetheless.

IS THAT YOUR FINAL ANSWER?

WHO WANTS TO BE A MILLIONAIRE
Lance Bass, Regis Philbin. ABC, 1999–2002
COVER: BY JOSEF ASTOR, NOVEMBER 6, 1999

It was the most extraordinary programming phenomenon in television history: This multiple-choice quiz show was such an instant, rival-slaying hit in 1999 that ABC—apparently regarding *Who Wants to Be a Millionaire* as the "final answer" to any of the network's ratings problems—ran it for an unprecedented 18 nights in a single month. But the carpet-bombing strategy ultimately exploded in its face. By late 2002, the much-copied franchise was downgraded from series to occasional special. Even so, by then host Regis Philbin (who already had a daytime talk-show hit) had once again proved, as TV GUIDE said early in the year, that he was "the most consistently entertaining presence on television."

FAMILY ALBUM

1) **THE ADVENTURES OF OZZIE & HARRIET**
Clockwise from top left: David Nelson, Ricky Nelson, Harriet Nelson, Ozzie Nelson. ABC, 1952-66

2) **FATHER KNOWS BEST** Kathy "Kitten" Anderson (Lauren Chapin), James "Bud" Anderson Jr. (Billy Gray), Jim Anderson (Robert Young), Margaret Anderson (Jane Wyatt), Betty "Princess" Anderson (Elinor Donahue). CBS, 1954-55; NBC, 1955-60

3) **LEAVE IT TO BEAVER** Ward Cleaver (Hugh Beaumont), Wally Cleaver (Tony Dow), June Cleaver (Barbara Billingsley), Theodore "Beaver" Cleaver (Jerry Mathers). CBS, 1957-58; ABC, 1958-63

4) **THE BEVERLY HILLBILLIES**
Clockwise from top left: Elly May Clampett (Donna Douglas), Duke, Daisy "Granny" Moses (Irene Ryan), Jethro Bodine (Max Baer Jr.), Jed Clampett (Buddy Ebsen). CBS, 1962-71

5) **THE ADDAMS FAMILY**
Clockwise from top left: Uncle Fester Frump (Jackie Coogan), Gomez Addams (John Astin), Grandmama Addams (Blossom Rock), Lurch (Ted Cassidy), Pugsley Addams (Ken Weatherwax), Morticia Frump Addams (Carolyn Jones), Wednesday Addams (Lisa Loring). ABC, 1964-66

6) **THE BRADY BUNCH**
Clockwise from top left: Greg Brady (Barry Williams), Mike Brady (Robert Reed), Carol Brady (Florence Henderson), Alice Nelson (Ann B. Davis), Marcia Brady (Maureen McCormick), Peter Brady (Christopher Knight), Bobby Brady (Mike

Lookinland), Cindy
Brady (Susan Olsen),
Jan Brady (Eve Plumb).
ABC, 1969-74

7) ALL IN THE FAMILY
Edith Bunker (Jean
Stapleton), Archie
Bunker (Carroll
O'Connor), Gloria
Bunker Stivic (Sally
Struthers), Mike Stivic
(Rob Reiner).
CBS, 1971-79

8) GOOD TIMES
Clockwise from left:
Michael Evans (Ralph
Carter), Thelma Evans
(BernNadette Stanis),
Willona Woods (Ja'net
DuBois), Florida Evans
(Esther Rolle), James
"J.J." Evans Jr.
(Jimmie Walker),
James Evans (John
Amos). CBS, 1974-79

9) FAMILY TIES
Clockwise from top right:
Steven Keaton (Michael
Gross), Mallory Keaton
(Justine Bateman),
Alex P. Keaton
(Michael J. Fox),
Jennifer Keaton (Tina
Yothers), Elyse Keaton
(Meredith Baxter-
Birney). NBC, 1982-89

10) THE COSBY SHOW
Denise Huxtable (Lisa
Bonet), Vanessa
Huxtable (Tempestt
Bledsoe), Dr. Heathcliff
Huxtable (Bill Cosby),
Rudy Huxtable (Keshia
Knight Pulliam), Clair
Huxtable (Phylicia
Rashad), Theodore
Huxtable (Malcolm
Jamal-Warner).
NBC, 1984-92

11) ROSEANNE
Becky Conner (Lecy
Goranson), Dan Conner
(John Goodman),
Roseanne Conner
(Roseanne Barr), D.J.
Conner (Michael
Fishman), Darlene
Conner (Sara Gilbert).
ABC, 1988-97

12) THE SIMPSONS
Bart Simpson,
Lisa Simpson,
Maggie Simpson,
Marge Simpson,
Homer Simpson.
FOX, 1989-

THE COSBY SHOW
NBC, 1984–92
COVER: BY MARIO CASILLI, OCTOBER 13, 1984

Just when experts were predicting the demise of the comedy format in the *Dallas*- and *A-Team*-dominated mid-'80s, *The Cosby Show* surfaced on NBC and singlehandedly rescued the genre. It ranked No. 1 for four consecutive years and finished in the Top 20 every year of its run. And yet, can you name a single catchphrase or running gag from the show? Probably not, because one of *The Cosby Show's* virtues was its aversion to comedy conventions and cheap gimmicks. Bill Cosby's creative control was so complete—his name appeared in the credits as many as six times for a single episode—that the show remained immune to producer meddling and gang-of-writers thinking. Cosby wanted a series about an upper-middle-class couple coping with the pleasures and challenges of raising a large family of kids, and he delivered it—as obstetrician Dr. Heathcliff Huxtable—with the cranky-amiable clown persona audiences already knew and loved. But what viewers were not prepared for, yet quickly embraced, was the show's determination to overturn stereotypes of African-Americans by portraying a financially comfortable black family in a loving household. The decor of the Huxtables' Brooklyn brownstone included antiapartheid posters and pictures of Martin Luther King Jr., but the "blackness" of the show was simply a given, not a battle cry. Speaking to TV Guide in 1984, Cosby seemed most concerned about influencing the way people thought about child rearing: "If this show can get to a parent who has never really thought about behaving differently and makes a change that works best for all, I'll be happy."

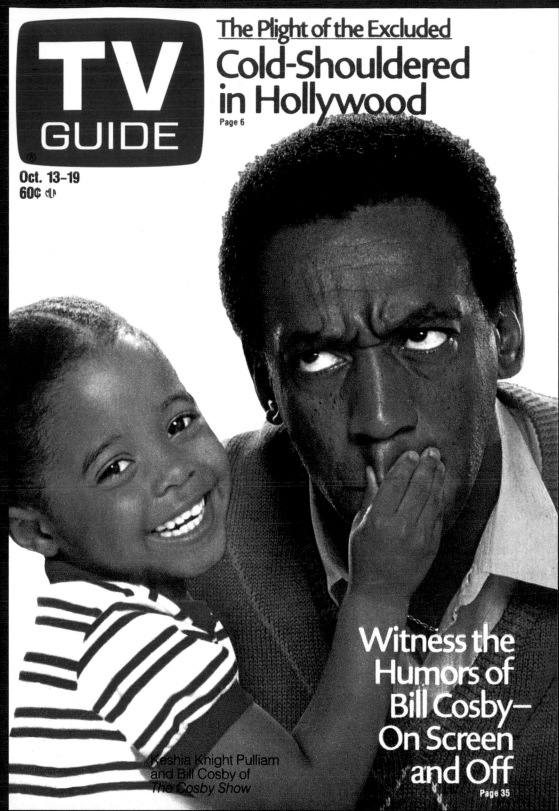

The Plight of the Excluded
Cold-Shouldered in Hollywood
Page 6

TV GUIDE

Oct. 13–19
60¢

Witness the Humors of Bill Cosby— On Screen and Off
Page 35

Keshia Knight Pulliam and Bill Cosby of *The Cosby Show*

THE FUNNIEST STORIES EVER TOLD ON TV
—SAY THE COMICS, SEE PAGE 22

TV GUIDE

15¢

Local Listings · Aug. 24-30

MARJORIE LORD / DANNY THOMAS

MAKE ROOM FOR DADDY
Rusty Williams (Rusty Hamer), Danny Williams (Danny Thomas).
ABC, 1953–57; CBS, 1957–64
COVER: BY GARRETT-HOWARD, AUGUST 24, 1957

After struggling to make it in television, comedian Danny Thomas famously dismissed the medium as "only for idiots." But then, in 1953, Thomas broke through with *Make Room for Daddy* (retitled *The Danny Thomas Show* after three seasons, with Marjorie Lord joining the cast soon after), about a nightclub entertainer whose absenteeism at home undermines his efforts to remain lord of his castle. "We honest-to-Pete got a hit!" Thomas exulted to TV Guide in 1954, before retracting his anti-TV remarks. "So I was an idiot myself," he said. "So I was wrong. That's a crime?" If it was, Thomas got off easy: 11 years' hard time on a successful comedy.

YABBA
DABBA
DOO!

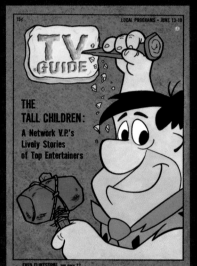

THE FLINTSTONES
Wilma Flintstone, Fred Flintstone, carhop. ABC, 1960–66
COVER: BY HANNA–BARBERA, JUNE 13, 1964

The arrival in 1960 of the first prime-time cartoon—set in the Stone Age and populated by characters who sounded suspiciously like ancestors of Ralph Kramden and *The Honeymooners*—delighted almost everybody, it seems, except critics like TV GUIDE. Tsk-tsking *The Flintstones* for its "flat jokes" and "stale" approach, the magazine lamented that the show was "better than nothing. But only the least bit better." Oh, well, when you're talking about prehistoric times, it's probably advisable to take the long view. *The Flintstones*, which held the record for the longest-running prime-time cartoon until *The Simpsons* stole it in 1997, eventually distinguished itself with a deft hand for using antiquity to parody modernity. Animation kingpins William Hanna and Joe Barbera conceived the cartoon for grown-ups after a survey showed that 65 percent of the audiences watching *Quick Draw McGraw* and *Huckleberry Hound* were adults. "We wanted to satirize suburbanites for nighttime TV, but nothing we drew in a modern setting was funny," Barbera told TV GUIDE in 1960. "Finally, we put our little man into a convertible with fins fashioned out of tree trunks and a thatched roof for a top. Looking at it, we all broke up." Fred worked as the operator of a dinosaur-powered crane, but most of the action in Bedrock took place back at home, where his dutiful wife, Wilma, vacuumed with a baby mammoth's trunk. Their neighbors, dim bulb Barney Rubble and sensible wife Betty, completed the *Honeymooners* comparisons. But unlike the Kramdens, Fred and Wilma had a baby girl, Pebbles; the Rubbles, keeping up with the 'stoneses, adopted an orphan boy, Bamm Bamm, soon after. *The Flintstones* went off the air in 1966 but earned a place in the morning-cartoon rotation that seemed as permanent as the cave paintings at Lascaux.

EVERYBODY LOVES RAYMOND
Marie Barone (Doris Roberts), Ray Barone (Ray Romano). CBS, 1996–
COVER: BY DARIEN DAVIS, FEBRUARY 20, 1999

"The year's most consistently hilarious comedy," TV GUIDE said in a roundup of critical favorites in 1999, "is also that rarest of shows: a smart family sitcom that lovingly but warily acknowledges the strangling ties that bind parents and children." The premise of *Everybody Loves Raymond* mirrored the life of its star, stand-up comedian Ray Romano: Like his character, sportswriter Ray Barone, Romano had three kids and a police-officer brother who lived with his parents. In the hands of skillful writers and gifted costars, including Doris Roberts and Peter Boyle as Ray's interfering parents, these elements coalesced into a winning comedy. Ray's level-headed wife, Debra (Patricia Heaton), was forever trying to get him to confront his parents, but as TV GUIDE observed in '96, "he inevitably chickens out because he's too nice and they're too nuts." (Ray's mom, for instance,

berates him for signing her up in a fruit-of-the-month club; the relentless arrival of succulent produce makes her shriek, "He's got us in some kind of cult!") The show adroitly evolved over time, finding a fresh supply of material in having Ray's big-lunk brother, Robert (Brad Garrett), finally move out of his parents' place, which added some empty-nest mania to their mom's lunacies and made Ray envy Robert's independence. But the heart of *Raymond* was his devoted relationship with his wife and affectionate guff-love with the kids (using the baby twins as barbells, for instance); they raise the show above the level of the typical, disposable comedy and provide some real tender-funny moments. "Miserable in each other's company," the magazine said of the Barone clan in '99, "they'd be even more so without it. And so would we."

THE ROCKFORD FILES
NBC, 1974–80
COVER: BY GENE TRINDL,
MARCH 6, 1976

If there's such a thing as comfort
food, is there comfort TV? That
would describe *The Rockford
Files* in the mid-'70s, a detective
drama featuring the solid, reassuring presence of James Garner
as Jim Rockford. The private eye
lived in a trailer home on a
California beach and was, as
TV GUIDE called him in 1974, a
"hero sandwich—part hero and
part antihero." Creator Stephen
J. Cannell told the magazine that
he intended "to break every rule
about a TV detective" when he
devised the character. For one
thing, Rockford occasionally
enlisted the help of his father,
"Rocky" (Noah Beery), a retired
trucker—that fact alone set him
apart from the Philip Marlowe
school of loner detectives. He
also hated violence and never let
his interest in solving cases over-
whelm his interest in making
money. So, naturally, Rockford
got slugged in almost every
episode and was routinely stiffed
by his clients. Garner's rendition
of the character was "*slow* funny,"
according to TV GUIDE. "In other
words, he grows on you." Keeping
the customers amused was in
line with Garner's philosophy of
acting. "We're the court jesters,"
he told the magazine in 1975.
"That's our function, to entertain
people. It's a hell of a lot better
than laying carpet." But not less
physically taxing, at least for
Garner, whose bad back and
painful knees—the result of a
variety of sports injuries and car
wrecks—made working an agony.
Garner quit *The Rockford Files*
abruptly in the middle of its sixth
season, finally opting for his own
personal comfort over that of
the audience.

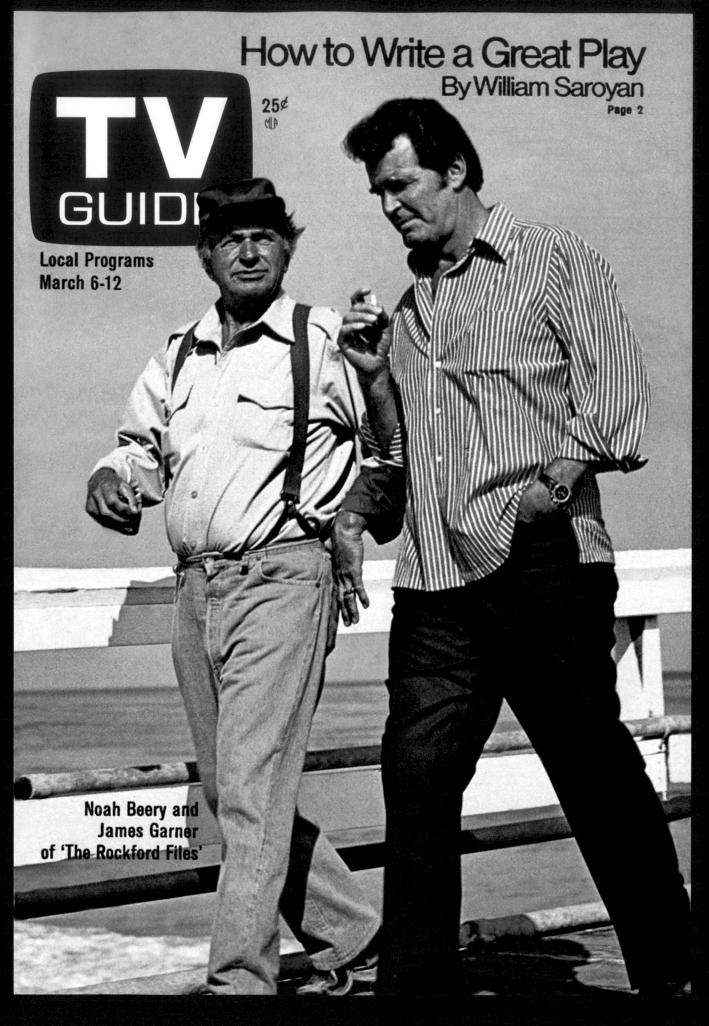

How to Write a Great Play
By William Saroyan
Page 2

TV GUIDE

25¢

Local Programs
March 6-12

Noah Beery and
James Garner
of 'The Rockford Files'

SANFORD AND SON
Lamont Sanford (Demond Wilson), Fred Sanford (Redd Foxx). NBC, 1972–77
COVER: BY GENE TRINDL, MAY 13, 1972

After shaking up American television by adapting a British series to create *All in the Family*, Norman Lear and Bud Yorkin hit a second home run a year later when they reinvented the U.K. comedy *Steptoe and Son*. The key change wasn't the new title, *Sanford and Son*, but the fact that the junk-dealing main character—and most of the rest of the cast—was African-American. "I've been working for 35 years to get three or four years of steady work in a row," Redd Foxx told TV GUIDE in '72, at the beginning of what would become five years as the star of the smash series. Though he was a stand-up comedy veteran ("Redd was the comedic father of us all," Bill Cosby told TV GUIDE in 1973) with a reputation for doing filthy jokes, Foxx translated seamlessly to television. One of his trademarks in the role as the doddering Fred Sanford was clutching his heart and crying out to his long-gone wife in heaven, "I'm coming, Elizabeth, I'm coming!"— usually when his devoted but impatient son, Lamont (Demond Wilson), seemed on the verge of leaving him. "The amazing thing" about Foxx, TV GUIDE said, is "that it's impossible, despite his outrageous disreputableness, not to love him."

THE DEFENDERS
CBS, 1961–65
COVER: BY CURT GUNTHER,
MARCH 17, 1962

With its first episode, *The Defenders* signaled that it was a complete departure from conventional legal dramas: A doctor went on trial for the mercy killing of a baby born with severe birth defects; after the show presented the arguments for and against a murder conviction, he was found guilty on a lesser charge of manslaughter. It was the sort of case you'd never see Perry Mason handle, TV GUIDE said. At a time when television preferred to skirt controversy, *The Defenders* embraced it, tackling topics from the debut episode's mercy killing to abortion rights for teenagers to the question of whether a pregnant Jehovah's Witness should be able to refuse a blood transfusion that would save her baby's life. (So many obstetrics-related issues came up they could have called the show *The Deliverers*.) "Certain issues in the news become hot copy, and you have to be sensitive to them. That's when I think the show is most effective," actor E.G. Marshall told TV GUIDE in 1964. Marshall starred as Lawrence Preston, the senior lawyer in the father-and-son team of Preston & Preston (Robert Reed played his son, Kenneth). The magazine criticized their intra-office quarrels and reconciliations during the show's initial season as coming "right out of the promptbooks of melodrama," but praised *The Defenders* the following year as "a show with a 'message' and a powerful dramatic technique for communicating it to the public." *The Defenders*, which lasted four seasons, also succeeded in delivering a powerful message to television itself: By '64, the medium had developed an appetite for more controversial fare, and as Marshall noted, "you have to give *The Defenders* at least part of the credit for that."

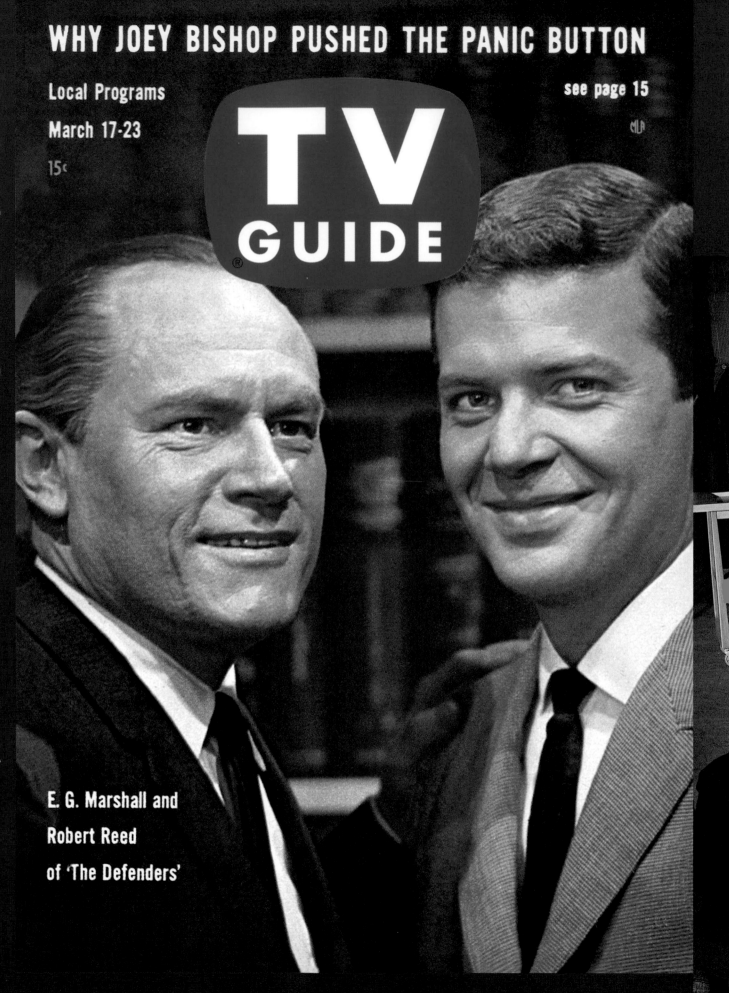

WHY JOEY BISHOP PUSHED THE PANIC BUTTON

Local Programs
March 17-23

15¢

see page 15

TV GUIDE

E. G. Marshall and
Robert Reed
of 'The Defenders'

PERRY MASON
Mason (Raymond Burr). CBS, 1957–66
COVER: BY YOUSUF KARSH, MARCH 4, 1961

Perry Mason may be the only lawyer in the world who's spent more time in the public eye than Alan Dershowitz. The character first appeared in the 1930s in the novels of lawyer-writer Erle Stanley Gardner, then moved on to a radio show that ran for 12 years, several TV-movies and two series. But from the moment Raymond Burr first appeared as Mason in 1957, every other incarnation seemed to fade away. The burly actor invested the character with such a sense of purpose in his pursuit of the truth that viewers never seemed to mind *Perry Mason*'s formulaic, eyebrow-raising courtroom scenes (last-minute discoveries of crucial evidence, sobbing witness-stand confessions). In 1958, TV GUIDE praised Burr's "rugged interpretation" of the character and the work of Barbara Hale as his devoted secretary, Della Street. But by 1965, the magazine wanted *Mason* thrown out of court, complaining about the "compulsion to cram into every episode not only a plot and a subplot, but also a sub-subplot," which complicated matters so much that viewers didn't have "a reasonable chance to guess who done it." A year later the magazine got its wish and the show was canceled. Still, Burr inhabited the role with such power that nearly 40 years later, all you have to do is mention the name Perry Mason and we all know who done it.

TV GUIDE

Big Man Big Heart
Big Troubles
RAYMOND BURR

Local Programs · March 4-10

15¢

by Richard Gehman

RAYMOND BURR
AS 'PERRY MASON'

THE FUGITIVE
Dr. Richard Kimble (David Janssen). ABC, 1963–67
COVER: BY RONALD SEARLE, JANUARY 22, 1966

Harrison Ford certainly made an acceptable Richard Kimble in the 1993 feature film *The Fugitive*, but David Janssen defined this role of a doctor wrongly convicted of his wife's murder, roaming the country searching for the one-armed man he'd seen fleeing the scene of the crime. Over the course of four years, Janssen's character was relentlessly chased by a detective, held dozens of odd jobs that allowed the altruistic doc to help others and suffered enough injuries to make an EMT wince—he was blinded by an explosion, hit by a car, stabbed four times, wounded by gunshots eight times and knocked unconscious 10 times. The punishment took its toll: Janssen told TV GUIDE in 1967 that he turned down half a million dollars to return for a fifth year. "I think I would have fallen apart," he said. The series ended with Kimble fighting the one-armed man atop a water tower, until Kimble's detective pursuer saved his life by shooting the bad guy. The finale drew 72 percent of the TV audience, a record not to be topped by any series until *Dallas*'s "Who Shot J.R.?" episode 13 years later.

SEARLE CAPTURES THE FUGITIVE—With a Pencil

SEE PAGE 11

TV GUIDE

Local Programs • January 22-28

15¢

DAVID JANSSEN

Ronald Searle

THE PRISONER
No. 6 (Patrick McGoohan). CBS, 1968–69

The Prisoner was a temporary replacement for *The Jackie Gleason Show* during the summer of '68, but it earned a permanent place in television's annals as one of the most fascinating dramatic series ever made. Patrick McGoohan, fresh from the action-adventure series *Secret Agent*, created and starred in this story of a spy who resigned his job and was immediately abducted–either by his own people or the enemy's, he was never sure–and installed in a strangely festive penal colony known as the Village (actually the Welsh seaside resort Portmeirion). In the Village, where the perimeter was patrolled by giant, menacing rubbery balls, everyone was known by a number and the inmates were ex-spies who'd been reduced to cheerful obliviousness by the techniques used to extract their secrets. But No. 6 (McGoohan) was too valuable to be handled so crudely; a succession of wardens known as No. 2 tried wilier ways of making the rebellious (or "unmutual," in Village parlance) prisoner answer the question "Why did you resign?" The show combined good, old-fashioned action/sci-fi with an eerily ambiguous surrealism that left fans and college professors alike debating the show's real significance. The loss of freedom? The dehumanization of society? The absurdity of existence? McGoohan himself told TV Guide in 1968 that he thought people were "being imprisoned and engulfed by a scientific and materialistic world," but refused to elaborate on the meaning of the series, which concluded after 17 episodes with No. 6 finally escaping. Or did he? *The Prisoner* left the answer, as usual, deliciously unclear.

MIAMI VICE
NBC, 1984–89
COVER: BY RICHARD AMSEL,
JULY 27, 1985

"We're not revolutionary," *Miami Vice* executive producer Michael Mann told TV GUIDE in 1985. "We're just current." *Miami Vice*'s debut the previous fall had certainly made every other cop show on television seem hopelessly antique. From the opening-title sequence—a headlong plunge into a luscious riot of flamingos, race-horses and bikini tops, all to the cool frenzy of Jan Hammer's theme song—you knew that episodic TV was going somewhere new. The still-fresh fast-cut, MTV pace and rock soundtrack gave *Miami Vice* a feel unlike anything else in prime time. And its under-cover detectives, James "Sonny" Crockett (Don Johnson) and Ricardo Tubbs (Philip Michael Thomas), whose work usually dealt with Miami's prodigious drug trade, looked like no one on TV who'd ever carried a badge: Crockett's two-day-old stubble and pastel jackets worn over T-shirts inspired a lamentable trend, and neither guy seemed to own a sock. Having vaulted to ninth in the ratings in its second season, *Miami Vice* was undone in its third as NBC pitted it against CBS's popular *Dallas* and the show inexplicably exchanged its signature palette for a grim color scheme. Viewers fled. "That's the thing about cutting edges," TV GUIDE said in 1987, two years before *Vice* was iced. "They're the first things to get dull."

TV GUIDE

July 27–Aug. 2
60¢

On Location With *Miami Vice*
Page 26

·AMSEL·

L.-r.:
Philip Michael Thomas and Don Johnson of *Miami Vice*

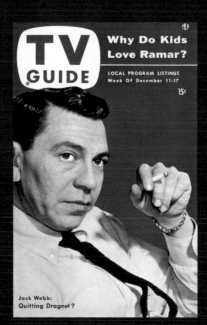

TV GUIDE

Why Do Kids Love Ramar?

LOCAL PROGRAM LISTINGS
Week Of December 11-17

15¢

Jack Webb:
Quitting Dragnet?

DRAGNET
Sgt. Joe Friday (Jack Webb), Officer Frank Smith (Ben Alexander). NBC, 1952–59
COVER: PHOTOGRAPHER UNKNOWN, DECEMBER 11, 1953

When *Dragnet* began on radio in 1949, police dramas were improbable shoot-'em-up tales of heroic law enforcement. Creator and star Jack Webb had a novel idea: that simply showing the workaday life of a detective—following leads, interviewing witnesses and solving crimes based on actual cases—could be fascinating. Audiences agreed, making *Dragnet*'s TV version a Top 10 ratings fixture in the mid-'50s. Elements of the show still instantly evoke Eisenhower-era pop culture, from the "dum, da-*dum*-dum" musical signature to LAPD sergeant Joe Friday's buzz cut. But the essence of *Dragnet*—summed up in its show-ending voiceover, "The story you have just seen is true. The names have been changed to protect the innocent"—remains as contemporary as the latest cop show that makes realism its goal.

THE '60s

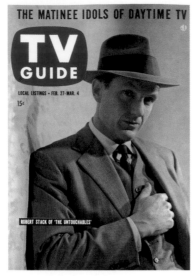

February 27, 1960
By Philippe Halsman
Robert Stack of *The Untouchables*

August 6, 1960
By Larry Fried
Esther Williams

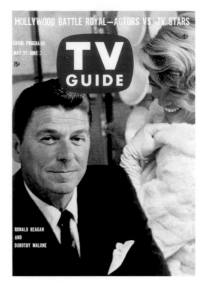

May 27, 1961
By Todd Walker
Ronald Reagan and Dorothy Malone of *General Electric Theater*

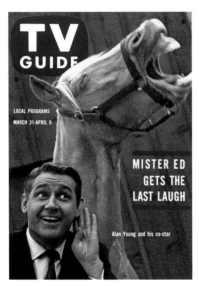

March 31, 1962
By Richard R. Hewett
Alan Young and Mister Ed of *Mister Ed*

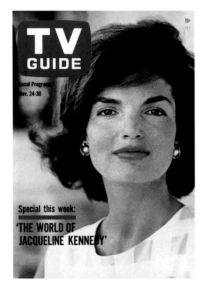

November 24, 1962
By Jacques Lowe
Jacqueline Kennedy

December 8, 1962
By Larry Schiller
Dick Van Dyke of *The Dick Van Dyke Show*

February 16, 1963
By Philippe Halsman
Princess Grace of Monaco

November 27, 1965
By Gene Trindl
Cynthia Lynn and Bob Crane of *Hogan's Heroes*

December 11, 1965
By Sheedy-Long
Cast of *F Troop*

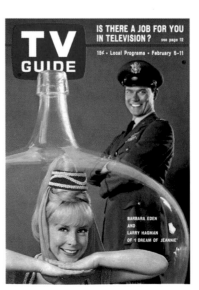

February 5, 1966
By Gene Trindl
Barbara Eden and Larry Hagman of *I Dream of Jeannie*

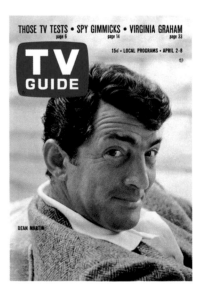

April 2, 1966
By Philippe Halsman
Dean Martin of *The Dean Martin Show*

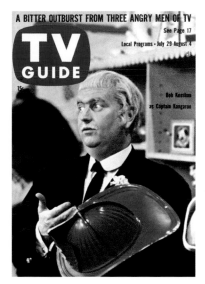

A BITTER OUTBURST FROM THREE ANGRY MEN OF TV
See Page 17

Local Programs • July 29-August 4

Bob Keeshan as Captain Kangaroo

July 29, 1961
By George E. Joseph
Bob Keeshan of *Captain Kangaroo*

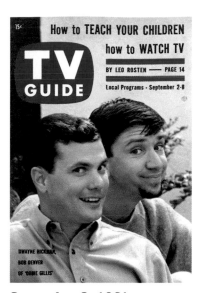

How to TEACH YOUR CHILDREN how to WATCH TV
BY LEO ROSTEN —— PAGE 14

Local Programs — September 2-8

DWAYNE HICKMAN, BOB DENVER OF 'DOBIE GILLIS'

September 2, 1961
By Gene Trindl
Dwayne Hickman and Bob Denver of
The Many Loves of Dobie Gillis

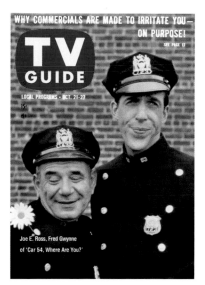

WHY COMMERCIALS ARE MADE TO IRRITATE YOU— ON PURPOSE!
SEE PAGE 13

LOCAL PROGRAMS • OCT. 21-27

Joe E. Ross, Fred Gwynne of 'Car 54, Where Are You?'

October 21, 1961
By George E. Joseph
Joe E. Ross and Fred Gwynne of
Car 54, Where Are You?

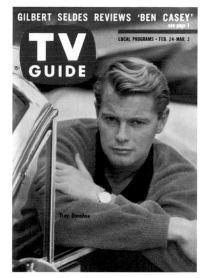

GILBERT SELDES REVIEWS 'BEN CASEY'
see page 1

LOCAL PROGRAMS • FEB. 24-MAR. 2

Troy Donahue

February 24, 1962
By Julian Wasser
Troy Donahue of *Surfside 6*

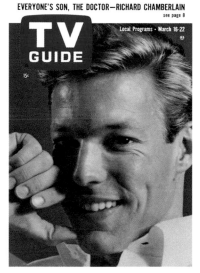

EVERYONE'S SON, THE DOCTOR—RICHARD CHAMBERLAIN
see page 8

Local Programs • March 16-22

March 16, 1963
By Gene Trindl
Richard Chamberlain of *Dr. Kildare*

THE KING FAMILY AND HOW IT GREW
see page 24

15¢ • LOCAL PROGRAMS • JULY 10-16

Yvonne DeCarlo, Fred Gwynne of 'The Munsters'

July 10, 1965
By Gene Trindl
Yvonne DeCarlo and Fred Gwynne
of *The Munsters*

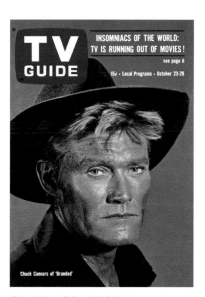

INSOMNIACS OF THE WORLD: TV IS RUNNING OUT OF MOVIES!
see page 6

15¢ • Local Programs • October 23-29

Chuck Connors of 'Branded'

October 23, 1965
By Sheedy-Long
Chuck Conners of *Branded*

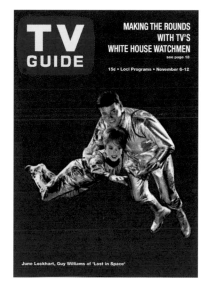

MAKING THE ROUNDS WITH TV'S WHITE HOUSE WATCHMEN
see page 18

15¢ • Local Programs • November 6-12

June Lockhart, Guy Williams of 'Lost in Space'

November 6, 1965
By Gene Trindl
June Lockhart and Guy Williams
of *Lost in Space*

DR. SPOCK'S ℞ FOR TV, YOUR FAMILY AND YOU
see page 8

15¢ • Local Programs • May 28-June 3

Sally Field of 'Gidget'

May 28, 1966
By Sheedy-Long
Sally Field of *Gidget*

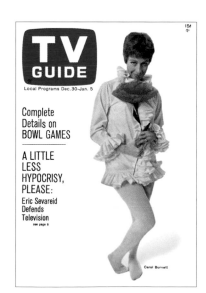

Local Programs Dec. 30-Jan. 5

Complete Details on BOWL GAMES

A LITTLE LESS HYPOCRISY, PLEASE:
Eric Sevareid Defends Television
see page 8

Carol Burnett

December 30, 1967
By Mario Casilli
Carol Burnett of *The Carol
Burnett Show*

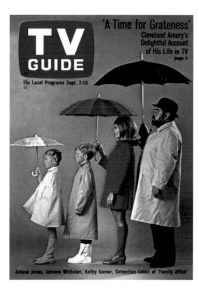

'A Time for Grateness'
Cleveland Amory's Delightful Account of His Life in TV
page 5

15¢ Local Programs Sept. 7-13

Anissa Jones, Johnnie Whitaker, Kathy Garver, Sebastian Cabot of 'Family Affair'

September 7, 1968
By Gene Trindl
Cast of *Family Affair*

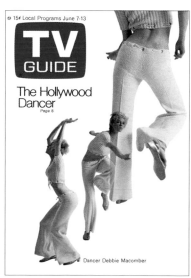

15¢ Local Programs June 7-13

The Hollywood Dancer
Page 8

Dancer Debbie Macomber

June 7, 1969
By Richard R. Hewett
Debbie Macomber

THE WALTONS
John-Boy Walton (Richard Thomas), Olivia Walton (Michael Learned), John Walton (Ralph Waite). CBS, 1972–81
COVER: BY JACOB KNIGHT, JUNE 25, 1977

Replying to readers who accused the magazine of never liking anything, TV GUIDE pointed out in 1972 that it regarded a new family drama called *The Waltons* as "a wise, warm, wonderful show.... There is, at last, a show about the poor." *The Waltons*, defying TV's custom of addressing only the concerns of the rich and middle class, chronicled the struggles of a family in Virginia's Blue Ridge mountains during the Depression. When we first met the extended clan, we saw them through the eyes of a high schooler, John-Boy Walton, the eldest of John and Olivia Walton's seven children and an aspiring writer (played with affecting intelligence and sensitivity by Richard Thomas). One of the virtues of the popular series was its realistic depiction of the passage of time: By series' end in 1981, John-Boy had gone to college, started his own local paper, sold a novel and become a war correspondent in London. Creator Earl Hamner Jr., a writer who based the show on his own boyhood memories, told TV GUIDE in 1973 that "if *The Waltons* is saying anything important, maybe it is just that ordinary people are capable of more nobility than they know."

LITTLE HOUSE ON THE PRAIRIE
Charles Ingalls (Michael Landon). NBC, 1974–83
COVER: BY SCOTT ENYART,
MAY 29, 1976

When it launched in 1974, *Little House on the Prairie* was considered a flatlander's knockoff of *The Waltons*' tales from the Blue Ridge mountains. But the series about a frontier family's hardscrabble life in 1870s Minnesota had two advantages: generations of viewers familiar with the Laura Ingalls Wilder books that were the inspiration for the series and a vast TV audience with a big thing for Michael Landon, who'd spent 14 years on *Bonanza*. It was his wife and daughter's love of the Wilder titles, though, that convinced Landon to produce, act in and often direct the show. "I thought, 'How wonderful if parents and children can watch this series together—and maybe it would start the kids *reading* the books,'" Landon said to TV GUIDE in '74. "'Imagine a TV show that would make kids read?'" The following year, the magazine described the series' plots as "pretty quiet" but called Landon "one of our favorites... particularly in the devastating-smile department." His grin got a little bigger over the next few years as *Little House* became a hit, surpassing *The Waltons* in the ratings.

BRIAN'S SONG
Gale Sayers (Billy Dee Williams), Brian Piccolo (James Caan).
ABC, November 30, 1971

In 1971, heartstrings were tugged, and maybe a few minds were opened, with *Brian's Song*, the story of the close friendship between Chicago Bears football teammates Gale Sayers, an African-American, and Brian Piccolo, who was white. The Emmy-winning TV-movie made stars of both Billy Dee Williams and James Caan. On the occasion of a 2001 remake, the real-life Sayers talked to TV GUIDE about his relationship with Piccolo, who lost his battle against a rare form of cancer at age 26: "People saw that a black and a white could get along together, could have a good time together and maybe be friends. It wasn't a big deal to Brian and me. We didn't think anything of it. We were teammates."

PLAYHOUSE 90
Mountain McClintock (Jack Palance) of "Requiem for a Heavyweight" (1956). CBS, 1956–60

In 1957, producer Martin Manulis told TV GUIDE that his only goals for this dramatic anthology show were "to bring the greatest variety possible to the series and to strive for excellence…. I feel that *Playhouse 90* should entertain the grown-ups." *Playhouse 90*'s reputation for excellence was established after just its second broadcast, with Jack Palance's performance as a broken-down boxer in "Requiem for a Heavyweight"—the first 90-minute drama written (by Rod Serling) specifically for television and the winner of five Emmy awards. As for variety, *Playhouse 90* presented a head-spinning assortment of productions—including "Judgment at Nuremberg," "The Days of Wine and Roses" and "For Whom the Bell Tolls"—and featured an all-star roster of performers, such as Errol Flynn, Jack Lemmon, Carol Channing, Jeanette MacDonald, Mickey Rooney, Paul Newman and Joanne Woodward. On top of that, many of the weekly performances were presented live. That helped make *Playhouse 90* a pricey proposition, as did paying for top-tier writers, directors and actors. Unfortunately, the show didn't attract enough grown-ups to register the sort of ratings that would support the expense. And even though in retrospect it is regarded as a paragon of the era of live, high-quality, New York City–based programming, the series—a latecomer to the dramatic-anthology genre—was fighting a losing battle as TV production increasingly shifted to the West Coast and to less-expensive formats. Late in *Playhouse 90*'s third season, TV GUIDE celebrated the show as "a symbol of television at its best—a program with a point of view, a program unafraid of controversy, a program alive with a sense of excitement. Long may it be with us." A few months later in '59, CBS cut the series back to every other week and shut it down completely the following spring.

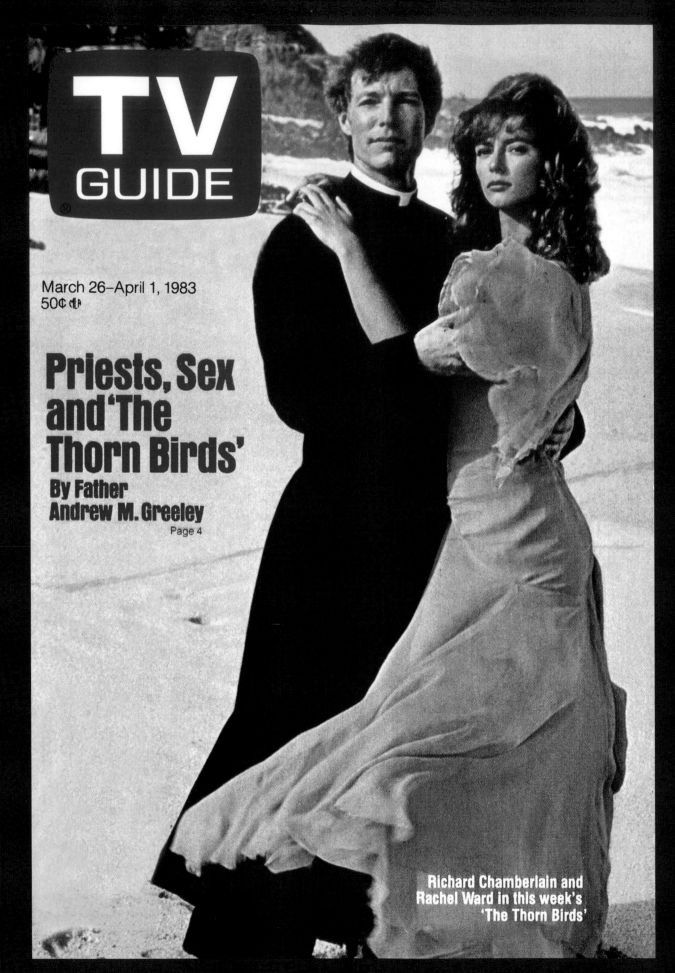

TV GUIDE

March 26–April 1, 1983
50¢

Priests, Sex and 'The Thorn Birds'
By Father Andrew M. Greeley
Page 4

Richard Chamberlain and Rachel Ward in this week's 'The Thorn Birds'

THE THORN BIRDS
ABC, 1983
COVER: BY DENNIS PIEL, MARCH 26, 1983

In the heyday of the miniseries, *The Thorn Birds* virtually ruled the ratings roost: The four-part, 10-hour adaptation of Colleen McCullough's massively popular novel ranks second only to *Roots* as the most-watched miniseries of all time. Set in Australia between 1920 and 1962, the epic drew protests for its depiction of an ambitious Catholic priest (Richard Chamberlain) falling in love with a beautiful woman (Rachel Ward). But the novelist Father Andrew M. Greeley, writing in TV Guide, pointed out that ultimately the series wasn't about "an uncontrollably passionate priest" so much as "a passionate God" who loves sinners as well as saints.

BRIDESHEAD REVISITED
Sebastian Flyte (Anthony Andrews), Julia Flyte (Diana Quick), Charles Ryder (Jeremy Irons). PBS, 1982

Great Performances waded into TV's miniseries competition in 1982, bringing the 11-part British production of *Brideshead Revisited* to PBS. The setting was lavish in this faithful adaptation of Evelyn Waugh's between-the-wars novel about friendship, art and religious faith. And the casting was equally sumptuous, from Jeremy Irons's career-making performance (as a young man whose life changes when he meets the family at Brideshead Castle) to John Gielgud and Laurence Olivier in supporting, yet masterful, roles. "In character, pace and acting," TV GUIDE said in 1983, *Brideshead Revisited* "is a television classic: worth watching again—and again."

HALLMARK HALL OF FAME
Jacob Witting (Christopher Walken), Sarah Wheaton (Glenn Close) of "Sarah, Plain and Tall" (1991). NBC, CBS, PBS, ABC and Hallmark Channel, 1952–

"I don't have a philanthropic attitude toward culture," Hallmark greeting-card company founder Joyce Hall told TV GUIDE in 1961, on *Hallmark Hall of Fame*'s 10th anniversary. He added: "The simple truth is that good TV is good business." Early productions relied on classic drama–a two-hour, live "Hamlet" in 1953 was the first full-length Shakespeare play broadcast on TV and, at the time, also the longest dramatic program ever aired. But subsequently, the *Hall of Fame* undertook everything from documentaries and comedies to contemporary drama ("Promise," in 1986, starred James Woods as a schizophrenic whose brother, played by James Garner, reluctantly becomes his caregiver; it won five Emmy awards). In its adventurous programming, "*Hallmark* has always leaped off the cliff," Glenn Close, the star of "Sarah, Plain and Tall," told TV GUIDE on the series' 50th anniversary. "That's why actors go back." Indeed, the *Hall of Fame* is itself a hall of fame–cast members have included George C. Scott, Jason Robards, Dame Judith Anderson and Julie Harris. With talent of this caliber, *Hallmark* has easily upheld the standard that Hall voiced to the magazine in '61: "I want to be able to look people in the eye without cringing the day after a show."

ROOTS
Kunta Kinte (LeVar Burton). ABC, 1977
COVER: BY ROMARE BEARDEN, JANUARY 22, 1977

For eight consecutive nights in January 1977, America was riveted as never before by a single television show: the miniseries *Roots*, a 12-hour dramatization of author Alex Haley's account of his African ancestry. At the time, it was the most-watched program ever made for TV, with the finale drawing more than 80 million viewers, or 71 percent of the entire television audience. The story began in 1750 and depicted the capture of a young African warrior, Kunta Kinte (LeVar Burton), by white slave traders and his transportation to America. Spanning 150 years, the epic followed Kinte (renamed Toby, and played by John Amos as an adult) and his descendants through the tragic story of slavery in the United States, ending with the slaves' emancipation and embrace of the opportunity to start life anew and free. The enormous cast, which included Edward Asner, Vic Morrow and Lloyd Bridges, was dominated by a remarkable gathering of African-American talent, including Cicely Tyson, Leslie Uggams, Louis Gossett Jr. and Ben Vereen (who memorably played Chicken George, a slave sent to England in the 1820s). "Television at its best is not only entertaining, it informs or even enlightens," Burton told TV GUIDE on the miniseries' 25th anniversary. By that time, four plagiarism lawsuits had cast a shadow on Haley's methods. The author won three and settled the other out of court, saying any similarities to another work were inadvertent. But what could never be undone was *Roots'* historic achievement: It took a nation too often riven by racial differences and bound it together with the power of storytelling.

ROOTS

In January 1977, my friend Warren Beatty and I caught up with each other in New York City for a long-standing dinner date. As it happened, that night was the premiere of the miniseries *Roots*, and Warren and I watched it together in his suite at the Pierre hotel. Neither of us spoke one word during those two hours. At the end, Warren stood up, looked at me and said, "Your life's changed as of tonight." He was so right.

The next morning, besieged for autographs at JFK airport, I missed my flight home. Within days, my usual weekly handful of mail had grown to three or more canvas bagfuls. And as dubbed versions of the film joined the translated book abroad, letters from afar bore such creative addresses as "Alex Haley, 'Roots,' U.S.A."

Invitations to visit every country imaginable poured in so thick and fast that I felt, metaphorically, as though I were hurtling over Niagara Falls in a barrel—quite a contrast to the beginning of *Roots*, back in my hometown of Henning, Tennessee.

I was a 5-year-old boy when my beloved Grandpa, a lumber dealer named Will Palmer, died. To soothe her grief, my

Grandma Cynthia invited her five sisters to come and spend the summer with us—which they did. Early evenings found us gathered on the front porch, as the sisters, their gray heads bobbing atop their rocking chairs, regaled the family with their reminiscing.

The stories always began with Grandma's strict blacksmith father, Tom Murray, who had "jumped the broom" (married) and raised a family. Next came the clucking and clacking over the "sinfulness" of the sisters' paternal grandfather, who was both the son and the slave of Tom Lea. A master gamecocker, George Lea was known far and wide by his indelible nickname: "Chicken George." Then came his mother, the much-venerated Miz Kizzy, and her mother, Bell.

Throughout that summer, I heard the family stories, in all their detail, until they became glued within my young memory—which is where they remained until some four decades later, when I found myself standing in front of the stately and imposing National Archives Building in Washington, D.C. Compelled by simple curiosity, I entered the Archives and asked to view the 1870 Census of Alamance County, North Carolina, where my grandmother said she'd been born and reared. I found there a record of the freed blacksmith Tom Murray and his family.

The chance visit set off nine years of research, an endeavor that took me from the dusty roads of Alamance County—where I found a deeply rusted old horseshoe that just couldn't have been made by anybody but my blacksmith great grandfather (I smuggled it to New York City, wrapped in a sheet of newspaper and stashed inside my shirt)—to a tiny village in Gambia, West Africa: the home of Kunta Kinte.

The end result of that endeavor was a phenomenon that neither I nor my publisher could ever have anticipated. Why did it happen? Reflecting now, I think that, without my intent, the book awakened a worldwide perception that genealogy isn't reserved for royalty. Quite the contrary, the peasant's family line is probably stronger than the prince's.

But more than that, people seemed to recognize that *Roots* symbolized their own ethnic struggles. In Beijing, *Roots* and I were feted by lineage masters who had traced families as far back as 1,000 years. In Tokyo, I was astounded to see my hugely enlarged photo displayed three stories high. The biggest crowd I ever drew was in Morocco, where people formed a human carpet over streets and housetops to meet the man who had dramatized the story of an African-Muslim youth who'd been kidnapped into slavery in the Christian West—and kept his Islamic faith intact until his death.

Just recently, the government of Egypt expressed interest in my writing an Egyptian equivalent to the Kunta Kinte saga. And the continuing classroom usage of *Roots* by West African educators is certainly one of my most gratifying experiences.

So it has been for 15 years now that, again and again, I've told the *Roots* story to hundreds of audiences, and responded to the unabating questions that the subject generates. (I'm always pleased to tell inquirers that my Henning boyhood home is now an official state of Tennessee museum.) I hope to bring forth other works, but my best hope is that *Roots* will find new viewers in future generations.

—ALEX HALEY, EXCERPT FROM TV GUIDE, FEBRUARY 29, 1992

The Plain Truth About Elvis Presley

LOCAL PROGRAM LISTINGS
WEEK OF SEPTEMBER 8-14

TV GUIDE

15¢

Elvis Presley

ELVIS
Elvis Presley.
NBC, December 3, 1968
COVER: BY WERTHEIMER,
SEPTEMBER 8, 1956

By 1968, Elvis Presley's heyday had passed—he was starring in corny movies while pop culture was grooving to the psychedelic era. But then, at 33, Presley returned to the medium that had helped make him a '50s icon, doing what he did best: singing and playing rock and roll. The electrifying "comeback special," as it came to be known among Elvisionados, was simply called *Elvis*, reflecting the stripped-down, raw nature of the performance. In the most memorable segments, Presley, clad entirely in black leather and never looking better, performed both alone and with some of his early band mates, ripping through his classic songs and reminding the world why the appalled curators of popular culture got so rattled when he first strutted onto the American scene. The King, TV GUIDE recalled of the special in 1996, had "reclaimed his throne."

MY NAME IS BARBRA
Barbra Streisand.
CBS, April 28, 1965
COVER: BY FIROOZ ZAHEDI,
JANUARY 22, 2000

In the early 1960s, record buyers knew her as a singer, and theater-goers knew her as the star of the hit Broadway musical *Funny Girl*. But it wasn't until her first television special that a national audience discovered what a potent force of nature Barbra Streisand could really be. In one segment, the quirky-looking Brooklyn waif waltzed through the fashion fortress Bergdorf Goodman, trying on outfits as she stunned viewers with her rendition of "Brother, Can You Spare a Dime?" It was that regal voice that would propel one of show business's most storied careers. *My Name Is Barbra* won five Emmy awards, a feat she repeated 30 years later with another special, HBO's *Barbra Streisand: The Concert*.

CHARLIE'S ANGELS
Sabrina Duncan (Kate Jackson), Jill Munroe (Farrah Fawcett), Kelly Garrett (Jaclyn Smith). ABC, 1976–81
COVER: BY PETER KREDENSER, SEPTEMBER 25, 1976

"When the show was No. 3, I figured it was our acting," said Farrah Fawcett, discussing the success of *Charlie's Angels* with TV GUIDE at the end of its instant-hit debut season. "When we got to be No. 1, I decided it could only be because none of us wears a bra." Bingo. The previous fall, the magazine had similarly divined the appeal of this show, about a trio of female private detectives who "drive race cars, stack decks, karate-chop 300-pound brutes…. Is any of this believable? Not remotely." Ditto the acting, which ranged "from adequate to preposterous. But with all that skin and hair on display, who notices?" If the series itself was popular, Fawcett was a bona fide phenomenon. "No one ever attained this kind of superstardom so fast," said the magazine. Though other actresses took over as relief Angels during the show's five-year run, the classic threesome was Fawcett, Jaclyn Smith and Kate Jackson. They fearlessly followed the instructions of their unseen boss, Charlie (the voice of John Forsythe), to investigate any dirty deed—as long as it also afforded an opportunity to don a bikini or maybe just a towel. Not that there was really much sex on *Charlie's Angels*—the show was all a big tease. Which also helps explain the hair.

BAYWATCH
C.J. Parker (Pamela Anderson). NBC, 1989–90; syndication, 1991–2001
COVER: BY JON RAGEL,
AUGUST 13, 1994

In 1994, when TV GUIDE selected "TV's Top 10 Guilty Pleasures," choosing No. 1 was "no contest," the magazine said. "It's *Baywatch*, the most popular TV show on the planet." That wasn't an exaggeration: Producer and star David Hasselhoff's syndicated series about the trials and titillations of stud-muffin and jiggly-minx lifeguards on Malibu Beach was being seen in 142 countries every week by an audience of more than one billion viewers. "I think there is this mystery about California that everybody in the world is sort of drawn to," costar Pamela Anderson told the magazine—the primary mystery being, of course, how long you would have to wait to see the next female lifeguard jog down the beach in slow-motion splendor.

DALLAS
J.R. Ewing (Larry Hagman), Cliff Barnes (Ken Kercheval), Bobby Ewing (Patrick Duffy). CBS, 1978–91

COVERS: BY ROBERT PHILLIPS, JUNE 16, 1979. BY GENE TRINDL, NOVEMBER 15, 1980. BY MARIO CASILLI, DECEMBER 29, 1984. BY TERESA FASOLINO, AUGUST 30, 1986

Dormant since the 1960s, the prime-time soap opera roared back to life like an oil-rig gusher with *Dallas*. Standing out even among such outsize characters as alcoholic Sue Ellen Ewing (Linda Gray) and upright Pam Ewing (Victoria Principal) was the gleefully amoral oilman J.R. Ewing. His attempted murder in a season-ending cliff-hanger inspired the burning question of the summer of '80: Who shot J.R.? "Villainy could be fun, and that's how I played it," Larry Hagman wrote of his character in TV GUIDE that year. In the article, Hagman also described how he fled to London in order to leverage his sudden popularity into a more lucrative contract—a successful ploy that surely would have made J.R. cackle with delight.

DYNASTY
Krystle Jennings Carrington (Linda Evans), Alexis Carrington Colby (Joan Collins). ABC, 1981–89
COVERS: BY ROBERT PHILLIPS, FEBRUARY 27, 1982. BY MARIO CASILLI, NOVEMBER 10, 1984; MARCH 23, 1985; AND DECEMBER 27, 1986

Big oil, big hair and big troubles were already proven winners on CBS's *Dallas* when ABC launched *Dynasty* as a challenger in 1981. "Trash with flash," TV GUIDE said of the new Denver-set prime-time soap. In addition to an eye-popping budget for extravagant clothing and furnishings, *Dynasty* also enjoyed one of television's great female rivalries: the pitting of lovely Krystle (Linda Evans), second wife of silky skunk Blake Carrington (John Forsythe), against his rapacious, vengeful-vamp first wife, Alexis, played to the hilt by Joan Collins. In 1985, *Dynasty* finished No. 1 in the ratings, having out-trashed and out-flashed even J.R. Ewing and Co.

THE MAD BUSINESS OF RUNNING FOR PRESIDENT
By Edward P. Morgan

TV GUIDE

15¢

LOCAL PROGRAMS
OCTOBER 3-9

MIA FARROW
OF 'PEYTON PLACE'

PEYTON PLACE
ABC, 1964–69
COVER: BY DENNIS CAMERON, OCTOBER 3, 1964

Daytime soap-opera mores moved to prime time in 1964 with the debut of *Peyton Place*, based on the popular novel by Grace Metalious. (The 1957 feature-film adaptation starred Lana Turner.) Airing twice a week and then three times a week in its second season, the series tracked the shenanigans of citizens in a small but prodigiously frisky New England town. Over the show's run, TV GUIDE's opinion paralleled the public's: A review in 1964 was enthusiastic—"We are not ones to equate bigness with goodness, but this show is, for once, both"—but by 1966, it had cooled toward the "single-minded monotony with which Peyton people face life, hunching over the ghastly sins and secrets that have taken place off screen and long ago." Still, the magazine asked, "who among us will deny the eternity in Mia Farrow's wide, wide eyes?" The show itself, however, would have far less than an eternity with its breakout star—Farrow quit shortly thereafter. Her character, Allison MacKenzie, mysteriously disappeared, and was kept alive by the arrival in town of other characters toting clues to her existence: a bracelet on one occasion, a baby on another. But even the mama Mia story line couldn't save *Peyton*'s place in the ratings—or ABC's schedule.

TWIN PEAKS
Laura Palmer (Sheryl Lee). ABC, 1990–91
COVER: BY MARIO CASILLI, SEPTEMBER 8, 1990

Who killed Laura Palmer? That was the question that millions of mesmerized fans wanted answered in the spring of 1990, when this astonishing, unearthly vision of life in a Pacific Northwest logging town shimmered into view. On the surface, the plot outline sounded at least reasonably conventional: The murder of a homecoming queen sparks an investigation led by FBI agent Dale Cooper (Kyle MacLachlan), who uncovers dark secrets in a town where characters are jumping in and out of one another's beds and where the rich folks are greedy and duplicitous. But that doesn't begin to suggest the hypnotic strangeness of creator David Lynch's vision, or the sense of warped normalcy conveyed by characters like Cooper. No one familiar with Lynch's truly twisted movies (*Eraserhead*, *Blue Velvet*) would ever have guessed he would turn up on television. But here he was, creeping us out with a fetishist's-eye view of everyday objects and reveling in his ability to manipulate the camera, his characters and the audience. Lynch rejected charges that he was merely perpetrating a camped-up soap opera: "Camp is not only not creative," he told TV GUIDE in '90, "it is putting yourself above something else that has already been done and poking fun at it. To me, that is a lower kind of humor." What Lynch was striving for, he said, was to create "a fantastic mood and sense of place...and hopefully you want to go back and feel it each week." Viewers did just that, and *Twin Peaks* was given a second season on ABC—which turned out to be a mistake. The stylish tricks and contorted plotlines quickly began to look like self-parody. That's too bad, because if the show had ended after its first six-week run, *Twin Peaks* might easily have been remembered as the coolest thing ever on television.

BEWITCHED
**Samantha Stephens (Elizabeth Montgomery), Endora (Agnes Moorehead), Darrin Stephens (Dick York).
ABC, 1964–72**
COVER: BY IVAN NAGY, MAY 29, 1965

Just in case some grad student in the semiotics of pop culture is contemplating a paper on the situation comedy and how it influences social evolution, here's an excellent candidate for deconstruction: *Bewitched*. Consider this: In 1964, as cultural upheaval was rocking the nation, we were presented with Darrin Stephens (Dick York), a '50s-style soldier in the gray-flannel army who diligently marched off to work every day while, back at home, *everybody else was on acid*. At least that's how it looked sometimes in this comedy about a straitlaced ad man who discovered that his well-scrubbed, all-American wife, Samantha (Elizabeth Montgomery), was really a witch. Darrin, worried about what his boss and neighbors would think, insisted that she suppress her nose-twitching power to alter the world. But Samantha couldn't resist using her magic to sort out a few

problems—and indeed, her supernatural family members *did* complicate life, like when Julius Caesar showed up instead of a Caesar salad. Audiences adored the show and especially Montgomery. But York may have had his own spooky powers. In a 1964 TV GUIDE article, he said there was only one way to tell for sure if he was overshadowed on the show by Montgomery because of his role or his acting ability: "Kill me off in one show, give the witch another husband and see if I'm missed." As it turned out, York, ailing with a chronic back injury, left the series in 1969 and was replaced by Dick Sargent—without an explanation to viewers. *Bewitched*'s ratings quickly eroded, and it was canceled in 1972. The show became a syndication favorite, as did the pastime of comparing the merits of old Darrin and new Darrin.

BUFFY THE VAMPIRE SLAYER
Buffy Summers (Sarah Michelle Gellar). WB, 1997–2001; UPN, 2001–
COVER: BY FRANK OCKENFELS 3, AUGUST 2, 1997

TV GUIDE had a thing for *Buffy the Vampire Slayer*, putting the show—OK, Sarah Michelle Gellar—on the cover twice in two and a half years, publishing an exhaustive guide to every episode of the first three seasons and even commissioning a five-page comic-book-style *Buffy* adventure. And why not? The series (based on the 1992 feature film of the same name) delectably combined the adolescent coming-of-age saga with horror-movie excess, then seasoned it with a dash of postmodern knowing-ness. Buffy Summers faced the usual trials of trying to fit in at a new school when the series began (a popular girl gave her this test: "John Tesh?" Buffy correctly answered: "The devil"), but she faced the added burden of being a vampire slayer in her spare time. Her assignment, which continued even after she moved on to college and beyond, was protecting Sunnydale, a town that had the misfortune of being located at the mouth

of hell itself. Guided by her "Watcher," the peculiar school librarian, and assisted by pals known as the Scooby Gang, Buffy battled various fiends with wooden stakes, crucifixes and the occasional kick upside their slavering heads. *Buffy*'s writing was a marvel, swinging easily from droll comedy to the moving romantic trauma of Buffy's ill-fated liaison with the dark Angel (David Boreanaz). Series creator Joss Whedon even memorably crafted an hour-long episode without a word of dialogue for 30 minutes and another composed almost entirely of original song-and-dance numbers. Gellar speculated in TV GUIDE in 2000 that girls liked her Buffy character because she's "not the smartest or the most beautiful. She's kind of awkward, but she is OK with who she is." Guys were attracted to the character, Gellar said, because "they see Buffy as a take-charge, kick-ass girl who has never lost her femininity."

THE TWILIGHT ZONE
Rod Serling; Virginia Gregg, Milton Selzer, Alan Sues, Brooke Hayward; Julie Newmar, Albert Salmi; William Shatner; Agnes Moorehead. CBS, 1959–64

Thanks to Rod Serling's sterling reputation as a drama writer in the 1950s, he was able to interest CBS in an anthology of half-hour shows that shared only one trait: an unadulterated love of the strange. Although Serling took advantage of the anything-eerie-goes format to delve into social issues—like neo-Nazism in an episode starring a young Dennis Hopper—more often *The Twilight Zone* just reveled in unnerving fables with dramatic plot twists. These are the shows that get kicked around whenever a group of baby boomers turns to that beloved parlor game, My Creepiest *Twilight Zone* Episode (bonus points: name the celebrity-to-be). Was it the one where a guy on an airplane (played by the then-unknown William Shatner) goes nuts thinking he sees a creature out on the wing trying to tear it apart? (As they lead him away to the loony bin, he looks up and sees the mangled evidence that he was not hallucinating after all.) Or maybe it was the one where we're told that a hideously deformed woman has undergone a last-chance operation to make her look presentable enough to live among "normal people." (The operation is a horrific failure when the bandages are peeled away to reveal that she's still a beautiful woman—it's the doctors and nurses who look like gargoyles.) As Stephen King wrote in *Danse Macabre*, a collection of his meditations on horror that was excerpted in TV GUIDE in 1981, *The Twilight Zone* "generated a kind of existential weirdness that no other series has been able to match."

There is a fifth dimension beyond that which is known to man. It is a dimension as vast as space and as timeless as infinity. It is the middle ground between light and shadow, between science and superstition, and it lies between the pit of man's fears and the summit of his knowledge. This is the dimension of imagination. It is an area which we call **The Twilight Zone**

XENA: WARRIOR PRINCESS
Xena (Lucy Lawless).
Syndication, 1995–2001
COVER: BY GARY HEERY, MAY 3, 1997

When Xena hurled her last razor-sharp chakram disk after six years of syndicated success, TV GUIDE noted "X Things We'll Miss" about her and Lucy Lawless, the actress behind the Amazonian sci-fi/fantasy babe. They included: "The Grrrl Power" (Xena once kicked the entire Persian army's collective butt); "The Fashions" ("We were always a sucker for a gal in a wrought-iron bra"); and "The Lesbian Subtext" (Xena's unstated relationship with comic-relief sidekick Gabrielle titillated many fans). As if those attributes weren't enough, the magazine also celebrated *Xena*'s message: "The show's plea for tolerance and its timeless advice—be true to yourself—are the ultimate cool."

STAR TREK: THE NEXT GENERATION
Capt. Jean-Luc Picard (Patrick Stewart). Syndication, 1987–94
COVER: BY MICHEL TCHEREVKOFF, MAY 14, 1994

Eighteen years after the original *Star Trek* succumbed to anemic TV ratings, but just eight years after the return of Captain Kirk et al. to boffo box-office movie success, the franchise returned to television in 1987 with *Star Trek: The Next Generation*. Far from a case of simple opportunism, the new series gave the ultimate starship commander, executive producer Gene Roddenberry, the chance to stage his trademark optimistic, intergalactic morality plays, but with a bigger budget and way cooler special effects. Advancing the story a hundred years, into the 24th century, Roddenberry posited a starship *Enterprise* twice the size of its predecessor, with an onboard barroom and a crew of more than a thousand. Calling *Next Generation* "a worthy successor" to the original series, TV GUIDE in 1988 said Roddenberry had "lost none of his ingenuity or his taste in selecting stories," which "carry a message of hope, a belief that mankind is growing—and maturing." Patrick Stewart, who as Capt. Jean-Luc Picard replaced Kirk's pugnacious, skirt-chasing ways with a more diplomatic, fatherly mien, was "terrific," the magazine said. He was supported by a "capable ensemble, all of whom understand the secret of acting in a science-fiction show—believe the story, no matter how wild." Far from doing some sci-fi slumming, the British Shakespearean actor Stewart told the magazine in 1993 that he was proud of the series. "Even though it's full of fun, high adventure, dazzling technology and all kinds of bizarre creatures, it's a very serious show," he said. Perhaps explaining the enduring appeal of *Star Trek* across the decades, Stewart added: "If you treat people as intelligent, sophisticated and cultivated as you can possibly imagine, chances are they just might be."

ANIMAL MAGNETISM

1) **THE LONE RANGER** (Clayton Moore) with Silver, Tonto (Jay Silverheels) with Scout. ABC, 1949-57

2) **THE ADVENTURES OF RIN TIN TIN** Native American (actor unknown), Rusty (Lee Aaker) with Rin Tin Tin. CBS, 1954-59

3) **THE PEOPLE'S CHOICE** Socrates "Sock" Miller (Jackie Cooper) with Cleo. NBC, 1955-58

4) **MY THREE SONS** Steve Douglas (Fred MacMurray) with Tramp. ABC, 1960-65; CBS, 1965-72

5) **THE JETSONS** George Jetson with Astro. ABC, 1962-63

6) **FLIPPER** Bud Ricks (Tommy Norden) with Flipper. NBC, 1964-68

7) **DAKTARI** Paula Tracy (Cheryl Miller), Bart Jason (Ross Hagen) with Clarence. CBS, 1966-69

8) **GENTLE BEN** Mark Wedloe (Clint Howard) with Ben. CBS, 1967-69

9) **LANCELOT LINK, SECRET CHIMP** Undercover simians. ABC, 1970-72

10) **BARETTA** Det. Tony Baretta (Robert Blake) with Fred. ABC, 1975-78

11) **MAD ABOUT YOU** Paul Buchman (Paul Reiser), Jamie Buchman (Helen Hunt) with Murray. NBC, 1992-99

12) **THE CROCODILE HUNTER** Steve Irwin, Terri Irwin with title creature. ANIMAL PLANET, 1996-

AN AMERICAN FAMILY
Clockwise from top left: Lance Loud, Delilah Loud, Grant Loud, Kevin Loud, Michele Loud, Pat Loud, Bill Loud. PBS, 1973

Long before *Big Brother* or *The Real World*, there was *An American Family*—a 12-part PBS documentary that riveted the country in 1973. For an hour every week, we stepped into the home of the Loud family of Santa Barbara, California, seeing first-hand the quotidian events and emotional dramas that occurred during the seven months that they lived under the unblinking gaze of the camera. The two signal moments of the series were the parents' breakup, when Pat Loud asked her philandering husband, Bill, to move out of the house, and Pat's trip to New York City. There, her son Lance—one of five Loud children—revealed he was gay, appeared on screen wearing blue lipstick and introduced his mom to the transvestite netherworld. Anthropologist Margaret Mead, writing in TV GUIDE, called the camera-as-witness programming "as new and as significant as the invention of drama or the novel—a new way in which people can learn to look at life." But *An American Family* also provoked a storm of criticism. The Louds themselves disavowed the documentary as a distorted view of their life. As TV GUIDE reported in a two-part investigation: "The family feels that [producer Craig] Gilbert and the editors were too eager to include pessimistic scenes." Pat added: "Knowing what I know now, I wouldn't go through it again." Other sniping came from critics who debated whether "the beleaguered family," as TV GUIDE called them, was being used "as an example of nearly everything that is supposedly going wrong with American society." For his part, Gilbert insisted that he wasn't trying to "propound universal truths" about families. But perhaps one universal truth of television did emerge from the affair: Whatever its controversies, "reality" programming—like a train wreck—holds an enduring fascination all its own.

THE OSBOURNES
Kelly Osbourne, Ozzy Osbourne, Sharon Osbourne, Jack Osbourne. MTV, 2002–

These things are hard to pin down, but TV GUIDE appears to have coined the subsequently ubiquitous phrase "Ozzy and Harried" to describe the cult TV hit of 2002, *The Osbournes*. That was the headline for a prescient late-February story about a show that didn't debut until March 5—and quickly became the biggest hit MTV had ever seen. Ozzy Osbourne, the middle-aged British heavy-metal star with a leaky brainpan, was the foul-mouthed, befuddled centerpiece of this genre salad: equal parts anti-*Ozzie and Harriet* family comedy, reality-TV show and special Beverly Hills edition of *This Is Spiñal Tap*. Osbourne worried aloud to TV GUIDE that fans of his old bat-gnawing excess might be disappointed to see him at home flummoxed by the remote control—"I wonder if it will crush their illusion about me"—but his wife and manager, the sardonic Sharon, reassured him: "People know you're not some mystical bloodsucking creature. You're a cottage-cheese eater." One of the Osbournes' teenagers, Aimee, opted out of the series, but second-generation rock and roll kids Kelly and Jack clomped through the dog-clogged Osbourne manse in a perpetual adolescent funk. "I have the foulest mouth on earth, and I don't really care," Kelly told TV GUIDE in April 2002, proving she's a *bleep* off the old block.

"It's 25 minutes of bleeps. It made me realize that we live in Beverly Hills and we sound like we live in a f---ing trailer park. What you see is the way it is; none of it's been doctored. None of it's hammed up. It's real. It's The Ozzy Osbourne Real World."
—Ozzy Osbourne

TV GUIDE

Behind Scenes Report:
THE PRESIDENT ON TV

LOCAL PROGRAM LISTINGS
Week Of May 7—13

15c

Nelsons—
Mother
And Sons

THE ADVENTURES OF OZZIE & HARRIET
Harriet Nelson, Ozzie Nelson, David Nelson, Ricky Nelson.
ABC, 1952–66
COVER: PHOTOGRAPHER UNKNOWN, MAY 7, 1954

Here's an idea for a reality-TV series: Lock a family of four in a house and come back with a TV camera once a week for 14 years to see what goes on. That's essentially what happened with *The Adventures of Ozzie & Harriet*, except the premise didn't inspire any secret alliances or backstabbing. Or, for that matter, much in the way of adventure. But the addictively pleasant comedy starring the real-life Nelson family enjoyed an epic run anyway (after eight years on radio) and provided a window for America into an idealized suburbia. The country watched as Ozzie and Harriet's two sons, David and Ricky, grew up in real time in a pleasant middle-class house modeled on the Nelsons' own Hollywood home. If one of the boys took up singing, it went into the show—and it turned Ricky Nelson into a pop star. If the boys got married, then their real-life wives joined their on-air family too. "Occasionally, critics have complained that everyone on our show is a nice person," Ozzie, the series' creator, director and cowriter, told TV GUIDE in 1963. "I don't understand this type of complaint. Most people are pretty nice." It was just such unquestioning optimism that would forever make *Ozzie & Harriet* the cultural archetype of its era.

JOHNNY CARSON AND HIS CHALLENGERS
See page 6

THE ADDAMS FAMILY
Gomez Addams (John Astin), Uncle Fester Frump (Jackie Coogan), Cousin Itt. ABC, 1964–66
COVER: ILLUSTRATION BY CHARLES ADDAMS, PHOTOGRAPHS BY IVAN NAGY, OCTOBER 30, 1965

When social change in the mid-'60s started chipping away at the institution of the traditional family, TV did its part by mocking Ozzie-and-Harriet values with two comedies launched in 1964: *The Munsters* (on CBS) and *The Addams Family*. Both shows wanted to wring laughs from the ghoul-next-door conceit, but as TV GUIDE pronounced at the time, "*The Addams Family* is far and away the most delectable." The show, inspired by Charles Addams's creepy-funny cartoons for *The New Yorker* magazine, stood conventional family life on its head: The morbid kids, Pugsley and Wednesday, skipped school because the class reading, *Grimms' Fairy Tales*, unfairly depicted cruelty to dragons, and their mother, the sepulchral Morticia, gushed wanly over her garden of deadly nightshade. Gomez, meanwhile, put a stake in the heart of the traditional neutered TV dad with a passionate, even carnal, devotion to his wife. Addams applauded what had become of his creations. "The casting has been superb," Addams wrote in TV GUIDE in 1965, "and Carolyn Jones and John Astin, as heads of this household, are beyond my reproach." The show left a pop-cultural legacy—two *Addams Family* feature films were released in the '90s—that lingered, like the undead, far beyond its two seasons on the air.

"WE HAPPENED TO HAVE A SHOW DURING A CULTURAL REVOLUTION

and a political revolution in this country. It was serendipitous, really. We were at the scene of the accident, and the times form you a little bit. And so we used comedy for our politics. Things had heated up in the Vietnam War and protests were out there, so we started reflecting more of what younger people were thinking. We were in our late twenties at that time and most of our writers were in their early twenties, so there was a certain passion there, and it showed up in sketches on the war and voter registration. And also in 1968, Martin Luther King Jr. was shot, Bobby Kennedy was shot, the riots at the Democratic Convention in Chicago—all that stuff happened during the time we were on the air. So basically, we expressed those alternative points of view that weren't being reflected, and it became a battle with the network censors. We'd put up a sign, ANOTHER MOTHER FOR PEACE. They'd say, well, you can't do that because it could be a Communist front organization or something like that. We played some games and had some fun. The last season, I said, 'If you're that unhappy with us, then don't pick us up.' They picked us up. But about three months later the election was over, Richard M. Nixon won over Hubert Humphrey, and in April we were fired. The Nixon administration wasn't going to have the Smothers Brothers critiquing their war effort."

—TOM SMOTHERS

THE SMOTHERS BROTHERS COMEDY HOUR
Tom Smothers, Dick Smothers. CBS, 1967–69
COVER: BY BOB PEAK, FEBRUARY 10, 1968

TV GUIDE applauded the arrival of *The Smothers Brothers Comedy Hour* in 1967, even though it wasn't sure if they were "folksinging comedians or comedy folksingers." Dick plucked the stand-up bass and was the level-headed foil for guitar-playing Tom's flights of fuzzy, convoluted logic—which somehow always led to his blurting out, "Mom always liked you better!" TV GUIDE's review, just a couple of months into the show, did issue a caveat: "One area in which this show could be improved is in the matter of taste." The magazine scolded the duo for using the rock group Paul Revere and the Raiders to lampoon Revolutionary War heroes. But if the magazine was sensi-tive about such matters, CBS was downright sore. The network fought to expunge anything controversial, particularly about religion or contemporary politics, despite the fact that the show's irreverence had made it immediately popular with viewers. The battles escalated until CBS canceled the series mid-hit after two seasons. The show "is much better in people's memories than it ever really was," Dick told TV GUIDE in 1988. Indeed, as the magazine noted, its martyrdom to the cause of free-dom of expression was "in its way, a blessing. The Smothers Brothers were forever fixed in public consciousness, a part of American cultural history."

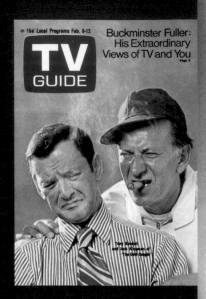

THE ODD COUPLE
Felix Unger (Tony Randall), Oscar Madison (Jack Klugman). ABC, 1970–75
COVER: BY GENE TRINDL, FEBRUARY 6, 1971

Neil Simon's conceit about two mismatched roommates, Felix the finicky photographer and Oscar the slobby sportswriter, played on Broadway and in movie theaters before moving to TV in 1970. Art Carney and Walter Matthau took the dueling duo on stage, while Jack Lemmon and Matthau were on the big screen. Tough acts to follow. But Tony Randall and Jack Klugman "are actually better than their predecessors" in the roles, said TV GUIDE, bringing subtler shadings to their characters: Randall delivered "something besides neurosis," and Klugman "something besides vulgarity." Those accomplishments aside, the magazine noted, "they never forget that the main point is to be funny."

MIKE JUDGE

HEH HEH
HEH

THE BEAVIS AND BUTT-HEAD SHOW
Butt-head, Beavis. MTV, 1993–97

"These characters are like guys I knew in junior high," *Beavis and Butt-head Show* creator Mike Judge told TV GUIDE shortly after its attention-grabbing debut on MTV. "Vulgar schoolyard humor is just the way they are." Critics deplored the proudly moronic duo's antics, such as using frogs for batting practice, urinating in swimming pools and starting fires (a rite of passage into juvenile delinquency that may have prompted copycat torchings among young viewers). But the cartoon cretins were in fact deftly satirizing the sex-obsessed, violence-fascinated, dumbbell layabouts in MTV's own audience. When the series ended, there was only one way to describe the announcement: It sucked.

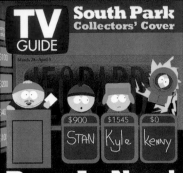

SOUTH PARK
Mrs. Broflovski, Kenny McCormick. Comedy Central, 1997–
COVER: BY *SOUTH PARK*, MARCH 28, 1998

A town that might be visited by aliens one day and a diarrhea epidemic the next. A school-cafeteria cook who croons his advice to schoolchildren in songs dripping with sexually explicit lyrics. A kid who vomits whenever he gets near the girl he adores; another who's a fat, foul-mouthed bully; and yet another who met a grisly death in nearly every episode (until his final gasp in the show's fifth season). Welcome to *South Park*, the playground of animation team Trey Parker and Matt Stone. "What we're trying to say is, nothing is sacred," Stone told TV GUIDE shortly after the show's 1997 debut. The Comedy Central series, with animation that was rivaled in crudeness only by its language, immediately provoked outrage from guardians of the culture—and sheer delight among fans. The *South Park* buzz was so strong that cable companies not carry-ing Comedy Central were deluged with phone calls demanding that they add it. Within months, T-shirts and other merchandise featuring *South Park*'s four third-graders—Kyle, Stan, Cartman and Kenny—were pouring out of stores, and in addition to countless obscenities, the show had its own catchphrase: "Oh, my God, they killed Kenny!" The quiet kid buried deep inside his hooded parka had to die over and over again, Stone told the magazine, because "we just like to kill him. And we really like the line." Despite the cartoon's joyously juvenile humor, TV GUIDE called *South Park* "one of the most sophisticated shows on TV these days" for its send-up of life in small-town Colorado. "There are some things that are kind of wholesome about *South Park*," Parker told the magazine. "The bottom line is that as insane as it gets, right always sort of wins."

LEAVE IT TO BEAVER
Wally Cleaver (Tony Dow), Theodore "Beaver" Cleaver (Jerry Mathers).
CBS, 1957–58; ABC, 1958–63
COVER: BY GARRETT-HOWARD, JUNE 28, 1958

This show achieved a minor miracle during its run: It built a TV franchise on a simple, gimmick-free depiction of the domestic life of a nice family in a pleasant small town. TV GUIDE called the half hours with the Cleaver family in mythical Mayfield "one of the most honest, most human and most satisfying situation comedies on TV." While Ward Cleaver (Hugh Beaumont) was the sensible dad and his wife, June (Barbara Billingsley), the sweet-tempered and patient mom, the heart of *Leave It to Beaver* was the kids—Wally (Tony Dow), who was 12 and on the cusp of adolescence as the series began, and Theodore (Jerry Mathers), aka Beaver, whose 7-year-old's perspective on the world suffused the show with the innocent joys of everyday life. Beaver was forever stumbling into one mild crisis after another, such as losing the

money entrusted to him by his father for a haircut and resolving to cut his own hair—a few days before appearing in a school play. Wally, impatient to grow up, fumed at being drawn back into Beaver's childish predicaments, but invariably helped out his brother despite the heckling of his friend Eddie Haskell (Ken Osmond). Though you sometimes still hear references to "June Cleaver" to describe the perfect mom, "Eddie Haskell" remains a vivid shorthand for a two-faced weasel, in this case a teenager whose elaborate politeness to adults ("*Good evening*, Mr. and Mrs. Cleaver") masks real contempt. *Leave It to Beaver* was a reliable performer, but it was during years of reruns that the show, with a characteristic lack of fanfare, gently won over viewers' affection.

THE LONG ARM OF THE LAW

1) THE MAN FROM U.N.C.L.E.
Napoleon Solo
(Robert Vaughn),
Illya Kuryakin
(David McCallum).
NBC, 1964-68

2) I SPY
Kelly Robinson (Robert Culp),
Alexander Scott
(Bill Cosby).
NBC, 1965-68

3) IRONSIDE
Robert Ironside
(Raymond Burr).
NBC, 1967-75

4) CANNON
Frank Cannon
(William Conrad).
CBS, 1971-76

5) KOJAK
Lt. Theo Kojak
(Telly Savalas).
CBS, 1973-78

6) STARSKY AND HUTCH
Det. Dave Starsky (Paul Michael
Glaser), Det. Ken "Hutch"
Hutchinson (David Soul).
ABC, 1975-79

7) QUINCY, M.E.
Dr. Quincy (Jack Klugman).
NBC, 1976-83

8) POLICE SQUAD
Det. Frank Drebin
(Leslie Nielsen).
ABC, 1982

9) MacGYVER
MacGyver
(Richard Dean Anderson).
ABC, 1985-92

10) WISEGUY
Vinnie Terranova (Ken Wahl).
CBS, 1987-90

11) MYSTERY!: "POIROT"
Hercule Poirot (David Suchet).
PBS, 1989-99

12) MYSTERY!: "PRIME SUSPECT"
DCI Jane Tennison
(Helen Mirren).
PBS, 1991-94

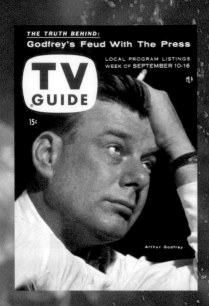

ARTHUR GODFREY

Date unknown
COVER: PHOTOGRAPHER UNKNOWN,
SEPTEMBER 10, 1955

It's probably safe to say that no one whose only talent was a charismatic personality will ever dominate television the way Arthur Godfrey loomed over TV in the early 1950s. In addition to his radio show, which was being televised, he hosted two monster hit series, *Arthur Godfrey's Talent Scouts* and *Arthur Godfrey and His Friends*, which in 1952–53 finished second and third in the ratings behind *I Love Lucy*. *Talent Scouts* was just what the name implied, a showcase for amateurs and rising pros (Pat Boone and the McGuire Sisters among them); *Friends* was a variety show of performers, mostly singers, who got their break with Godfrey. But in both cases, the real attraction was the host himself, whose avuncular charm made him famous on '40s radio and translated deftly to television. Godfrey's championing of unknown performers, and his needling of corporate sponsors, established "the old redhead" as the little guy's best friend—a bond that endured until 1953, when Godfrey fired singer Julius LaRosa on the air. "That, folks, was Julie's swan song," Godfrey said after the unsuspecting LaRosa finished a number. LaRosa was an unknown when Godfrey discovered him, but had become a recording star and fan favorite on *Friends*. The press reaction to his canning was thunderously negative, particularly after Godfrey explained that LaRosa had been dumped for lacking "humility." The host then lashed out at his disapproving critics and started firing more stars and staff. The affair "ultimately shrank his TV empire almost to the dimensions of a doghouse," TV GUIDE said in '63, noting that "the conflict of amiability and ill temper has always raged within Godfrey." For his part, Godfrey may have learned the first lesson of modern celebrity, telling the magazine, "I did not have a well-organized public relations outfit."

TV GUIDE

Daylight Time Starts: TV Headaches For You?

15¢

Red Skelton

THE RED SKELTON SHOW
NBC, 1951–53 and
1970–71; CBS, 1953–70
COVER: BY GARRETT-HOWARD,
APRIL 28, 1956

Kindhearted, tirelessly inventive clown Red Skelton appeared on TV GUIDE covers five times over the course of his comedy-variety show's 20-year history. The comedian may have kept a file cabinet full of tens of thousands of jokes, but Skelton was most beloved for the characters he created, including the hobo Freddie the Freeloader, country bumpkin Clem Kadiddlehopper, and the excessively bird-brained seagulls Gertrude and Heathcliffe. When Skelton died in 1997, frequent collaborator Marcel Marceau wrote in TV GUIDE: "Red Skelton brought joy, happiness and poetry to millions of children and grown-ups. In his field he had no peer."

'My Wife Jayne,' By Steve Allen

TV GUIDE

LOCAL PROGRAM LISTINGS
WEEK OF DECEMBER 1-7

15¢

George Burns
Gracie Allen

THE GEORGE BURNS AND GRACIE ALLEN SHOW
CBS, 1950–58
COVER: BY AL HIRSCHFELD, DECEMBER 1, 1956

By the time George Burns and Gracie Allen took their act to television—he was the cigar-puffing, bemused straight man to her endearing scatterbrain—it had been refined to perfection by decades of work in vaudeville and on radio. They could have easily coasted on the goodwill of their built-in audience, but *The George Burns and Gracie Allen Show* proved that they didn't need to: They had an apparently bottomless well of humor on which to draw. Only Gracie's decision to say good-night for the last time in '58 ended the show—though four years later, TV GUIDE was still celebrating the couple for finding so much comedy in "a husband and a wife who (miracle of miracles in these days!) seem to love each other."

THE SONNY AND CHER COMEDY HOUR
Sonny Bono, Cher Bono. CBS, 1971–74 and 1976–77
COVER: BY ROGER PRIGENT, JUNE 5, 1976

Yes, there was plenty of controversy (Cher Bono's outlandish, flesh-revealing Bob Mackie out-fits), lots of talent (guest stars like Teri Garr and Steve Martin) and dependable fun (regular skits such as "Sonny's Pizza" and Cher's vamp segment). But the heart of *The Sonny and Cher Comedy Hour* was the husband-and-wife ribbing between the puppyish Sonny Bono and sardonic Cher. "In a word, it's terrific," TV Guide said of the show in 1972, singling out Cher for praise: "Is there anything she can't do?" Yes, apparently: get along with Sonny. The couple's 1974 divorce scuttled *Sonny and Cher* at the height of its popularity. The two tried solo shows and then reunited two years later for a reprise of the original series, but the divorced duo never recap-tured the magic of the "I Got You, Babe" years.

MONTY PYTHON'S FLYING CIRCUS
John Cleese. BBC, 1969–74

In 1974, just as it was ending a five-year stint on the BBC, *Monty Python's Flying Circus* rolled into America, bringing its brilliantly loony brand of humor to public television. No subject was safe from the freewheeling, smarty-pants slapstick of the five British Oxford and Cambridge grads (Graham Chapman, John Cleese, Terry Jones, Eric Idle and Michael Palin) and their rarely seen American pal, Terry Gilliam, who provided the show's crudely executed but wickedly funny animated segments. Pretentious TV talk-show hosts, stuffy bureaucrats, Hollywood directors, harridan housewives, sadistic shop clerks—they all got skewered in sketches, blackouts, faux documentaries and anything else the troupe could cram into half hours that were the comic equivalent of five years' worth of *Saturday Night Live* episodes. "The fact that our satire was never specific makes it last," Gilliam told TV GUIDE in 1990. "Our targets are cosmically silly forever." To its eternal shame, TV GUIDE back in 1975 just didn't get the joke. "It was all so far-fetched that it was pathetic," the magazine said, singling out for criticism "The Ministry of Silly Walks," a now-classic Cleese performance. "Plodded on endlessly," the magazine harrumphed, just begging for someone to apply the trademark Python silencer, a smack in the face with a large fish.

THE ERNIE KOVACS SHOW
CBS, 1952–53; NBC, 1956
COVER: BY PHILLIPE HALSMAN, MAY 14, 1960

It's difficult to say which was more stunning: *The Ernie Kovacs Show* itself, or the fact that it only ran for a grand total of eight months (five in 1952-53 and three in 1956). Kovacs, still regarded by many as one of the most inventive, iconoclastic and funny comedians in television history, flouted virtually every convention of the medium, then and now. There was simply no one else on television to whom it would occur, for instance, to let the screen go black—except for the lines of an oscilloscope undulating to the sound of "Mack the Knife" sung in the original German. Further absurdist adventures in musical comedy included regularly convening the Nairobi Trio: Three guys, always dressed in gorilla suits, slowly played the same tune until one got bonked on the head. They would pause, then return to their song. Kovacs's sense of humor was indeed lost on some people—he was never a ratings giant—but anyone who saw his work never forgot it. He parodied other TV shows and commercials, brilliantly adapted TV technology to create surreal special effects and dreamed up recurring characters like the pricelessly fey poet Percy Dovetonsils. "While Sid Caesar and Imogene Coca were keeping millions in stitches over a domestic quarrel," Chevy Chase wrote in a TV GUIDE tribute in 1977, "Ernie was tilting sets, doing entire specials with no dialogue whatsoever and daringly working without a studio audience. He was, and remains, fresh and innovative, and above all—because this is the bottom line—funny." Although his series was short-lived, Kovacs was wonderfully prolific, bringing his trademark comedy to *The Tonight Show* as a fill-in for Steve Allen, creating TV specials and even hosting a game show. Kovacs's life was cut short: He died in 1962, at age 42, in a car accident in Los Angeles.

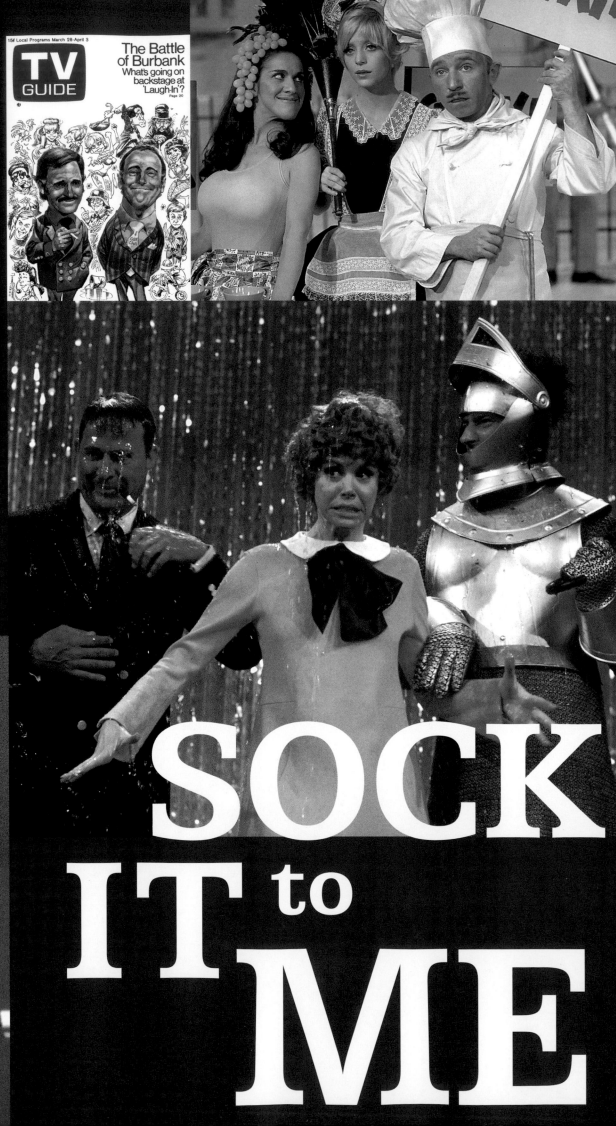

ROWAN AND MARTIN'S LAUGH-IN
Clockwise from top right: Ruth Buzzi, Goldie Hawn, Henry Gibson; Dick Martin, Judy Carne, Dan Rowan; Arte Johnson. NBC, 1968–73
COVER: BY JACK DAVIS, MARCH 28, 1970

Early in the second season of *Rowan and Martin's Laugh-In*, hosts Dan Rowan (the suave one) and Dick Martin (the goofy playboy) presented a plaque to executive producer George Schlatter that read: IN SKATING OVER THIN ICE—OUR SAFETY IS OUR SPEED. *Laugh-In* was nothing if not fast: a whirling kaleidoscope of pratfalls, trapdoors, one-liners, bikini-clad and body-painted dancers, and joke-spouting celebrity guests that slipped daring (for the time) humor about politics and sex into scripts teeming with pure silliness. The show went to No. 1 in the ratings in its first two full seasons at the end of the '60s. Then it imploded as stars departed, behind-the-scenes bickering escalated and, most likely, the frenetic show simply wore out its welcome and its audience. But for two exhilarating years, *Laugh-In* was a major pop-cultural presence. (The show's reach was vividly demonstrated when presidential candidate Richard M. Nixon appeared on *Laugh-In* saying, "Sock it to *me*?") Judy Carne as the sock-it-to-me waif, Goldie Hawn as the endearingly giggly dumb blond, Lily Tomlin's coyly snorting telephone operator, Arte Johnson's "Verrrry interesting" Nazi—these characters became instant classics of American comedy. "Whatever happens to the show now," TV GUIDE said in 1970, "it has earned its niche as a genuine phenomenon of the 1960s, breaking the stale old mold of the standard host-guest-comic-choreography variety show, and substituting, instead, irreverence, bawdiness and topical 'today' humor, aimed like buckshot at children and intellectuals alike." Hawn was already feeling nostalgic in 1972, two years after leaving the show and a year before it ended: "The farther away I get, the more beautiful it becomes," she told TV GUIDE. "When I look at the old pictures, I could cry."

IN LIVING COLOR
Clockwise from near left: Jim Carrey; Damon Wayans, David Alan Grier; Wayans; the Fly Girls. Fox, 1990—94

The upstart Fox network, anxious to distinguish itself from the TV big boys in the early '90s, accomplished just that with *In Living Color*. It was the anti–*Saturday Night Live*: mostly black instead of mostly white, and a half hour crammed full of funny sketches instead of 90 minutes of sometimes spotty humorous moments. Creative multi-tasker Keenen Ivory Wayans was the engine behind the show and its main star, though he was surrounded by plenty of talent, from his brother Damon to Fly Girl dancer Jennifer Lopez to force-of-nature comedian Jim Carrey (working under the name James). Sketches to look forward to every week included "Men on Film," with the gayest cineasts around ("Two snaps up!"), and Damon's humorless Homey the Clown ("Homey don't play that"). Unfortunately, *In Living Color* went on life support after just two seasons when Keenen quit the show (followed by four of his siblings on the payroll) because of a dispute with Fox over the network's use of reruns, which he felt damaged the show's value in syndication. *In Living Color* left the air in '94 after one more season, but the memory remains: a dazzling example of a comedy-variety series brimming with energy and take-no-prisoners humor.

MILTON BERLE
Date unknown
COVER: BY AL HIRSCHFELD,
JANUARY 10, 1959

If you were one of the few hundred thousand people in America who owned a television set in 1948, on Tuesday nights at 8 P.M. you were almost by definition watching—probably in the company of a few friends and neighbors—*Texaco Star Theater*, better known as *The Milton Berle Show*. Berle would himself soon become better known as Mr. Television, or Uncle Miltie, as consumers anxious to watch the anything-for-a-joke-comedian sent the sale of TV sets soaring across the country. Municipalities reported drastic surges in water usage the moment the comedy-variety series left the air at 9 P.M. One theater owner in Ohio hung a sign in the lobby that said: CLOSED TUESDAY. I WANT TO SEE BERLE TOO. And what was everyone so excited about seeing? A vaudeville and radio veteran madly exploiting the new television medium with an avalanche of puns, one-liners and, above all, sight gags. Berle would black out his front teeth, don a dress, take a shot of seltzer or a pie in the face, stumble into a juggler's act or come out on stage as a caveman after being introduced as "the man with the jokes from the Stone Age." The frantic shows were all live, with Berle so completely involved in the production that he was often shot from the waist up so the TV audience couldn't see his hands signaling the cameras. In 1959, three years after his phenomenal run ended, Berle told TV GUIDE, "I'm the kind of greasepaint bum—not 'bum'; make that 'ham'—who likes to hear the sound of applause."

I'M SO GLAD WE HAD this TIME TOGETHER

THE CAROL BURNETT SHOW
CBS, 1967–78
COVER: BY AL HIRSCHFELD, APRIL 11, 1970

One of the secrets of Carol Burnett's immense appeal was that she always imagined herself performing for a very specific middle-American couple that she named "Fred and Marge." The couple was "smart, they know everything," Burnett told TV GUIDE in 1972. You couldn't play down to them, she said, you couldn't be too risqué and you couldn't get away with a mediocre production. Hence *The Carol Burnett Show*, television's last great variety series. By 1963, TV GUIDE had already dubbed Burnett "America's most raucous female comic," but her gifts for clowning, singing and dancing found their ideal showcase in the variety show that launched four years later. The series was packed with marvelous performers, including Harvey Korman, Lyle Waggoner, Tim Conway and Vicki Lawrence. Among the many terrific regular features, the movie parodies got some of the biggest laughs. "Went With the Wind," a satire of a certain Civil War classic, itself became a classic with moments like the one where "Ratt" admires the dress that "Starlett" has made out of curtains (including the rod) and she replies, "I saw it in a window and I just couldn't resist it." The shows often started informally, with Burnett and that week's guest star answering the studio audience's questions; each broadcast ended with Burnett singing "It's Time to Say Goodbye" and tugging on her earlobe, originally a secret signal to her grandmother. The public's affection for Burnett endured long after the show left the air. A CBS special 23 years later in November 2001, with the former cast members chatting in between old outtakes, was the week's top-rated show, drawing 30 million viewers.

15¢ • Local Programs April 11-17

TV GUIDE

Don't blame us for bad news: A TV news director's plea Page 3

Carol Burnett

THE '70s

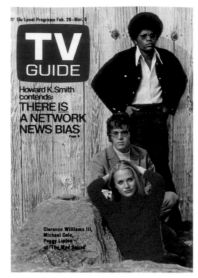

February 28, 1970
By Raphael
Clarence Williams III, Michael Cole and
Peggy Lipton of *The Mod Squad*

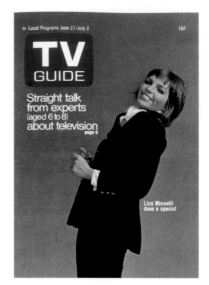

June 27, 1970
By Raphael
Liza Minnelli

October 31, 1970
By Gene Trindl
Mike Connors of *Mannix*

May 18, 1974
By Bob Peak
Lee Majors of *The Six Million Dollar Man*

November 16, 1974
By Jack Davis
Cast of *The Godfather*

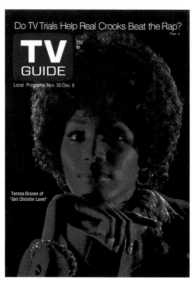

November 30, 1974
By Philippe Halsman
Teresa Graves of *Get Christie Love!*

May 3, 1975
By Al Hirschfeld
Valerie Harper and David Groh of *Rhoda*

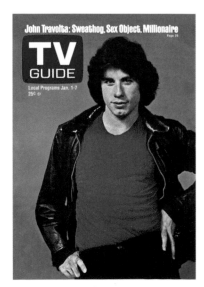

January 1, 1977
By Gene Trindl
John Travolta of *Welcome Back, Kotter*

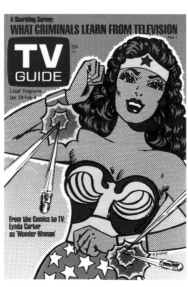

January 29, 1977
By William Goldberg
Lynda Carter of *Wonder Woman*

May 21, 1977
By Douglas Kirkland
Farrah Fawcett-Majors of *Charlie's Angels*

May 20, 1978
By Richard Amsel
Suzanne Somers, Joyce DeWitt and
John Ritter of *Three's Company*

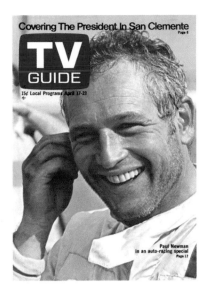

April 17, 1971
By Raphael
Paul Newman

July 14, 1973
By Prigent
Sonny Bono and Cher Bono of
The Sonny and Cher Comedy Hour

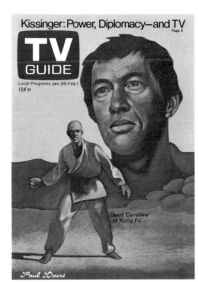

January 26, 1974
By Paul Davis
David Carradine of *Kung Fu*

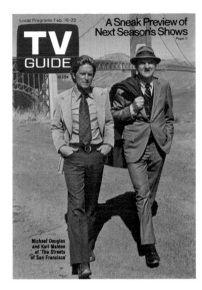

February 16, 1974
By Curt Gunther
Michael Douglas and Karl Malden
of *The Streets of San Francisco*

June 21, 1975
By Mario Casilli
Sherman Hemsley, Isabel Sanford and
Mike Evans of *The Jeffersons*

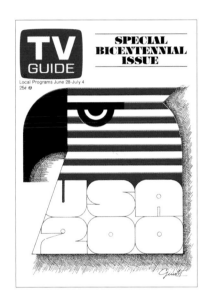

June 28, 1975
By George Giusti
Bicentennial

May 22, 1976
By Dorthy Tanous
Cindy Williams and Penny Marshall
of *Laverne & Shirley*

August 7, 1976
By Peter Kredenser
Marie Osmond and Donny Osmond
of *Donny & Marie*

September 16, 1978
By David Byrd
Dirk Benedict, Lorne Greene and
Richard Hatch of *Battlestar Galactica*

October 21, 1978
By Robert Phillips
Cast of *WKRP in Cincinnati*

October 28, 1978
By Peter Kredenser
Pam Dawber and Robin Williams of
Mork & Mindy

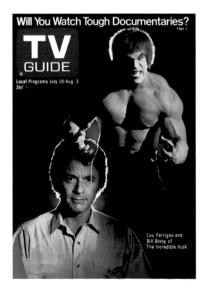

July 28, 1979
By Pete Turner
Bill Bixby and Lou Ferrigno of
The Incredible Hulk

ROLLER DERBY
Gerry Murray (No. 22) of the New York Chiefs in New York City, 1958

For sheer good-versus-evil theatrics with a sweaty subtext—not to mention a rabid TV following—pro wrestlers Stone Cold Steve Austin and the Rock ain't got nothing on the Roller Derby stars of the 1950s and '60s. San Francisco Bay Bombers Charlie O'Connell and Joanie "the Blonde Bomber" Weston were superstars of the men's and women's divisions, and hell-on-wheels Midge "Toughie" Brasuhn an early antihero of the banked-track oval. "Hostile Roller Derby women," TV GUIDE recalled in 1971, "meant as much to the early growth of television as Gorgeous George, Howdy Doody and Uncle Miltie."

MONDAY NIGHT FOOTBALL
Howard Cosell.
ABC, 1970–
COVER: BY JACK DAVIS,
NOVEMBER 29, 1980

The history of sports in America can be divided into two eras: pre- and post-*Monday Night Football*. Before *MNF*'s debut in 1970, football on TV looked like it was being broadcast through a 7-Eleven security camera. The president of ABC Sports, Roone Arledge, perceived that the Sunday-afternoon staple of NFL football could instead be presented as flashy nighttime entertainment. That insight—which has since spread to other sports and remade the industry into the multibillion-dollar marketing and entertainment juggernaut it is today—found its ideal packaging with the *MNF* broadcast team of Howard Cosell, "Dandy" Don Meredith and Frank Gifford. Meredith's folksy-cowboy shtick was the perfect antidote to Cosell's obnoxious "telling it like it is" style, a pleasure for millions to hate, and Giff's smooth neutrality made him the perfect play-by-play guy between them. "Sports is maybe the primary means in the United States for sustaining illusion and delusion," Cosell told TV GUIDE in 1971, explaining his mission to puncture those fantasies. But even as Cosell pursued his prickly crusade, *MNF* was building a myth about itself, and football in general, that would remake the sports business in America.

TV GUIDE

'Monday Night Football': The Booth Is Often Hotter Than the Game

40¢ Local Programs
Nov. 29–Dec. 5, 1980

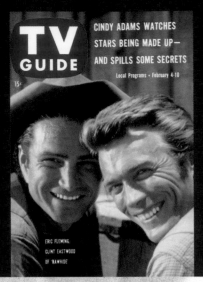

RAWHIDE
Rowdy Yates (Clint Eastwood). CBS, 1959–66
COVER: BY RUSS HALFORD, FEBRUARY 4, 1961

For once, the herd mentality in television was a good thing: *Rawhide* depicted life on the cattle drives of the 1860s, telling the low-key stories of the cowpokes and the folks they encountered along the way. Eric Fleming played the leather-tough trail boss Gil Favor, but the main attraction was the man who portrayed ramrod Rowdy Yates, his second-in-command. "We're doing stories as they pretty much happened," Clint Eastwood told TV GUIDE in 1961. "Oh, occasionally I guess we hoke one up for dramatic purposes, but generally speaking we're doing the kind of things that guys on the cattle drives really did." Head 'em up, move 'em out!

WRESTLING
The Rock, Stone Cold Steve Austin, 1999
COVER: BY MARK HANAUER, DECEMBER 5, 1998

Beefy guys engaged in titanic battles of good and evil have been a TV staple almost since the first ratings-hungry television producer landed a job. In the 1940s and '50s, viewers watched cartoonish characters such as Gorgeous George, Argentina Rocca and Lou Thesz sweating their way through scrapes "as rigidly stylized as a Greek tragedy," TV GUIDE wrote in 1959. It was a bonanza for promoters—though they caught flak for solemnly insisting that the matches weren't rigged, a fiction that kept the skeptical out of their audiences. In the 1980s, however, Vince McMahon had the brilliant idea to embrace the fakery and reposition pro wrestling as "sports entertainment," plunging wholeheartedly into all-out spectacle. That decision "was the turning point," McMahon told TV GUIDE in 2000, when his World Wrestling Federation (later World Wrestling Entertainment) was virtually minting money from its pay-per-view events. The phenomenon created superstars out of musclebound hams like Stone Cold Steve Austin, the Rock and a menagerie of "babyface" good guys and "heel" bad guys who acted out story lines involving sex, homophobia and racism, and made old-time wrestling look like episodes of *Romper Room*. "Once you say you're an entertainment," McMahon told the magazine, in a rare understatement, "it allows you to entertain in a much broader spectrum."

CAST YOUR VOTE FOR
THE FIRST TV GUIDE AWARDS
BALLOT INSIDE!

TV GUIDE

December 5-11

nWo

The incredible story of how wrestling became TV's biggest sensation!

HOLLYWOOD HOGAN

Hollywood Hulk Hogan

$1.49

1 of 4 signature covers this week

Members of the cast of *The A Team*

THE A-TEAM
B.A. "Bad Attitude"
Bosco Baracus (Mr. T).
NBC, 1983–87
COVER: BY MARIO CASILLI,
MARCH 10, 1984

Pity the fool who underestimated the joys of a show about blowing stuff up. George Peppard as Col. John "Hannibal" Smith was the putative centerpiece of this hit, in which a group of heavily armed Vietnam vets shuttled around the world righting wrongs. But the scowling, gold-chained Mr. T was its breakout star. TV GUIDE wondered in 1983 about the effect of *The A-Team*'s unabashed love of destruction, but acknowledged that this "blue-collar *Mission: Impossible*" could be "an uncomplicated diversion." If you didn't say that with a smile, you better watch out, sucka!

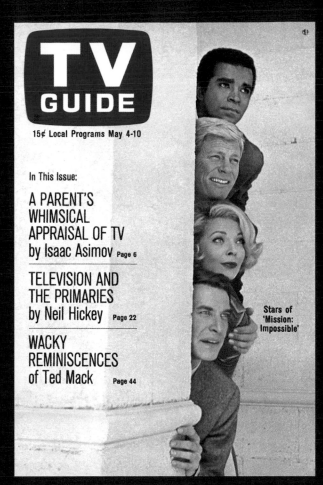

MISSION: IMPOSSIBLE
CBS, 1966–73
COVER: BY PHILLIPE HALSMAN,
MAY 4, 1968

Mission: Impossible had just about everything to satisfy the '60s taste for spy dramas: ingenious gadgetry, noble missions to throw a monkey wrench into the plans of America's enemies, Martin Landau as a master of disguise and an about-to-self-destruct tape giving the Impossible Missions Force its marching orders. What the show didn't have, despite its seven years on the air, was stability. Peter Graves replaced the first-year team leader, Steven Hill; Landau and his wife, Barbara Bain (who played sexy spy Cinnamon Carter), left in 1969 over a contract dispute; and even Landau's replacement, Leonard Nimoy, ditched after two seasons. But two actors—Greg Morris, as electronics pro Barney Collier, and Peter Lupus, as brawny Willie Armitage—decided to accept all seven seasons' worth of missions. Perhaps it was the cool theme song?

"WHEN I WAS A KID, WE DIDN'T HAVE A TV,

so I went to my neighbor's house and hoped he wanted to stay inside and watch television. I really liked *The Untouchables* with Walter Winchell doing the narration. But [mainly] we liked to watch Westerns like *The Wild Wild West*, *Wanted—Dead or Alive* with Steve McQueen, *The Rebel* with Nick Adams and *Gunsmoke.* The best action shows had characters who were likable, so people could feel in that character's shoes. [Shows have] got to be exciting—that's the key.

"Coolness, I think, is better than violence. We would watch them get the bad guys and then we would laugh a little bit, but nobody said, 'I want that type of gun.' At that time, we just saw it as entertainment, and we left it on the TV. We didn't fight with guns. I could watch action at my neighbor's house and then go back home and just forget about it."

—MR. T

BATMAN
Clockwise from top right: Penguin (Burgess Meredith), Riddler (Frank Gorshin),
Joker (Cesar Romero); Batman (Adam West), Robin (Burt Ward). ABC, 1966–68
COVER: BY SHEEDY-LONG, MARCH 26, 1966

By the mid-'60s, comic-book heroes had already been adopted by artists Roy Lichtenstein and Andy
Warhol in an ironic embrace of lowbrow sensibility. It didn't take long for TV to follow suit in '66 with
ABC's tongue-in-cheek *Batman*. Throwing "Pow!" and "Thud!" graphics across the screen and splashing
colors everywhere, the show—breathless but snickering—followed Batman and Robin (aka the Caped
Crusader and Boy Wonder, aka millionaire Bruce Wayne and his young ward, Dick Grayson) as they battled
a series of extravagantly overacting evildoers. "Possibly the best thing about this show," TV GUIDE said,
was the cast of crooks, especially Burgess Meredith and his "superb waddling through his role as the
Penguin." *Batman* was an immediate ratings, er, "Smash!" Even so, TV GUIDE was already wondering how
long the hit could last: Children loved it, but "for the adults the joke could very quickly run thin." Holy
prescience! By the show's second season, the numbers were dropping, and in '68 the Batmobile was
towed off the TV schedule.

TV GUIDE

Can Sportscasters Spot A Curve?

VIEWING GUIDE TO WORLD SERIES
15¢

COMPLETE LOCAL PROGRAM LISTINGS
Week of Sept. 25 to Oct. 1

GEORGE REEVES——
MAN and SUPERMAN

THE ADVENTURES OF SUPERMAN
Lois Lane (Phyllis Coates), Superman (George Reeves). Syndication, 1952–57
COVER: PHOTOGRAPHER UNKNOWN, SEPTEMBER 25, 1953

Superman has demonstrated his superpowers in every media, but for many people it was George Reeves's performance in *The Adventures of Superman* during the '50s that became the definitive portrayal of the defender of truth, justice and the American way. Certainly, only a real Man of Steel could get away with wearing those tights and that cape. And as TV GUIDE said in 1953, Reeves "carries the *Superman* role on his broad shoulders with a delicate sense of balance, kidding himself when among adults but taking it dead seriously when among the younger fry."

051.60

JORDAN
23

NBA

NBA
Michael Jordan (No. 23), June 14, 1998
COVER: BY GREGORY HEISLER, APRIL 12, 1997

In the 1940s and '50s, TV sports was all about baseball. In the 1960s and '70s, the medium discovered football. Then, in the 1980s, basketball finally scored a slam dunk. Suddenly, people who'd never even watched a game before were gripped with an undeniable urge to watch the National Basketball Association. Well, not the NBA so much as two superstars: Los Angeles Laker Earvin "Magic" Johnson and Boston Celtic Larry Bird. The league expertly promoted the rivalry between these two charismatic players, and in the process mightily expanded its fan base in the United States and around the world—preparing the ground, as it turned out, for the dazzling decade of Michael Jordan. In 1994, TV GUIDE observed that "from Madison Avenue to Main Street, basketball has bypassed baseball and set its sights on football in the quest to be America's most popular sport." It certainly seemed that way at the time. The Jordan dynasty had plenty of riches yet to offer, including his storybook final shot in '98 against the Utah Jazz to complete the Chicago Bulls' second championship three-peat. Although the NBA's buzz soon subsided, hardcore fans knew that the game would continue to offer jaw-dropping moments of athletic achievement. And TV would still be there to witness them.

MAJOR LEAGUE BASEBALL
Carlton Fisk, October 21, 1975
COVER: BY ROBERT GUISTI, OCTOBER 6, 1979

The New York Giants' Willie Mays making his fabled over-the-shoulder catch to rob the Cleveland Indians' Vic Wertz of an extra-base hit in Game 1 of the '54 World Series. Carlton Fisk, in the bottom of the 12th, *willing* his long ball to stay fair and win the Boston Red Sox the sixth game against the Cincinnati Reds in the '75 series. Kirk Gibson hobbling to the plate and drilling the game-winning homer for the Los Angeles Dodgers in the first game of the '88 series with the Oakland Athletics. Great, Hall of Fame moments— amazing to have seen in person, to be sure, but known to the world, savored over and over again, thanks only to television. Of course, the national pastime wasn't truly nationwide until every small town in America could see the sport. Writing in TV GUIDE in 1954, pitcher-turned-broadcaster "Dizzy" Dean described a recent trip to his home state, Arkansas: "I'm a son of a buck if they didn't have television. People can see big-league games now that never could before." Not that they had major-league owners to thank for that. For years, the proprietors of the sport were leery of giving the game away for free on television. TV GUIDE even ran editorials during the '50s urging these "obstacles to the 20th century" to understand that "exposing as many people as possible to baseball— through television—will make the future take care of itself." Football, better able to exploit the development of TV technology, learned the lesson quickly and eventually surpassed baseball in popularity. Even so, nowadays baseball's future does indeed take care of itself. Whether you're on the sofa or in the next room, you know the rhythm of a ball game on television just as surely as you know the pulse of American life.

HILL STREET BLUES
Sgt. Henry Goldblume (Joe Spano), Officer Bobby Hill (Michael Warren), Officer Andy Renko (Charles Haid). NBC, 1981–87
COVER: BY GENE TRINDL, JUNE 19, 1982

Hill Street Blues never cracked the Nielsen ratings' Top 20 during its six years, but creator Steven Bochco's innovative approach to the ossified cop-show genre paved the way for such '90s hits as *NYPD Blue* and *Homicide: Life on the Street*. In fact, *Hill Street* did make one Top 20 list: TV GUIDE's best shows of the '80s. What earned the magazine's admiration was its "new style of gritty, grimy urban realism" and "one of television's great ensemble casts. On *Hill Street*, viewers learned to expect the unexpected—hilarity could turn to horror in an instant—but the writing and acting were consistently fine." Capt. Frank Furillo (Daniel J. Travanti) was the calm eye in the hurricane of life at the Hill Street station in a seamy, drug-infested district of an unidentified city. When he wasn't dealing with the squad room full of vividly drawn cops or the puffed-up bureaucrat Chief Daniels (Jon Cypher), he was coping with the hectoring of his bitter ex-wife, Fay (Barbara Bosson) or escaping into the arms of pretty, no-nonsense public defender Joyce Davenport (Veronica Hamel). (Sharp-eyed fans will also recall that future *NYPD Blue*s-man Dennis Franz played not one but two separate rabid cops over the series' lifespan.) As it turned out, the show's backstage dramas were as chaotic and acrimonious as its on-screen ones, and a year before its demise, TV GUIDE was already writing the show's epitaph: "*Hill Street* wasn't about events but about how people responded to them," the magazine said, "so there were never any simple answers, any neat endings." It was an approach that, long after *Hill Street Blues*'s own ending, still endures.

"WHEN HILL STREET BLUES CAME ON,

it set a new standard for television drama. When I go back and look at *Hill Street*—then look at any shows prior to it—there's nothing that matches it in terms of the complexity of the storytelling or the abundance of characters we can invest in. They had flaws that we could identify with. They came to life as human beings, as opposed to TV characters.

"On *NYPD Blue*, we have stayed with that tradition and taken it a step further with our character studies. We've gone deeper into what makes up these people's personal lives, seeing them as troubled at times and perhaps having difficulty doing their jobs and living their lives. I think viewers enjoy investing in characters they can relate to.

"Some shows get criticized for playing up the realities of life, but those are the shows that set new benchmarks, the shows that everybody seems to watch. We say there is too much vulgarity and sexuality and violence on TV, and then we talk about the brilliance of *The Sopranos* and *The Shield*. We are very hypocritical as an audience.

"Television dramas have evolved with our society. If we look back at a show like *Dragnet* now, it's like looking at a black-and-white movie. Earlier dramas are enjoyable to watch as an artifact of their time. Now we try to make them more realistic; the characters aren't black-and-white—there are more shades of gray. I think the more gray matter there is, the more interesting the show is.

"My character [on *NYPD Blue*, Det. Andy Sipowicz] would have died off in the first episode if the show had been in the *Dragnet* days. I don't fit the mold—my character has too many problems and doesn't always show himself in the best light. Yet those types are the ones viewers are often most interested in. We're a wiser audience now. We have evolved as television has evolved."

—DENNIS FRANZ

LAW & ORDER

Assistant D.A. Ben Stone (Michael Moriarty), Det. Mike Logan (Christopher Noth),
Det. Phil Cerreta (Paul Sorvino), Assistant D.A. Paul Robinette (Richard Brooks). NBC, 1990–

COVER: BY MICHAEL DAKS, MARCH 28, 1998

In the spring of 2000, NBC signed a deal with *Law & Order*—which at 10 years old was already gray in TV terms—that would keep it on the air through 2005, making it second only to *Gunsmoke* in prime-time-drama longevity. It was a remarkable accomplishment for a series that took five years to crack the weekly Nielsen Top 20, and it further burnished *Law & Order*'s reputation for not only surviving major cast changes, but getting better with the passage of time. (The show even spun off two series, *Law & Order: Special Victims Unit* in 1999 and *Law & Order: Criminal Intent* in 2001.) The bust-'em-and-try-'em approach had been attempted before, in the early '60s with *Arrest and Trial* (starring the unlikely duo of Ben Gazzara and Chuck Conners), but *Law & Order* offered something unusual in police dramas: almost zero interest in the personal lives of its characters. The show preferred instead to concentrate on a realistic depiction—heightened by handheld camera-

work and a bureaucratically drab palette—of the step-by-occasional-misstep legal process. "There's an unspoken desire on a lot of people's parts to go back to a more understandable morality," creator Dick Wolf told TV GUIDE in 1996, explaining *Law & Order*'s building popularity. "And cop shows are morality plays." The series' keystones were Jerry Orbach, as the seen-it-all Det. Lennie Briscoe, and Sam Waterston, as Assistant D.A. Jack McCoy; they joined in '92 and '94 respectively and—unlike several other stars, such as Benjamin Bratt and Carey Lowell—never left. The show stayed fresh by ripping many of its plotlines from the headlines, presenting its own versions of real-life stories like the Mike Tyson rape trial. And there was one other ingredient in the success of *Law & Order*, which was shot on the streets of the Big Apple. As TV GUIDE said in 1990: "There's even something of a New York attitude in the show's style: Hey, ya want crime? Here it is. Now shuddup."

PHIL CERRETA
DETECTIVE SERGEANT

ER

Dr. Elizabeth Corday (Alex Kingston), Dr. Kerry Weaver (Laura Innes), Dr. Peter Benton (Eriq La Salle), Dr. Doug Ross (George Clooney), Dr. Mark Greene (Anthony Edwards), Head Nurse Carol Hathaway (Julianna Margulies), Physician's Assistant Jeanie Boulet (Gloria Reuben), Dr. John Carter (Noah Wyle), Dr. Anna Del Amico (Maria Bello). NBC, 1994–

COVER: BY LANCE STAEDLER, OCTOBER 14, 1995

"The reason our show took off," George Clooney told TV GUIDE in 1995, "was because it was something you hadn't seen before." Sure, portraits of overworked but heroic doctors and nurses were nothing new to television. But no audience this side of a cable documentary had ever seen as much blood, guts and chaos as there was in this emergency room, where gurneys were forever bursting through doors as the camera careened down the halls. Michael Crichton, the *Jurassic Park* author, drew on his real-life experience as a hospital intern to create the Chicago-set series, but was unsure whether the idea would work. So he showed it to a friend: "He said, 'It doesn't follow any of the rules—but you're not going to be able to take your eyes away from it,'" Crichton recalled in TV GUIDE in 1994. That's what backer Steven Spielberg thought, too, as he sat at home screening the unedited *ER* footage, which was even bloodier than what aired: "I don't want my kids to watch it," he told TV GUIDE. As it turned out, it was hard to say which action was more riveting: the operating-room ordeals or the bedroom romance between Clooney's hard-partying, self-redeeming screwup, Dr. Doug Ross, and suicidal head nurse Carol Hathaway (Julianna Margulies). When Clooney left *ER* in 1999, it had been first in the ratings for three out of its five years. By 2002, thanks to its inventive writing and strong, revolving ensemble cast, the show was still in the Top 10—proof that viewers still couldn't take their eyes away from it.

TV GUIDE Oct 14–20 99¢

SPECIAL REPORT:
Did Television Acquit
O.J. Simpson? See page 37

Love in the ER

Should TV's sexiest soul mates
turn up the heat on their
passion? George Clooney and
Julianna Margulies say...

ST. ELSEWHERE
Dr. Victor Ehrlich (Ed Begley Jr.), Dr. Mark Craig (William Daniels).
NBC, 1982–88

St. Elsewhere broke with TV's tradition of depicting the medical profession as a well-scrubbed haven for virtuous miracle workers. Instead of paging Drs. Kildare or Welby, the hour-long drama called on a gritty ensemble cast to portray the rough goings-on in a Boston city hospital disparagingly known as St. Elsewhere, a dumping ground for patients shunned by fancier medical centers. The series came from the same MTM Productions shop that produced *Hill Street Blues*, and it was rightly likened to that groundbreaking cop show for its lack of a major star (though cast member Denzel Washington certainly went on to become one), its multiple story lines that carried over from week to week and its roaming camera, which picked up snippets of conversation in a simulation of life in an intense workplace. TV GUIDE singled out William Daniels's performance as the arrogant heart surgeon Dr. Mark Craig for praise a few months after the show's 1982 debut (he "plays this impervious boob to perfection"). While not exactly raving about *St. Elsewhere*, calling it only "interesting," the magazine did "hope it survives." That was certainly in doubt after the first season, when it finished 86th out of 98 prime-time series. But as TV GUIDE reported after the show was miraculously renewed for a second season, *St. Elsewhere* set a precedent that would have far-reaching implications for the industry. NBC had decided not to cancel the series after newfangled audience-composition reports revealed that the show's fans were high-income viewers between the ages of 18 and 49, a fact that could be hyped to advertisers. "Thank God for people who like cleansers," actor Ed Begley Jr., who played the clumsy Dr. Victor Ehrlich, told the magazine. "It is programming by a new kind of numbers," TV GUIDE said. "Maybe that will be *St. Elsewhere*'s legacy."

Local Programs Feb. 24–Mar. 2

TV GUIDE
15¢

Pay Television:
The Big Push Is On Page 6

Cast of 'M*A*S*H'

Mr. Ford's China Trip: TV's Hits and Misses

TV GUIDE
Local Programs Jan 24–30
25¢

CONEY ISLAND
SAN FRANCISCO
INDIANAPOLIS
LOS ANGELES
BUR

Alan Alda, Mike Farrell,
Henry Morgan of 'M·A·S·H'

TV GUIDE
400 Local Programs
April 25–May 1 1981

Fun and Games
Behind the Scenes
at 'M·A·S·H' Page 34

TV GUIDE

So Long,
M·A·S·H

Local Programs Feb. 12–18

M*A*S*H
Cpl. Maxwell Klinger (Jamie Farr). CBS, 1972–83
COVERS: BY SHERMAN WEISBURD, FEBRUARY 24, 1973. BY SCOTT ENYART, JANUARY 24, 1976. BY AL HIRSCHFELD, APRIL 25, 1981. BY MARIO CASILLI, FEBRUARY 12, 1983

When TV GUIDE asked Alan Alda in 1983 to write about his favorite episode of *M*A*S*H*, he couldn't limit himself to just one—instead he described more than a dozen. Many fans certainly felt the same way regarding this black comedy about the insanity of war—specifically, the Korean War—as seen through the eyes of the troops in the 4077th Mobile Army Surgical Hospital. "Clearly, even in our most antic moments," Alda wrote, "death is usually lurking just behind the door, even if sometimes he's wearing a fright wig and carrying a pig's bladder." The fighting in Korea, of course, was a surrogate for the Vietnam War in a series that began in 1972 (two years after Robert Altman's feature film of the same name), when antiwar sentiment had moved into the mainstream. *M*A*S*H* entertained, even as it appalled, with tales that centered around Alda as the gifted but rebellious surgeon-prankster, Capt. Benjamin Franklin "Hawkeye" Pierce. Over the course of the show's 11 years, he and the rest of the colorful crew became utterly familiar to TV audiences. As Alda—who won Emmys for acting, writing and directing—proudly pointed out in TV GUIDE, *M*A*S*H* experimented in its storytelling. One episode was presented as a black-and-white war documentary, for instance, and another was told in real time, with a clock ticking in the corner of the screen as the doctors performed a vein-graft operation. The final episode, a two-and-half-hour special called "Goodbye, Farewell and Amen," was seen in 77 percent of the households watching television that night. In terms of number of viewers, it's the most-watched program of all time. The show's "multitude of fans," TV GUIDE said, could take some comfort in knowing "that on TV, at any rate, old soldiers never die...they just go on rerunning from here to eternity."

LT. COL.
HENRY BLAKE
COMMANDING
OFFICER
4077th MASH

M*A*S*H WAS
ONE OF A KIND

It is one of the unsolved mysteries of American television that *M*A*S*H*, a tragicomedy about an unpopular war almost as dire in its effects as Vietnam, should have retained for more than a decade a popular rating way up there in a catalog of trash of many varieties. Night after night, week after week, year after year, its siren song of "incoming wounded!" beckoned 33 million or so away from teary soaps, drug sagas, frantic sitcoms and marshmallow porn. It is not the intention of this piece to unravel the knotty problem, except to identify some of the elements that made *M*A*S*H*—as the song says—"an isle of joy" in an ocean of junk.

War movies of two sorts—the knockabout farce and the grimly sentimental "pity-of-it-all" epic—have been standard products of the American film industry from *Shoulder Arms* to *Apocalypse Now*. Their usual elements were predictable enough to guarantee for each kind an audience that knew exactly what it was going to get. In most of the epics, against a background of artillery fire and ruined woods (World War I), or mopped-up villages and Pacific jungles (World War II), we had half a dozen or so familiar types: the solemn colonel, the hip-hup sergeant, the rough diamond, the goldbrick, the gentle weakling, the company comic, the plucky kid and his mentor—our hero—the clean-limbed star, played by John Gilbert, Gary Cooper, Kirk Douglas, Burt Lancaster, et al. In the farces, the blood-and-guts action had to be indicated as unpleasantness far in the future, while Wheeler and Woolsey or Bob Hope made adorable asses of themselves in basic training.

Apart from a glut of shameless morale-builders made during WWII—in which the Nazis were always bullies, the Japanese always shifty and our chaps decent and heroic, if in cantankerous ways—most war movies were made in retrospect, when the real thing was comfortably over. The fact that Chaplin's *Shoulder Arms* came out while WWI was still on can now be seen as one freakish consequence of a frontline censorship so ironclad that the chuckling audiences had only the faintest notion of the scale and hideousness of the enormous slaughter. Offhand, I don't recall any uproarious comedies about Vietnam. So, all right, *M*A*S*H* started, also, when the Korean War was all over. Even so, Ring Lardner Jr.'s original movie script, filmed and shown 17 years after the fighting ended, was enough of a shocker (joking surgeons whose hands, just below the frame, were fiddling with intestines) to cause the British film historian Leslie Halliwell to call it "the great anti-everything film, certainly very funny for those who can take it"; and Judith Crist to write: "The laughter is blood soaked and the comedy cloaks a bitter and terrible truth." Not, you would say, the sort of thing likely to spawn a television series that would last 11 years.

But we have come to take its "blood-soaked" scene for granted and to adopt a whole family of characters who were novel and astonishing in many ways. Let me count the ways.

First, instead of a commanding officer who looks like a gray-flecked "man of distinction" in a whiskey ad, we had, first, Henry Blake, half-dolt, half locker-room buddy; and then Sherman Potter, a sentimental, bandy-legged holdover from WWI. Both of them, however, were soldiers of much horse sense who knew—

as COs came to know in any war later than WWII—that parade and discipline are impossible to maintain in conscripts bogged down in a jungle clearing. The colonels' tolerance of Klinger's idiotic transvestism was a big shock to early viewers. But it provided a constant reminder of how much eccentricity had to be put up with in a small group of often overworked human beings pushed to the limit of sanity by nothing but boredom. One veteran doctor of a Mobile Army Surgical Hospital unit recalled to me that above everything else boredom was the pitiless enemy, so that childish entertainment, dressing up, lotteries, cartoon movies, casual sex, petty racketeering and practical jokes became essential therapy.

(The actual boredom came to include hideous routines—having to do with the disposal of human wastes and the daily examination of the Korean "service" girls on the line—that even M*A*S*H chose to sidestep.)

This basic condition of life in the 4077 must have been grasped by the writers early in the series, and it made us accept a wildly varied cast of characters and wildly unmilitary behavior that the training manuals and all previous army scripts had never imagined. Thus, the CO's ranking subordinates offered the startling novelties of a woman major and her light of love, the asinine chauvinist and reluctant husband, Maj. Frank Burns—both, I should guess, impossible bits of casting in any previous war movie. And, just to ram home the lesson that excessive devotion to "loyalty" and "security" was an almost obscene nuisance, we had the paranoid CIA snooper.

Offsetting these weirdos was a group of comparative innocents such as every soldier has encountered, though perhaps not in the movies: Father Mulcahy, no heroic priest he, in the mold of Bing Crosby or Pat O'Brien, but a limited, slow-witted nice man; Radar, befogged, unsure even of his virginity; Dr. Freedman, the sensible, believable psychia-

trist, a million miles away from the Hollywood fusspot with the Viennese accent; the absurd Winchester, to remind us of another world—ours—and other values, preposterous maybe, but the values we all pretend to aspire to. Finally, Trapper and B.J.—two amiable variations on the smart-ass's sidekick, the smart-ass being no one but Hawkeye.

Hawkeye was the hinge. Played less well, by an actor less high-strung, less deeply forlorn, the whole series could have expired in its infancy. Somebody had the wit to spot him at the beginning as Hamlet and Horatio rolled into one: the brilliant neurotic and the normal antihero. He was the one who kept the place in a happy ferment: the enviable expert surgeon and also the mischief maker all pent-up soldiers yearn to be.

And yet. Hawkeye represented, more than most, the one quality that held the whole family together, the quality of fundamental decency. This was the sheet anchor of a crew awash in exhaustion, emergencies, bad temper, physical peril. The patient came first, the patient of either side and any color. And the only golden rule that everybody recognized was that no big brass, no visiting congressman, no CIA inquisitor or other busybody must be allowed to forget it. It was here that every viewer, according to personal taste and judgment, had to decide how often the series ignored the messiness of life and spilled over into the neatness of sentimentality.

All in all, the series was remarkable, something of a marvel, in staying so close to ordinary life and peopling a formula with what in television is something of a curiosity: a company of recognizable human beings. Let us stifle a starting tear and bid farewell to M.A.S.H. 4077, and pray that no Hollywood smarties are licking their chops and drafting some carbon-copy series. M*A*S*H, like The Honeymooners and Upstairs, Downstairs, was one of a kind. Let it stay that way.

—ALISTAIR COOKE, EXCERPT FROM TV GUIDE, FEBRUARY 12, 1983

THE '80s

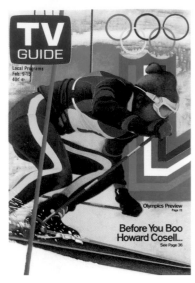

February 9, 1980
By Wilson McLean
The Olympics

April 12, 1980
By Herb Ritts
Olivia Newton-John

May 31, 1980
Illustrator unknown
Cast of *Vegas*

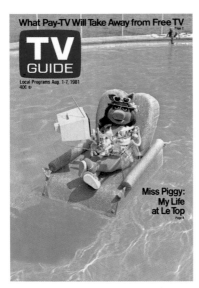

August 1, 1981
By John E. Barrett
Miss Piggy of *The Muppet Show*

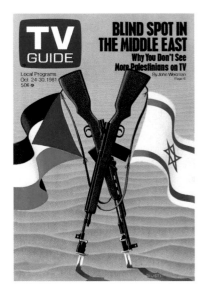

October 24, 1981
By Robert Giusti
"Blind Spot in the Middle East"

November 21, 1981
By Richard Hess
John Lennon

January 9, 1982
By Richard Hess
Michael Landon of *Little House on the Prairie*

July 7, 1984
By Mario Casilli
Valerie Bertinelli of *One Day at a Time*

November 3, 1984
By Braldt Bralds
"Tales of Election Night Drama"

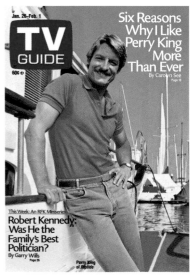

January 26, 1985
By Jim Shea
Perry King of *Riptide*

March 9, 1985
By Richard Amsel
Angela Lansbury of *Murder, She Wrote*

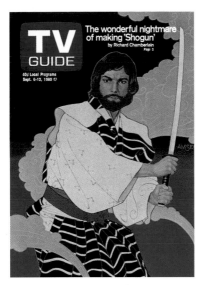

September 6, 1980
By Richard Amsel
Richard Chamberlain in *Shogun*

January 31, 1981
By Gene Trindl
Bob Hope, George Burns and
Johnny Carson

February 7, 1981
By Peter Kredenser
Jane Seymour in *East of Eden*

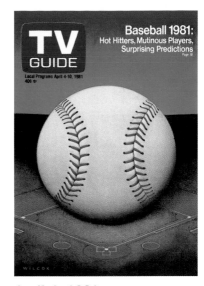

April 4, 1981
By David Wilcox
"Baseball 1981"

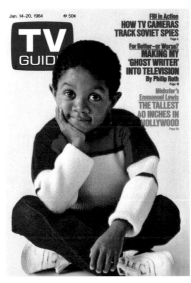

January 14, 1984
By Ken Whitmore
Emmanuel Lewis of *Webster*

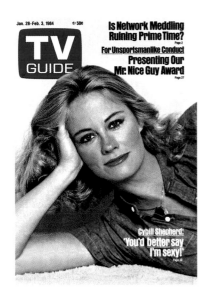

January 28, 1984
By Peter Kredenser
Cybill Shepherd of *The Yellow Rose*

March 3, 1984
By Mario Casilli
Ann-Margret and Treat Williams in
A Streetcar Named Desire

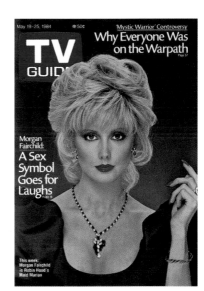

May 19, 1984
By Robert Phillips
Morgan Fairchild in *The Zany
Adventures of Robin Hood*

May 4, 1985
By Roger Prigent
Phoebe Cates in *Lace II*

April 18, 1987
By Tony Costa
Tony Danza of *Who's the Boss*

August 15, 1987
By John Eggert
ALF of *ALF*

August 20, 1988
By Tony Costa
Johnny Depp and Holly Robinson
of *21 Jump Street*

THAT GIRL
ABC, 1966–71
COVER: BY KEN WHITMORE,
NOVEMBER 12, 1966

That Girl "is not exactly going to keep you on the edge of your chair," TV GUIDE said in 1966 about the comedy starring the "very pretty and very funny" Marlo Thomas. She played the upbeat but struggling actress Ann Marie, who dated nerdy magazine exec Donald Hollinger (Ted Bessell) while trying to make it in New York City. The show aired for five years, but it had a more dramatic and lasting effect in Hollywood: Its success paved the way for such independent-woman comedies as *The Mary Tyler Moore Show* and *Rhoda*.

How Television's Rich Actors Stay That Way

see page 14

LOCAL PROGRAMS · NOVEMBER 12-18

TV GUIDE

15¢

MARLO THOMAS OF 'THAT GIRL'

"THE MOST
REVOLUTIONARY THING
ABOUT THAT GIRL

was that my father on the show would continually say to me, 'When are you going to get married?' and I would say, 'Daddy, I don't want to get married yet. I want to have my career.' That was the single most radical element of the show, even more than having her living on her own. In essence, we were saying out loud that a woman didn't have to get married in order to be fulfilled. Not that you shouldn't get married, but you didn't *have* to—there were others things you could do. This was groundbreaking at the time.

"You can really see the progression of women in comedies after *That Girl*. There were single mothers in *Kate & Allie*. Murphy Brown was a not-so-perfect woman who was a drinker, screamed at people and had a baby without being married. Even Rachel on *Friends*—who also is not married—talks about sex and had a baby.

"Ironically, in real life, young people in the '60s were behaving exactly how the characters on *Friends* are behaving now. It's not like we were any more pure than girls are today. But we weren't reflecting that

behavior—or even talking about it—on TV comedies. I remember we did a whole episode on *That Girl* about the fact that Donald's dry cleaning was quite innocently hanging in my closet, and my father came over and saw it and it became this big deal. These were people in their twenties—come on!

"There was a certain dishonesty about all this. Remember Lucy and Ricky didn't sleep in the same bed? And when she got pregnant, they used all sorts of phrases to describe her condition because you couldn't say 'pregnant' on TV? They even called the episode in which she finds out she's expecting 'Lucy Is *Enceinte*'—which is French for pregnant—just to get around using the word. Since when did pregnancy become a bad word? It was all really backward, and it infantilized the audience.

"Now, of course, reality has caught up with television and television has caught up with reality. Now *The Vagina Monologues* is on TV. At last!"

—MARLO THOMAS

COMPLETE INFORMATION ON THE BOWL GAMES

LOCAL PROGRAMS · DEC. 28-JAN. 3

TV GUIDE

15¢

PATTY DUKE

THE PATTY DUKE SHOW
Frank Sinatra Jr., Patty
Duke. ABC, 1963–66
COVER: BY PHILLIPE HALSMAN,
DECEMBER 28, 1963

Patty Duke turned from her movie
triumph in 1962's *The Miracle
Worker* to perform a mini-miracle
of comedy on TV. She was the
youngest performer, at 17, ever to
get her name in the title of a
prime-time show. For three years,
she portrayed identical cousins:
Cathy, a serious Scot who had
lived "ev'rywhere from Zanzibar
to Berk'ley Square"—as the show's
theme song explained—and Patty,
the quintessential pre-hippie '60s
teen, who had "only seen the
sights a girl can see from Brooklyn
Heights." Cathy lived with Patty's
family, and the girls' frequent
identity swapping seemed to
flummox everyone within a 10-
block radius. Duke did such a
delightful job that TV GUIDE said in
'64: "As far as we are concerned,
she could play *all* the parts."

MY SO-CALLED LIFE
Angela Chase (Claire Danes), Jordan Catalano (Jared Leto). ABC, 1994–95

For all the grown-ups who ever lectured a miserable teenager about these being *the best years of your life*, here was the ultimate retort. *My So-Called Life* "is adolescence as adolescents see it: gritty, mean, real and only occasionally fun," TV GUIDE said in 1994. "It's the scholastic *NYPD Blue*." Actress Claire Danes, as 15-year-old Angela Chase, seemed like teen agony incarnate, electrified by life's possibilities but apprehensive as she balanced awkwardly on the cusp between childhood and young adulthood. "School is a battlefield for your heart. You are lucky to get out alive," she said. Angela started hanging out with a dicey crowd and found herself drawn—in the classic good-girl/bad-boy tango—to Jordan Catalano (Jared Leto), who sang in a rock band but was otherwise inscrutable. At home, Angela had to deal with a sniping mother and a father who was beginning to withdraw from her as she began to mature sexually. *My So-Called Life*, from Ed Zwick and Marshall Herskovitz, the creators of *thirtysomething*, scored well with critics and teens but wasn't lucky enough to graduate to a second season. MTV astutely picked up the episodes and replayed them for three years to an audience for whom Danes's poignant portrayal must have resonated like no other young actress's on television.

Members of the cast of *Cheers*

CHEERS
**Sam Malone (Ted Danson), Diane Chambers
(Shelley Long). NBC, 1982–93**
COVER: BY BRUCE STARK, MAY 10, 1986

A few months after the show's debut, TV GUIDE tried to convey how
terrific the dialogue among the *Cheers* patrons was by citing their
colloquium on the sweatiest movies of all time—"*Body Heat*"? "*Cool
Hand Luke*"?—but then concluded: "The jokes don't reproduce on paper,
mostly because they arise out of character instead of out of a gag file.
It's a healthy sign. This one should be around awhile." Although it took
more than three years for *Cheers* to catch on with audiences, the
characters did indeed become some of the most familiar in TV history.
They included Sam (Ted Danson), the cocky ex–Red Sox pitcher who
owned the Boston bar; Diane (Shelley Long), the pretty and pretentious
grad student/waitress; Carla (Rhea Perlman), the tough-talking broad
who delivered as many insults as drinks; lovable but dim bartender
Coach (Nicholas Colasanto), who was followed by the younger but just
as clueless Woody (Woody Harrelson); and Norm and Cliff (George
Wendt and John Ratzenberger), the Tweedledee and Tweedledumber
accountant and postal worker who were bar-stool fixtures. At what
appeared to be the height of the show's popularity, in 1987, Long left
to pursue a movie career. It seemed like a disaster for *Cheers*—the
mercurial relationship between Sam and Diane had been one of the
great antagonistic TV romances, a fact made abundantly clear when
their long-anticipated first kiss seemed to electrify the entire nation
as well as the couple. But Long's departure turned out to be disastrous
only for the actress's own fortunes. *Cheers* thrived with the arrival of
Kirstie Alley as Rebecca Howe, the corporate climber who became
Sam's boss after he sold the bar. The only indispensable player was
Danson: *Cheers* finally ended with his departure in 1993, when it was
still one of the top-rated shows in television—a testament to the powerful
pull of a place where you were so well-acquainted with the characters,
you'd swear everybody knew *your* name.

FRIENDS
Rachel Green (Jennifer Aniston), Ross Gellar (David Schwimmer). NBC, 1994–
COVER: BY DAVIS FACTOR, SEPTEMBER 23, 1995

Critics groaned at the debut of *Friends* in 1994—TV GUIDE called the comedy about a bunch of pals sitting around cracking jokes just another *Seinfeld/Cheers* hybrid that was "born more of marketing than of imagination." The only part of *Friends* that seemed original was the focus on twentysomethings who were ambivalent about plunging fully into the grown-up world of careers and commitment. But the show also had two secret weapons: truly first-rate writing, led by series creators David Crane and Marta Kauffman, and a talented cast of six actors, who also just happened to be insufferably attractive. The combo captivated viewers, and critics soon came along, too. A year into the show, TV GUIDE admitted that you "just couldn't resist liking these guys." Led by ravishing amateur den mother Monica (Courteney Cox Arquette), the gang—Monica's brainiac brother Ross (David Schwimmer), aromatherapized ditz Phoebe (Lisa Kudrow), spoiled rich kid Rachel (Jennifer Aniston), good-hearted meathead Joey (Matt LeBlanc) and jokester Chandler (Matthew Perry)—all got together to kvetch entertainingly about dating, sex, work, parents and one another. "When the six of us filmed the pilot, there was something inexplicable about the chemistry among us, like we were six pieces of a puzzle that naturally came together," Schwimmer told TV GUIDE in 2001. Indeed, the palpable affinity between cast members helped make *Friends* a ratings hit in its first season. It remained at or near the top of the Nielsens for eight years, and in 2002 its popularity showed no signs of flagging. New plotlines kept viewers hooked (Monica and Chandler were married, Ross and Rachel were on-again, off-again; she had his baby). But as Perry told TV GUIDE in '95: "The show is really at its best when it's just the six of us in a room talking, making each other laugh."

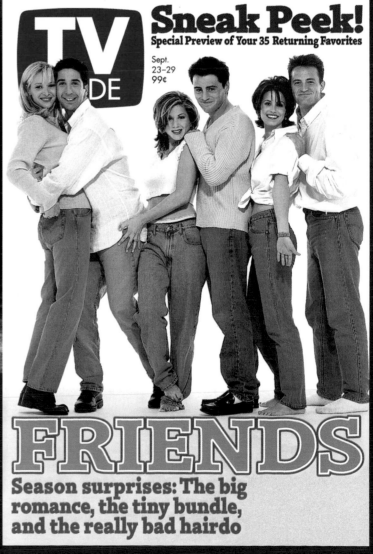

WHY I CONSIDER CAGNEY & LACEY
THE BEST
SHOW ON TELEVISION

I consider *Cagney & Lacey* the best show on television. Launched as a CBS TV-movie in 1981 and as a series in 1982, it honors women's friendships and represents a radical departure from the myth that women can't get along.

Before that, women on TV tended to be tokens in a man's world or else rivals for a man's affections. In the few instances when women were permitted to be friends (e.g., Lucy Ricardo and Ethel Mertz), the relationship was comedic and often catty. And the women weren't working together. Christine Cagney and Mary Beth Lacey, two New York City police officers, are work buddies in a way that only male characters have been in the past.

The quality of their friendship has humanized cop shows. In fact, along with NBC's *Hill Street Blues*, *Cagney & Lacey* has brought a human resonance to TV police work that renders the simple good-guy/bad-guy cop shows of the past hopelessly obsolete.

I particularly like the fact that the scripts usually don't take the easy way out. Some scripts are so strong that they might actually change people's attitudes.

The most authentic touches are found in the wonderfully strong acting of Sharon Gless, as Cagney, and Tyne Daly, as Lacey. The characters are so convincing that one can imagine them growing and changing, like real people. It's this human accuracy that makes the show attractive to women, who tend not to care for the usual cop shows.

In fact, one hears that women identify strongly with both the very married Lacey and the very single Cagney. After all, even though few women are police detectives, most women have demanding jobs, whether inside or outside the home, and they rely for support on close women friends. *Cagney & Lacey* is one of those rare shows that reflect the reality of women's lives.

—GLORIA STEINEM, EXCERPT FROM TV GUIDE, JANUARY 16, 1988

CAGNEY & LACEY
CBS, 1982–88
COVER: BY DAVID BYRD, JANUARY 16, 1988

If it had simply come and gone like other series, *Cagney & Lacey* would have earned a place in TV history as the first buddy cop show that starred two women. But *Cagney & Lacey* was also notable for the very fact that after it came and went, it came back again—stronger than ever, thanks to a letter-writing campaign that persuaded CBS to reverse its decision to cancel the show in 1983 after one season. Sharon Gless was the fun-loving but ambitious Christine Cagney, and Tyne Daly the more settled wife and mom, Mary Beth Lacey. The show eagerly tried to approximate real life, embracing the personal struggles—not just the jobs—of its two New York City police detectives. That approach won it no shortage of well-known champions: *Ms.* magazine founder Gloria Steinem and *Love Story* author Erich Segal both wrote valentines to *Cagney & Lacey* in TV Guide. Segal praised the show upon its return to the air for offering "real characters with real emotions," calling it "one of the best series ever to hit the tube." As Segal might have put it, loving *Cagney & Lacey* meant never having to change the channel.

Jan. 16–22
75¢

Why I Consider *Cagney & Lacey* the Best Show on TV
By Gloria Steinem
Page 4

L.-r.: Sharon Gless and Tyne Daly of *Cagney & Lacey*

BYRD

Dec. 23-29   75c

TV's real newswomen give THUMBS UP TO MURPHY
Page 4

Candice Bergen of CBS's *Murphy Brown*

Scott Bakula: Hopes are high for a quantum career leap
Page 14

MURPHY BROWN
CBS, 1988–98
COVER: BY BERNARD BOUDREAU, DECEMBER 23, 1989

This comedy ("put together like a fine watch," TV Guide said in 1989) about a TV newsmagazine called *FYI* had many memorable elements: Candice Bergen as a glam-but-tough journalist, her glacially slow housepainter-in-residence, the stream of Murphy's hapless secretaries. But despite a 10-year run, the show is most likely to be remembered for a single plot development—Murphy's single parenthood—and its denunciation in 1992 by Vice President Dan Quayle as an example of Hollywood's hostility toward family values. "I'm the last person to think fathers are obsolete," Bergen told TV Guide at the time, but having the baby was "absolutely the right decision," she said. "For Murphy and the show."

1) **77 SUNSET STRIP**
Merry Anders
(Herself), Stuart
Bailey (Efrem
Zimbalist Jr.) with
1961 Thunderbird.
ABC, 1958-64

2) **CAR 54, WHERE
ARE YOU?**
Officer Francis Muldoon
(Fred Gwynne), Officer
Gunther Toody (Joe E.
Ross) with Car 54.
NBC, 1961-63

3) **MY MOTHER THE CAR**
Dave Crabtree (Jerry
Van Dyke) with 1928
Porter. NBC, 1965-66

4) **GIDGET**
Francine "Gidget"
Lawrence (Sally Field)
with 'board.
ABC, 1965-66

5) **LOST IN SPACE**
Jupiter II. CBS, 1965-68

6) BATMAN
Batman (Adam West)
with Batmobile.
ABC, 1966-68

7) ADAM-12
Officer Jim Reed (Kent
McCord), Officer Pete
Malloy (Martin
Milner) with 1968
Plymouth Belvedere.
NBC, 1968-75

8) SCOOBY-DOO,
WHERE ARE YOU?
Shaggy, Scooby-Doo
with Mystery Machine.
CBS, 1969-73; ABC, 1976-77
and 1979-86

9) THE PARTRIDGE FAMILY
Shirley Partridge
(Shirley Jones),
Christopher Partridge
(Jeremy Gelbwaks),
Tracy Partridge
(Suzanne Crough),
Laurie Partridge (Susan
Dey), Danny Partridge
(Danny Bonaduce),
Keith Partridge (David
Cassidy) with school
bus. ABC, 1970-74

10) CHiPs
Officer Jon Baker (Larry
Wilcox), Officer Frank
"Ponch" Poncherello
(Erik Estrada) with
Kawasakis. NBC, 1977-83

11) THE DUKES OF HAZZARD
Luke Duke (Tom
Wopat), Bo Duke
(John Schneider) with
the General Lee.
CBS, 1979-85

12) MURDER, SHE WROTE
Dr. Seth Hazlitt
(William Windom),
Jessica Fletcher
(Angela Lansbury)
with two-wheeler.
CBS, 1984-96

TAXI
Latka Gravas (Andy Kaufman), Louie De Palma (Danny DeVito). ABC, 1978–82; NBC, 1982–83
COVER: BY BOB PEAK, JULY 26, 1980

It might have been known as the Sunshine Cab Company, but when Elaine Nardo (Marilu Henner) showed up for her first day of work there, she nailed the mood of the place when she asked: "Why is everyone here just a little bit angry?" Perhaps it was because like her—an aspiring art-gallery owner—several of her fellow drivers regarded their jobs as nothing more than annoying pit stops on the way to great success. Tough guy Tony Banta (Tony Danza) pursued a boxing career even though he'd been knocked down so many times he had "a cauliflower back," and bushy blond Bobby Wheeler (Jeff Conaway) dreamed of unlikely fame and fortune as an actor. As it turned out, the show proved to be an excellent showcase for several performers who did indeed go on to bigger and better things. Danny DeVito shined as a short, stout tyrant whose sadistic barbs were issued from inside the dispatcher's cage—he was Lou Grant with a whiff of Hannibal Lecter. Christopher Lloyd played "Reverend Jim" Ignatowski—a wobbly, recovering '60s burnout—to perfection. And

the extraordinary Andy Kaufman created the gentle immigrant mechanic Latka. But the show truly revolved around the one driver, Alex Reiger, who actually worked full-time there and thought of himself as nothing more than a cabby. Judd Hirsch played the role with good-hearted grimness: "His delivery is flat as a slab but somehow wonderful," TV GUIDE said after *Taxi*'s 1978 debut. For all of its supposed animus, the show had a heart of gold, reflected in its prickly yet always sweet-natured scripts, as when Alex, mercilessly ribbed by his coworkers, follows through on his blind date with an obese woman whom he ends up hugging. "Come to think of it, *Taxi* often ends with someone hugging someone else," the magazine noted. Viewers, however, didn't exactly embrace the show. ABC canceled it after four years; NBC gave it a try for one more and fared no better. But the proof was in the prizes: *Taxi*'s sparkling ensemble acting and sharp writing won it three Emmy awards for Outstanding Comedy Series.

BARNEY MILLER

Capt. Barney Miller (Hal Linden), Det. Stanley Wojehowicz (Maxwell Gail), Det. Phil Fish (Abe Vigoda), bomber (actor unknown). ABC, 1975–82
COVER: BY AL HIRSCHFELD, OCTOBER 25, 1980

The early returns weren't good, and you didn't have to be a detective to pick up the clues: First, TV GUIDE (among others) panned this 1975 mid-season replacement about a New York City precinct house ("an awful lot going on, and most of the lot is awful"). Then, in a profile, it dubbed the show's sweet-tempered star, Hal Linden, "an optimist in the midst of disaster" because "practically nobody" was watching. But Linden's faith paid off: *Barney Miller* soon climbed into the Nielsen ratings' Top 20 and stayed there for four years as audiences—and critics—managed to get past the show's contrivances (a rigorously multiethnic mix of characters and a formula that required three plotlines in each half hour). The atmosphere was more social club than police headquarters, a hangout for a few guys with a crime-fighting hobby: Abe Vigoda's Detective Fish was the epic complainer, Maxwell Gail's "Wojo" an earnest striver, Jack Soo's Detective Yemana a hilarious deadpan philosopher. When viewers finally wandered away, the series ended with a plot about the city declaring the precinct house a landmark and dispersing the cops to new assignments. Nevertheless, *Barney Miller* itself remained a landmark for reminding us that comedy doesn't have to be mean-spirited.

THE LARRY SANDERS SHOW
Sanders (Garry Shandling). HBO, 1992–98

For six years in the 1990s, comedian Garry Shandling administered the definitive antidote to the age of celebrity with this lacerating satire of Hollywood self-loathing. Shandling played Larry Sanders, the host of a late-night show who managed to simulate Johnny Carson–like amiability on camera, but who backstage—and even on stage, during commercial breaks—was a wreck of insecurity and anxiety. Clustered around him was a pitch-perfect choir of Tinseltown types, particularly the brilliant Rip Torn as Artie, a glad-handing, string-pulling producer, and Jeffrey Tambor as Larry's repellent sidekick, Hank (catchphrase: "Hey, now!"), who was equal parts preening arrogance and pathetic desperation. *The Larry Sanders Show* so hilariously skewered the bitter, backstabbing insincerities of show business that real-life celebrities clamored to appear on the show, playing themselves in some sort of cathartic truth telling about the industry. Two of the most memorable guest appearances came in the dazzling final episode in 1998, when Shandling decided to quit while he was ahead. David Duchovny reprised a previous appearance when his tenderly solicitous treatment of Larry drove the host batty trying to figure out if Duchovny was coming on to him. And Jim Carrey belted out an over-the-top "Dreamgirls" anthem in a farewell tribute—and then, the moment after the cameras switched off, icily said to the host, "What are you going to do now? Movies? I'll *crush* you." For all the belly laughs *Larry Sanders* inspired, its star found a moral in all the amoral grasping. "I think it's a metaphor for a wrong way to live," Shandling told TV Guide near the end of the series. "Worrying too much about what people think and wanting to appeal to the most number of people" was a bad idea whether you are "in show business or in high school." There is no doubt, however, that it made for fabulous television.

FRASIER
Dr. Frasier Crane (Kelsey Grammer). NBC, 1993–
COVER: BY KATE GARNER, OCTOBER 3, 1998

Quick, name the only five-time winner of the Emmy award for best comedy. *The Dick Van Dyke Show*? *Cheers*? *All in the Family*? Nope. They all pulled down four. *Frasier* won five Emmys in a row in the mid-'90s, cementing its reputation as the most successful comedy spin-off ever. Frasier Crane (Kelsey Grammer) afforded us plenty of laughs on *Cheers* as a pompous psychiatrist bumping up against regular-guy sensibilities. The genius of *Frasier* was to relocate him to Seattle as a radio call-in therapist and pair him with his brother, Niles (David Hyde Pierce), also a psychiatrist and, if anything, even pickier and more pretentious. "Such unlikely characters," Grammer told TV GUIDE in 1998, "so forbidding and elite, and yet we are so adrift in the same sea of pettiness that all brothers go through." Frasier's cranky ex-cop father, Martin (John Mahoney),

who lived with Frasier in his gorgeous high-rise apartment, had a retirement hobby of puncturing the Crane brothers' effete balloons, while Daphne (Jane Leeves), the English home-care worker who tended to Martin, unwittingly pierced the shy Niles's heart. That infatuation simmered for years, peaking in a grand, *Graduate*-like gesture in which Niles stole away with bride-to-be Daphne in a Winnebago. In 1998, executive producer Christopher Lloyd described the essence of *Frasier* to TV GUIDE: "It's really about these guys who have an idea of this utopian world where people are polished and smart and treat each other well, and every week they get strong evidence to the contrary. It's very winning to root for them." When it comes to Emmys and audiences, winning is clearly the right word.

"PEANUTS" HOLIDAY SPECIALS
A Charlie Brown Christmas (1965). CBS, 1965–
COVER: BY CHARLES SCHULZ, OCTOBER 28, 1972

Charles Schulz was never really comfortable translating his "Peanuts" comic strip to television. "In TV there is no time for talk," he griped to TV GUIDE in 1972. "Everything has to lead to action." And eight years later, he wrote an article in the magazine complaining that too little "low-key poetry finds its way into the script." None of that mattered to audiences, who embraced his first foray into the medium, *A Charlie Brown Christmas* (which seemed to be graced with plenty of low-key poetry in its tale of Charlie Brown's homely tree and the true spirit of Christmas). Charlie Brown, Snoopy and friends quickly became something of a TV staple. As the magazine reported in '72, the first seven "Peanuts" specials each averaged a 40 to 44 percent share of the television audience, with about 35 million households tuned in–and, amazingly, drew similar numbers on their first few reruns. "I'll say this: The specials have brought children in more," Schulz grudgingly told TV GUIDE. Thirty years later, many of those children have their own families and still make viewing a vintage "Peanuts" special–say, the Halloween classic *It's the Great Pumpkin, Charlie Brown*–a holiday tradition.

TV GUIDE

Entry Rules For All Giveaway Shows

LOCAL PROGRAMS
JAN. 26-FEB. 1

15¢

Bob Hope

BOB HOPE
Date unknown
COVER: BY AL HIRSCHFELD,
JANUARY 26, 1957

"What's an American institution?"
TV GUIDE asked in 1965. "Well,
there's Mount Rushmore...baseball...
Mom's apple pie...and Bob Hope."
Hope thrived in vaudeville, on stage,
in radio and in feature films—
particularly in the marvelous *Road*
movies with Bing Crosby—but found
his greatest success on television.
The star-laden Christmas shows he
put on to entertain troops deployed
around the world kept soldiers and
TV audiences laughing from World
War II all the way through the Gulf
War. As the perfect, classy-yet-
teasing host, Hope was practically a
permanent fixture at the Academy
Awards throughout the '50s and
'60s. His countless other specials,
guest appearances and TV series
were for decades simply an
essential element of television
entertainment, as were his needling
topical humor and jibes at
politicians. But of all the great
moments show business afforded
him, Hope told TV GUIDE that the
greatest ones were with the GIs. "If
only they knew," he said, "what *they
do for me.*" One of the comedian's
most enduring contributions, the
magazine said in 1996, was that
"Hope made it possible to be
irreverent *and* patriotic."

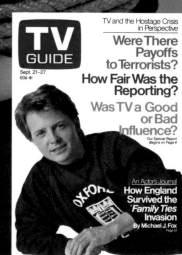

TV and the Hostage Crisis in Perspective

Were There Payoffs to Terrorists?

How Fair Was the Reporting?

Was TV a Good or Bad Influence?

Our Special Report Begins on Page 6

An Actor's Journal

How England Survived the *Family Ties* Invasion

By Michael J. Fox
Page 37

Michael J. Fox of *Family Ties*

FAMILY TIES
Alex P. Keaton (Michael J. Fox), Elyse Keaton (Meredith Baxter-Birney), Jennifer Keaton (Tina Yothers), Steven Keaton (Michael Gross), Mallory Keaton (Justine Bateman). NBC, 1982–89
COVER: BY PETER KREDENSER, SEPTEMBER 21, 1985

The quintessential television comedy of the Reagan era showed us just how far the culture had traveled since the days of *All in the Family* in the early '70s: Now, instead of an old grouchy reactionary versus a young liberal, we had *Family Ties*, where the parents were leftover lefties continuously needled by their *Wall Street Journal*-reading Republican teenage son, Alex P. Keaton. *Family Ties* became a hit after surviving several "squalls," TV GUIDE said in 1985. They included initially sorry ratings and Michael J. Fox's "unexpected, potentially disconcerting burst into stardom." The public's infatuation with him and his character spurred a "realignment of the show's dramatic thrust," the magazine said, a move that helped cement its status as one of the biggest hits of the 1980s. Talking to TV GUIDE in 1985 about his newfound fame, Fox said: "I'm afraid someone will take it away if I'm a jerk about it." It was that sort of self-policing modesty that made Fox such an appealing actor, despite Alex's undeniable obnoxiousness. The goodwill he earned from viewers did not wane: Seven years after *Family Ties* left the air in 1989, they were delighted to see Fox return to television as the even more politically savvy star of ABC's *Spin City*.

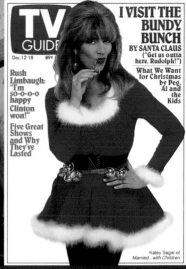

MARRIED... WITH CHILDREN

Front row: Al Bundy (Ed O'Neill), Peg Bundy (Katey Sagal). Back row: Kelly Bundy (Christina Applegate), Bud Bundy (David Faustino). Fox, 1987–97

COVER: BY E.J. CAMP, DECEMBER 12, 1992

Every time *Married...With Children* aired in the late 1980s, the fledgling Fox channel sent a shot across the bow of the established networks. In an era ruled by *Cosby Show* coziness, *Married...* chronicled the unholy Bundy household. It was less a family than it was a nest of rabid backbiting and viciousness, moronic gloating and sexual ridicule. The show seemed intent not only on breaking every law of old-school TV censorship (even Fox balked at running the 1988 season premiere episode in which all three women on a camping trip start menstruating at the same time; it aired later in the season), but also breaking Hollywood's golden rule that every script have at least one character the audience can root for. Nevertheless, it all somehow worked. "It's packed with sharp, funny lines and comic acting," TV GUIDE said during the debut season. The show ran for 10 years, defying the efforts of well-connected Michigan housewife Terry Rakolta to cripple it with an advertiser boycott. As it happened, that was long enough for son Bud (David Faustino) to finally lose his virginity—on the series that may have marked the deflowering of network television.

THE '90s

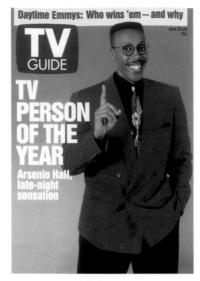

June 23, 1990
By Charles William Bush
Arsenio Hall of *The Arsenio Hall Show*

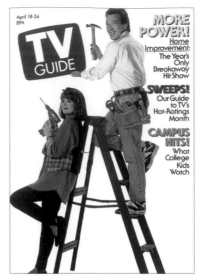

April 18, 1992
By Philip Saltonstall
Patricia Richardson and Tim Allen of
Home Improvement

February 6, 1993
By Timothy White
Katie Couric of *Today*

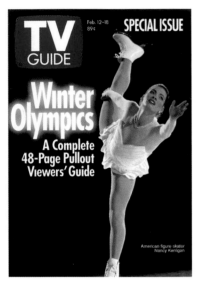

February 12, 1994
By Nancie Battaglia
Nancy Kerrigan

April 23, 1994
By Jeffery Newbury
Jason Alexander of *Seinfeld*

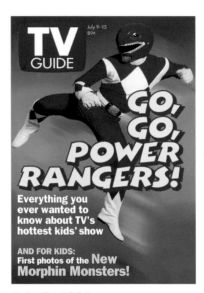

July 9, 1994
By Jeff Katz
Red Ranger of *Mighty Morphin
Power Rangers*

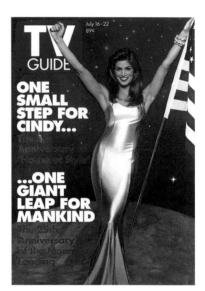

July 16, 1994
By Deborah Feingold
Cindy Crawford of *House of Style*

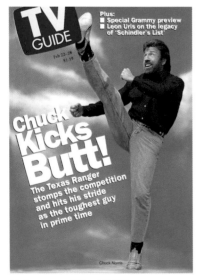

February 22, 1997
By Wyatt McSpadden
Chuck Norris of *Walker, Texas Ranger*

March 1, 1997
By Greg Lavy
Cast of *3rd Rock From the Sun*

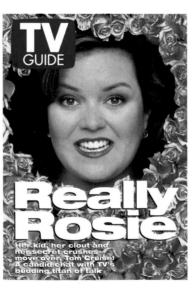

April 5, 1997
By Michael Daks
Rosie O'Donnell of *The Rosie
O'Donnell Show*

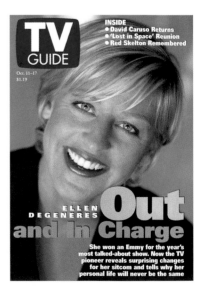

October 11, 1997
By Gregory Heisler
Ellen DeGeneres of *Ellen*

March 27, 1993
By Theo Westenberger
Billy Crystal

May 29, 1993
By Timothy White
Richard Simmons

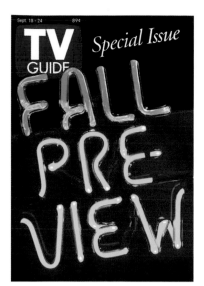

September 18, 1993
Photographer unknown
Fall Preview

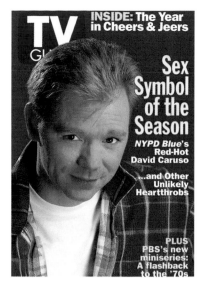

January 8, 1994
By Jeff Katz
David Caruso of *NYPD Blue*

February 25, 1995
By Jeffery Newbury
George Clooney of *ER*

May 27, 1995
By Steve Wayda
Pamela Anderson of *Baywatch*

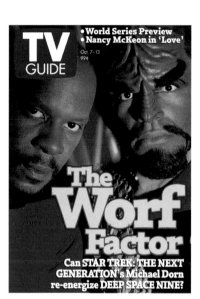

October 7, 1995
By Darryl Estrine
Avery Brooks and Michael Dorn of
Star Trek: Deep Space Nine

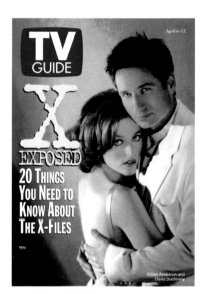

April 6, 1996
By William Hawkes
Gillian Anderson and David
Duchovny of *The X-Files*

March 7, 1998
By Fergus Greer
Katie Holmes of *Dawson's Creek*

October 31, 1998
By John-Frances Burke
Steve Burns and Blue of *Blue's Clues*

June 5, 1999
By Jose Molina
Ricky Martin

July 10, 1999
By Frank W. Ockenfels 3
Chris Rock in *Bigger & Blacker*

"L.A. LAW
WAS ONE OF THE FIRST

hour-long dramas with so much humor in it. When I think back to *All in the Family*—one of the shows that I loved so much—I realize it was the opposite. It was a comedy that was very dramatic. To me, the mix is more realistic, it's what life is about. In the worst moments, there can still be humor.

"Grace was tough and she was serious, and yet there was this vulnerable side that was dying to come out but was so afraid to. She has a line where she says, 'You know, I always wanted to be taken seriously. All my life, that's all I wanted, and now that's the only way people take me.' That's a great line, isn't it?"

—SUSAN DEY

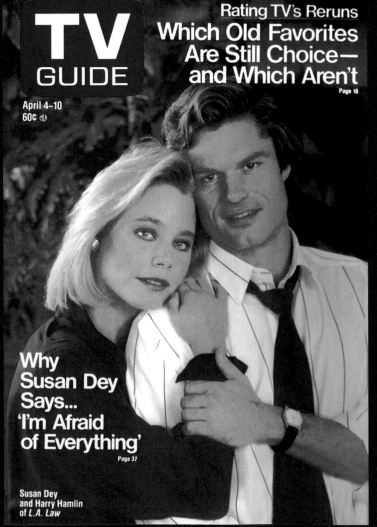

L.A. LAW
NBC, 1986–94
COVER: BY GENE TRINDL, APRIL 4, 1987

L.A. Law was hardly the first series about the legal profession, but as creator Steven Bochco told TV GUIDE in 1986, he envisioned his show as a departure from the *Perry Mason* tradition. Old-school legal dramas were too "earnest," Bochco said, with "precious little humor," and "the cases were all resolved, usually heroically, by the end of each episode." The *Hill Street Blues* executive producer lifted many of that show's techniques out of the dank police precinct and transferred them to the bright, cool *L.A. Law* offices: an ensemble cast, intertwined story lines that sometimes spanned several episodes, lots of humor, thinly veiled variants on headline-grabbing real-life cases (dwarf tossing, the outing of closeted homosexuals) and plenty of on-the-job romantic tension. Middle-aged viewers everywhere rooted for dumpy tax lawyer Stuart Markowitz (Michael Tucker) and his use of the never-explained Venus Butterfly sex maneuver to win over colleague Ann Kelsey (real-life wife Jill Eikenberry), but the major loveline involved good-looking younger partner Michael Kuzak (Harry Hamlin) and fetching assistant district attorney Grace Van Owen (Susan Dey). The only hotter romance on the show was the infatuation of sleazy divorce lawyer Arnie Becker (Corbin Bernsen) with himself. Just two months after *L.A. Law*'s launch in late '86, TV GUIDE was championing the show, urging readers to support it and send a message to Hollywood that "this is the right direction for television."

TV GUIDE

Writer Studs Terkel Says:
**Let's Get Rid of TV's Pundits
—They're Dangerous** Page 2

June 11-17
75¢ ◎

Why *thirtysomething*
Is So Good
By Dan Wakefield
plus
**The Fears of
Ken Olin**
Pages 35 and 238

L.-r.: Mel Harris, Brittany Craven
and Ken Olin of *thirtysomething*

THIRTYSOMETHING
**Front row: Nancy Weston
(Patricia Wettig), Elliot Weston
(Timothy Busfield), Ethan Weston
(Jason Nagler). Back row: Ellyn
Warren (Polly Draper), Prof. Gary
Shepherd (Peter Horton), Janey
Steadman (Brittany and Lacey
Craven), Michael Steadman (Ken
Olin), Hope Murdoch Steadman
(Mel Harris), Melissa Steadman
(Melanie Mayron). ABC, 1987–91**
COVER: BY TONY COSTA, JUNE 11, 1988

Not many television shows have their
very titles enshrined in the language—
we'll be hearing people described as
"thirtysomething" long after the characters in this show reach fiftysomething.
And it was just as unusual for a series to
provoke such a love-hate passion from
TV audiences: You were either riveted by
the emotional lives and often low-anxiety
domestic dramas of its seven financially
comfortable friends, or you were "one of
those who say they have enough troubles
without having to watch a show about
yuppie angst," as TV GUIDE put it in 1988.
Over the course of its four years, buddies
Michael and Elliot opened up their own
ad agency and forever pondered if they
were making the right choices in life,
while their wives, ambitious Hope and
artistic Nancy, raised the kids and forever
wondered if *they* were making the right
choices in life. Such was the confidence
of *thirtysomething*—in its writing and in
its hold on viewers' attention—that story
lines that might be resolved in a single
episode on other series here were allowed
to unfold over months. (Nancy spent an
entire season in the slow-motion collapse
of her relationship with Elliot, and another
in her struggle with ovarian cancer.)
Though each character represented some
aspect of not-old/not-young adulthood,
Ken Olin's Michael was the mouthpiece
for creators Ed Zwick and Marshall
Herskovitz. Rather than worrying about
his daughter's eventual first date, Olin
told TV GUIDE, Michael "is filled with self-
questioning and self-doubts. How often do
you see a father like that on television?"
It was that accomplishment—defining the
young ambivalent professional—that
would establish *thirtysomething* as a
monument to the 1980s.

TV GUIDE

Dec. 28–Jan. 3

The Cybill War
The sitcom star talks about turbulence on her set

The Best Show You're Not Watching

The Case for Homicide

$1.19

Michelle Forbes,
Andre Braugher,
and Kyle Secor

HOMICIDE: LIFE ON THE STREET
NBC, 1993–99
COVER: BY STEVE DANELIAN, DECEMBER 28, 1996

There have been more popular cop shows, but none better than
Homicide: Life on the Street, where gunfights were infrequent, car chases
almost unheard of and corpses plentiful. Not every case from the drug-
ravaged inner city of Baltimore was solved—the killing of a child named
Adena Watson haunted the squad room—but every new murder was
approached with a *Homicide*-al mixture of missionary zeal, mordant
humor and Sisyphean doggedness by the show's vivid collection of
sharply observed characters. If *Miami Vice*'s detectives were "MTV cops,"
Richard Belzer told TV Guide in 1993, then *Homicide*'s were "Tolstoy
cops." Belzer, a stand-up comedian, eagerly signed up to play the squad's
foul-tempered cynic, John Munch: "It's the difference between being
Zippy the dumb neighbor in a sitcom or a fully realized homicide cop
working in a very gritty, real situation." Though many actors performed
brilliantly in the Barry Levinson-produced series—Ned Beatty as the
veteran "Big Man" Det. Stanley Bolander, for instance, and Yaphet Kotto
as the perfect no-nonsense boss—Andre Braugher topped them all. As
TV Guide said in '98, Braugher's "electrifying" performance as Det. Frank
Pembleton made him "*Homicide*'s most provocative and prickly detective,
a master of intuition and intimidation. His operatic interrogations in 'the
box' rank among the blistering highlights of any TV season." Despite
almost uniformly ecstatic reviews, the show never drew ratings that
measured up to the stature of its writing or performances. After seven
years, NBC finally and officially closed the *Homicide* case for good.

COPS
Zane Schuberger, John Cosgrove. Fox, 1989–

Crime never looked more deglamorized than on *Cops*, the ride-along documentary series showing police officers on the job. Since its 1989 beginning, the show has been filmed in more than 100 American cities, as well as overseas precincts like London and Hong Kong. But no matter where the cameras went, the message was always the same: Police officers are by and large dedicated, low-key heroes, and criminals—whether a wife-beating drunk or a drug-dealing sleazeball—are almost uniformly miserable numbskulls. You just couldn't take your eyes off the banal but enthralling struggle between the good guys in blue (and gray and brown) and these car wrecks of humanity.

Local Programs Sept. 4-10

TV GUIDE

15¢

Miss America Fights Back
Page A

Jack Lord of
Hawaii Five-O

HAWAII FIVE-O

Det. Steve McGarrett (Jack Lord).
CBS, 1968–80
COVER: BY BOB PEAK, SEPTEMBER 4, 1971

Brooklyn-born Jack Lord always looked like a film-noir refugee who had wandered onto the set of a beach-blanket movie. He was Det. Steve McGarrett, wearing a suit and a scowl, battling crime in the land of leisurewear. And it worked. In 1971, three years into what would become one of television's longest-running cop shows, Lord told TV GUIDE: "People wonder why he doesn't get himself more girls. Our form is as rigid as a sonnet. Romance just doesn't work." Ah, but there was the romance of luscious Hawaii itself, and the irresistible theme song, which could keep you sitting around for an hour, waiting for the final credits just so you could hear it again.

BOOK 'EM, DANNO

134

COLUMBO
Lt. Columbo (Peter Falk). NBC, 1971–77; ABC, 1989–93
COVER: BY AL HIRSCHFELD, AUGUST 14, 1976

The only mystery in the detective drama *Columbo* was how, precisely, a shambling cop who appeared to sleep in his raincoat could outfox his wealthy, polished adversaries (one possibility: Columbo's deceptively casual request for "just one more thing"—the question that often tripped up his suspects). Even so, it wasn't the "how" as much as the "who" that explained the lasting appeal of this show. Director John Cassavetes talked to TV GUIDE in 1972 about series star Peter Falk: "He's archaic. He's deep. He's gentle. He's 2,000 years old. He's also somebody everybody falls in love with." That included the magazine, which lauded him as the "highly irregular—and highly wonderful—Mr. Peter Falk."

Republican Convention
Complete Details of TV Coverage

TV GUIDE
Local Programs Aug. 14-20
25¢

Peter Falk of 'Columbo'

MAGNUM, P.I.
Thomas Magnum (Tom Selleck). CBS, 1980–88
COVER: BY GENE TRINDL,
JANUARY 2, 1982

CBS decided it needed a crime-fighting series set in the Aloha State to pick up where *Hawaii Five-O* left off in 1980. But its chosen star, Tom Selleck, wasn't happy with the overly macho-heroic tenor of the pilot script he was shown. "I wanted the guy to make mistakes, to have flaws," Selleck told TV GUIDE shortly after *Magnum, P.I.*'s debut. That turned out to be a masterstroke—Selleck looked the part of a hunky private investigator, but as the magazine noted, he was endearing as "a guy who, running from a gang of thugs, forgets where he parked his car."

"PEOPLE REALLY UNDERSTOOD MAGNUM AND THEY RELATED TO HIM.

He didn't always get the girl. In fact, most of the time he did what most guys do, which is screw it up. Magnum said that one day he woke up as a Navy SEAL at age 33 and realized he'd never been 23. So the eight years represented in *Magnum* were the least responsible period in that character's life. He owed everybody money. He was always having to trick his friends into doing him favors. He was living for free and he drove somebody else's really expensive car. But the show seemed to have this universal audience where women found Magnum very attractive and men weren't offended by him. And I think that his fallibility and his humanness were big keys to the success.

"*Magnum* was really an ensemble piece about four characters and their relationships. But Hawaii was also a character in the show, and we treated it as such. *Hawaii Five-0* and *Magnum, P.I.* literally followed each other—*Five-0* went off the air and we came on—and both were hugely successful series. Hawaii is a state of mind for some people. If you're in Minnesota in the winter, it's kind of nice to watch this guy running around in a Hawaiian shirt and shorts.

"*Magnum, P.I.* was like *The Rockford Files*, because it dealt with problems of the human condition. Rockford was a neat character, and he influenced me a lot. He was an ex-con; people forget that. Magnum was a Navy SEAL—highly trained, highly lethal if he wanted to be—and had a lot of tragedy and heartache in his life. There's a timelessness to shows like *Rockford* and *Magnum*. I meet a lot of high school kids who know more lines from the show than I knew. I'm proud of the fact that the show has been around for so long and they still think Magnum is cool.

"I was fortunate enough to win an Emmy as best dramatic actor, but it was a show with an enormous amount of humor. I know somebody told me you have to find the comedy in tragedy and the tragedy in comedy, and I think *Magnum* did that pretty well. And we're in the Smithsonian. Magnum's Hawaiian shirt, his Detroit Tigers hat and his ring are all in there along with Archie Bunker's chair. And we were recognized officially by the Smithsonian as the first show that [portrayed] Vietnam veterans in a positive light. We did something right."

—TOM SELLECK

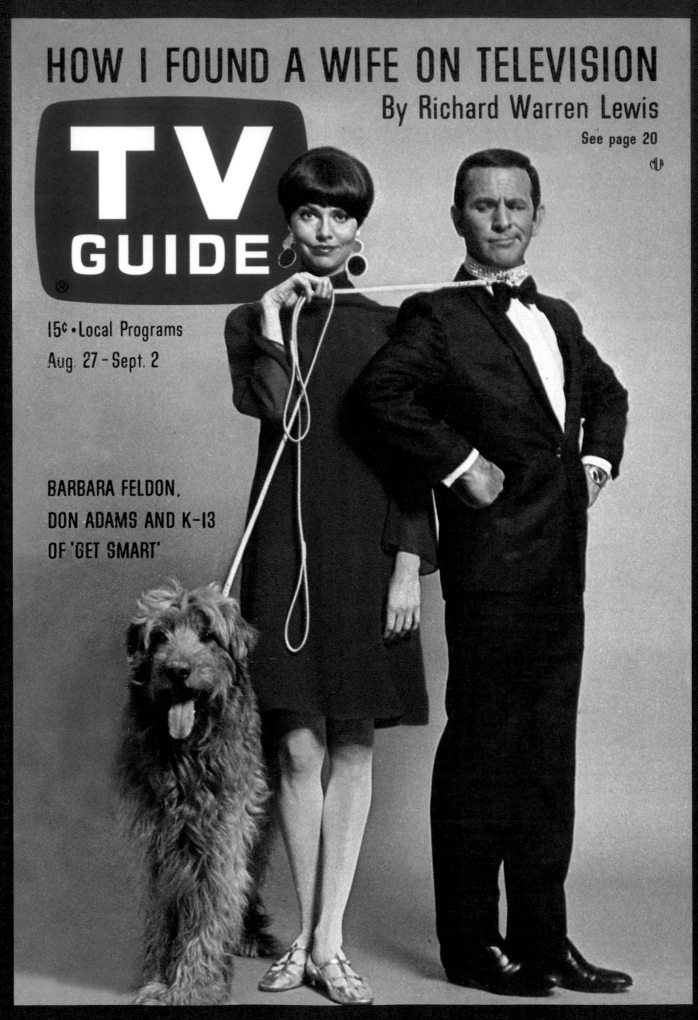

GET SMART
NBC, 1965–69;
CBS, 1969–70
COVER: BY KEN WHITMORE,
AUGUST 27, 1966

The 007-fueled secret-agent fad of the 1960s begged for lampooning, and comic masters Mel Brooks and Buck Henry obliged with *Get Smart*, about the world's dimmest spy. They found the ideal Maxwell Smart in comedian Don Adams, who could keep a straight face while talking into his shoe-phone or endlessly milking catchphrases like "Sorry about that, Chief." "I don't want to change the thinking of the world," Adams told TV GUIDE in 1965. "I just want to make people laugh." Sure enough, with the help of Barbara Feldon as brainy beauty Agent 99, he had the country in stitches.

HOW I FOUND A WIFE ON TELEVISION
By Richard Warren Lewis
See page 20

TV GUIDE

15¢ • Local Programs
Aug. 27 – Sept. 2

BARBARA FELDON,
DON ADAMS AND K-13
OF 'GET SMART'

Jan. 14-20   75¢

TV GUIDE

Cybill and the Moonlighting Mess—

Behind the Feuding That Almost Killed the Show

Delta Burke and Gerald McRaney

Their First Screen Kiss Turned into Real-Life Love

Memo to President Bush: How to Use TV— and Not Be Abused by It

By Richard Nixon

Cybill Shepherd and Bruce Willis of *Moonlighting*

MOONLIGHTING
ABC, 1985–89
COVER: BY ABC, JANUARY 14, 1989

Moonlighting's ostensible focus was the Blue Moon detective agency, but the cases were incidental to the exhilarating verbal sparring between Cybill Shepherd, as reluctant owner and glam ex-fashion model Maddie Hayes, and pre-*Die Hard* Bruce Willis, as cocksure detective David Addison. "Few television shows had ever been so heralded by audiences and critics alike," TV GUIDE said in 1987, already speaking in the past tense about a series just two years old. As it happened, production delays and backstage acrimony on *Moonlighting* would take another two years to actually bring the show down.

THE DICK VAN DYKE SHOW
Laura Petrie (Mary Tyler Moore), Rob Petrie (Dick Van Dyke). CBS, 1961–66
COVER: BY MARIO CASILLI, MARCH 27, 1965

When this show made its 1961 debut, TV GUIDE was so sure that readers would be unfamiliar with the comedian who supposedly merited name-in-the-title treatment that it ran an article called "What's a Dick Van Dyke?" (Answer: "He is a long, elegant string bean of a man with a knack for doing almost everything interestingly, whether playing a love scene or taking the most explosive falls since Buster Keaton.") By the end of the show's five-year run on CBS, of course, millions of people knew not only Van Dyke and his portrayal of Rob Petrie, head writer for a comedy-variety series in New York City, but also Mary Tyler Moore, as his high-strung but lovable wife, Laura, and his writing partners, played by Rose Marie and Morey Amsterdam. Though plenty of action took place behind the scenes of the fictional *Alan Brady Show* (*Your Show of Shows* vet Carl Reiner, who played the egomaniacal Brady, created *The Dick Van Dyke Show*), the moments that endeared a generation of viewers to the series occurred back home in suburban New Rochelle, New York. There, Rob was forever plunging into situations armed with the wrong information or a missing vital fact: Laura actually hates the gaudy piece of jewelry he thinks she loves; after an embarrassing display of jealousy, Rob discovers that a former suitor of Laura's is now a priest; Rob demands to meet a couple he is certain got the Petries' baby by mistake at the hospital—and discovers they are black. "We found it unfunny," TV GUIDE said in 1964 of the hospital mix-up episode, "but the producers undoubtedly felt it was all very modern and adult." On the whole, though, the magazine agreed that the show was "fresh, fast and frolicsome"—thanks primarily to the lucky fact that this series about a comedy writer happened to enjoy terrific comedy writing.

ROSEANNE
Roseanne Conner (Roseanne Barr), Dan Conner (John Goodman). ABC, 1988–97
COVER: BY TIMOTHY WHITE, AUGUST 29, 1992

In 1988, before the crotch-grabbing national anthem, before the startling declaration of multiple personalities and before the less than salutary marriage to Tom Arnold, there was simply Roseanne—star of a new comedy that was so resonantly "real" that it rose to second place in the Nielsen ratings in its fourth week (and stayed in the Top 5 for the next six years). "I'm not Lucy tryin' to hide 20 bucks from Ricky or June Cleaver glidin' around a dust-proof house in pearls and heels," Roseanne Barr told TV GUIDE during her show's first season. "I'm a woman who works hard and loves her family, but they can drive her nuts." It was precisely that unsentimental view of family and married life that had propelled the sarcastic "domestic goddess" to fame as a stand-up comedian in the mid-'80s. With *Roseanne*, she also wanted to create "a portrait of working folks with a little warmth and dignity, not buffoons. Bad grammar doesn't mean you're an idiot." The working folks in this case were Roseanne and Dan Conner of Lanford, Illinois: overweight, underpaid and trying to make ends meet while raising three kids. Dan, adeptly played by John Goodman, was a small-time contractor, and Roseanne was a production-line drone at a plastics factory (reflecting the way people really live, both changed jobs over the years). But the focus was usually back home, on the thorny but loving relationships between mom, dad and the kids. Other comedies had working-class premises, of course, but not even *The Honeymooners* or *All in the Family* nailed what it was like to be a blue-collar family in America as effectively as *Roseanne*.

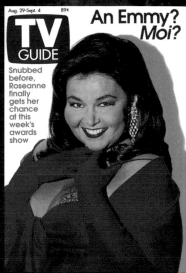

Aug. 29-Sept. 4   89¢
TV GUIDE
An Emmy? *Moi?*
Snubbed before, Roseanne finally gets her chance at this week's awards show

TO THE
MOON,
ALICE'

THE HONEYMOONERS

Above, left: Ralph Kramden (Jackie Gleason), Alice Kramden (Audrey Meadows), Ed Norton (Art Carney), Trixie Norton (Joyce Randolph). CBS, 1955–56
COVERS (FROM TOP): BY TOM CAFFREY, MARCH 19, 1955, AND MAY 21, 1955

"To the moon, Alice." "One of these days, Alice, one of these days: Pow! Right in the kisser." "Baby, you're the greatest." These lines have been repeated so many times on television over the past five decades that they're practically ingrained in our DNA. But it wasn't just the sheer repetition of *The Honeymooners* that made Jackie Gleason's trademark phrases so familiar; it was the vividness of his performance as Ralph Kramden, the pop-eyed, big-bellied bus driver who stormed around his grim Brooklyn, New York, apartment scheming to strike it rich, raging at the world and chafing at the skepticism of his sardonic wife. TV GUIDE loved *The Honeymooners* ("a rollicking, slapsticky, fast-paced situation comedy, played for the big reaction") but was so perplexed by its popularity in light of Ralph's aspiring-wife-beater shtick that the magazine consulted a psychiatrist to help explain its success. "The psychiatrist thinks that the American male has a feeling he is being submerged by his mate," the magazine reported in 1955, when the show moved from being a segment on *The Jackie Gleason Show* to its own half-hour slot on CBS, "and that he recognizes his own submission in Ralph Kramden's comic exasperation." That, plus the fact that the show was simply damned hilarious, week after week. There's an argument to be made that the real genius of *The Honeymooners* lay not in the relationship between Ralph and Alice (Audrey Meadows), but between him and his pal and upstairs neighbor, sewer worker Ed Norton, played by the incomparable Art Carney. There was an inherent comedy in big baby Ralph having to take care of someone else even more handicapped in life than he was (even in sleep, "Nah'en" needed Ralph to save him from his night walking). They were alike in their burning desire to get rich quick—and in the brain-cell deficit that kept them from accomplishing the dream—but where Ralph almost frantically veered between pure hope and utter despair, Norton seemed to glide through life with an improbable confidence. It's surprising Ralphie-boy never sent *him* to the moon.

Text within images:

The Chordettes: 'Who's Mr. Godfrey?'
TV GUIDE
LOCAL PROGRAM LISTINGS
WEEK OF MARCH 19-25
15¢

Kefauver: 'Reduce Crime On TV!'
...See Page 10
TV GUIDE
LOCAL PROGRAM LISTINGS
WEEK OF MAY 21-27
15¢

Are you taking care of yours?
BUY U.S. SAVINGS BONDS

SEX AND THE CITY

Miranda Hobbes (Cynthia Nixon), Samantha Jones (Kim Cattrall), Charlotte York (Kristin Davis), Carrie Bradshaw (Sarah Jessica Parker). HBO, 1998–

COVERS: BY DAH LEN, JUNE 17, 2000

Sure, *Sex and the City* featured four comely women whose frank sexual chat turned chic New York City bistros into the female equivalent of a guys' locker room, and of course it *had* to be on cable, because there's no way characters on a broadcast network could have gotten away with saying and doing the graphic stuff routinely showcased here. But as TV GUIDE said in 2000, HBO "also got a sharply written, seamlessly acted and, at times, poignant adult comedy." The show revolved around newspaper columnist and self-titled "sexual anthropologist" Carrie Bradshaw (Sarah Jessica Parker) and her three frisky friends: publicist Samantha (Kim Cattrall), lawyer Miranda (Cynthia Nixon) and art dealer-turned-museum volunteer Charlotte (Kristin Davis). Though only Samantha was as promiscuous as the hype suggested, the women certainly upended conventional depictions of relations between the sexes. "The men are playing all the women's roles in this show," Parker told TV GUIDE in 1998. "The women are in control." Among their potential dates—"toxic bachelors," "modelizers" and others—a guy occasionally broke out of the pack (Chris Noth's Mr. Big, for instance), but generally, Parker said, "men are objectified the way we often are." In terms of ratings, it was a *Sex* technique that worked.

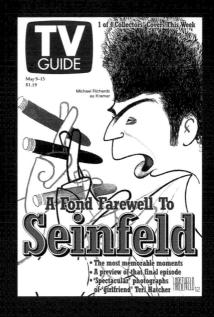

SEINFELD
George Costanza (Jason Alexander), Elaine Benes (Julia Louis-Dreyfus),
Cosmo Kramer (Michael Richards), Jerry Seinfeld (Jerry Seinfeld). NBC, 1990–98
COVERS: BY AL HIRSCHFELD, MAY 9, 1998

Mary Tyler Moore, who knows a few things about television comedy, summed up her thoughts about *Seinfeld* for TV GUIDE in 1996: "The unexpected turns, the complete dedication to the multiple layers of the characters, the chances that each actor takes— it's like watching each one of them on the high wire, and when they make it to the end, you cheer." Neil Simon, who knows a few things about *writing* comedy, was more succinct: "It's a terrific show. It's just *funny*." As put forth on the series itself, *Seinfeld* was a comedy about nothing. But in reality it was about the very worthy subject of modern manners—waiting interminably for a table at a Chinese restaurant, for instance, or trying to find your car in a parking garage—and it addressed these issues with all the acute observation and satirical brilliance of a Restoration comedy. It's just that the manners of Jerry (Jerry Seinfeld), George (Jason Alexander), Elaine (Julia

Louis-Dreyfus) and Kramer (Michael Richards) were often atrocious. Seinfeld told TV GUIDE in 1992 that it was "micro-concept TV," as if, the magazine said, they had taken "the fourth wall off not just the apartment, but the *life* of an urbane 38-year-old, and invited the audience in." What you saw wasn't always pretty, but it was almost uniformly hilarious. (Has any show ever contributed more catchphrases to the national discourse? "Not that there's anything wrong with that," "sponge-worthy," "master of my domain," "yada, yada, yada"—if you need them explained, you missed the '90s.) When *Seinfeld* finally signed off in '98, TV GUIDE said: "In the end we're left with nothing. Nothing but a comic afterglow: echoes of shamelessly loud guffaws, laugh lines etched over years of sustained smirking at the unlikely fates and unseemly follies of four chronically maladjusted Manhattanites."

IS SEINFELD THE BEST COMEDY EVER?

In the beginning was *The Honeymooners*. Then *I Love Lucy*. It's about time to elect *Seinfeld* to the Sitcom Hall of Fame. Now that half the shows on prime time bear a striking familial resemblance to the show about Jerry and his friends, it behooves us to honor this *Citizen Kane* of situation comedies, and to propose that it may be—as Ralph Kramden would say—the greatest.

I wish to go on record as saying that the first time I saw *Seinfeld* I predicted that it would die a quick and quiet death. Not because I didn't think it was great; I just thought it was way too good to be on TV. I thought they'd cancel it. Generally, if I like a new television show, it's quickly devoured by a mid-season replacement. And *Seinfeld* seemed too weird to survive on the tube. Or rather, too much like real life, which is actually far more peculiar than life in sit-com land. It was also outrageously funny, the humor arising out of mundane situations of failed communication and everyday embarrassment, like being caught picking your nose by your new girlfriend. *Seinfeld* pays homage to the fact that embarrassment is funny. Men probably laughed louder than women at the episode in which Elaine discovered that her nipple was exposed on her Christmas-card photo, while women presumably had a huge laugh when George was caught with his pants down after a dip in a cold swimming pool. This stuff happens to all of us. And it's funny—particularly when it happens to someone else. But who ever thought they'd put it on TV?

It's easy to forget after seven seasons just how strange *Seinfeld* seemed at first. Remember the show in which Jerry and George are trying to come up with an idea for a TV show to pitch to NBC? George suggests that they pitch a show about nothing: "No story, just talking." Kramer, on the other hand, proposes a show in which Jerry plays a circus manager. The characters will be circus freaks. "People love to watch freaks," says Kramer. Like the candy mint that is also a breath mint, *Seinfeld* is both of these things. It's a show about nothing in particular, which is to say, everyday life as we know it. And Jerry is the bemused ringmaster of a genuine freak show.

"We are all queer fish," F. Scott Fitzgerald once said. The revelation of *Seinfeld*, as distinct from most sitcoms, is that normal life is actually quite peculiar. Kramer, lurching around Jerry's apartment like a cross between Baby Huey and Frankenstein's monster, isn't the only freak; Newman, the Pillsbury Sourdoughboy, certainly qualifies. And George is neurotic enough to make Woody Allen seem positively serene and WASPy. I know people like this. But before *Seinfeld*, I don't recall anyone like George or Elaine or even Jerry on TV.

Yankees owner George Steinbrenner, who will have a cameo on the show next season, declared recently, "George Costanza is a nice guy." He was also quoted as saying, "This Seinfeld is the nicest young man." Steinbrenner is wrong as usual. One of the nicest things about *Seinfeld* is its portrayal of George and Jerry and Elaine in their not-so-niceness. Unlike your average sitcom protagonists, George and Jerry are not especially nice to the women they date, or even to sweet little old ladies, like the one who happens to have purchased the last loaf of rye bread from the bakery right before Jerry tries to buy one; Jerry knocks her over on the street and steals it. Mind you, he had a good reason, as we all do when we do something lousy. But let's not rob Jerry of his own obnoxious charm by calling him a nice guy. He'd sell Kramer down the river in a minute for a date with the buxom heiress to the O'Henry candy fortune. As would many of my closest friends. And George, in last month's season finale, doesn't see any harm in calling Marisa Tomei for a date just hours after learning that his fiancée has died.

As a New Yorker, I appreciate the fact that although it's filmed in L.A., *Seinfeld* actually has the lumpy texture of life in the city, the random looniness of the street, the idioms (Jerry waits on line, not in line) and speech inflections of Manhattan. But I don't necessarily expect the rest of the country to share my taste. Perhaps there is something inherently funny about the claustrophobia of New York apartment living, which is the backdrop that the three greatest sitcoms of all time—including *The Honeymooners* and *I Love Lucy*—have in common. (My only complaint vis-à-vis *Seinfeld*'s authenticity is the fact that all the characters seem to own and drive cars. This is nuts. No New Yorker in his right mind drives a car around the city. We ride around in foul-smelling yellow limos with bad shocks.)

Car quibbles aside, I still don't know how Jerry Seinfeld and cocreator Larry David managed to talk the network into a show about nothing except a bunch of neurotic New Yorkers. But from my own experience meeting with network types around the time *Seinfeld* was hatched, I can only assume they must have kidnapped an NBC executive and held him hostage until they got the green light. It presumably made things easier for the creators of subsequent quirky New York shows. *Mad About You*? No sweat—like *Seinfeld*, except Jerry and Elaine are married. *Friends*? *Seinfeld* with great-looking actors. *Caroline in the City*? Jerry Seinfeld with breasts.

However Jerry and Larry pitched the show, you have to hand it to the person who approved the *Seinfeld* pilot, which wasn't like *anything* on the tube. That's the most frightening concept in Hollywood—a genuine original.

—JAY McINERNEY, EXCERPT FROM TV GUIDE, JUNE 1, 1996

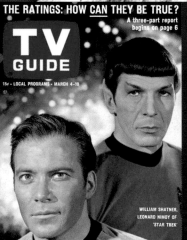

STAR TREK
Capt. James T. Kirk (William Shatner), Spock (Leonard Nimoy). NBC, 1966–69
COVER: BY SHEEDY-LONG, MARCH 4, 1967

With its debut in 1966, *Star Trek* boldly went where no television adventure series had gone before. Sure, other shows, like *Captain Video*, had ventured into outer space, but none combined special effects with an interest in social commentary. Series creator Gene Roddenberry made the U.S.S. *Enterprise* the vessel of his '60s idealism, and Capt. James T. Kirk (William Shatner) his spokesman. That is, except when Kirk was too busy fending off the attacks of enemy Klingons, trying to goad a smile out of the reserved Mr. Spock (Leonard Nimoy) or requesting a hailing frequency from communications officer Uhura (Nichelle Nichols, a rare African-American on '60s TV but in keeping with *Star Trek*'s One World sensibility). Writing in TV GUIDE in 1967, science-fiction master Isaac Asimov called the show a "noble and successful effort to present good science fiction to the American public." The American public—at least the adult segment—did not appreciate the gesture; the foundering series was canceled by NBC after just three seasons. But the phasers-set-on-stun gadgetry and abundance of women in skin-tight synthetic mini-dresses were catnip for teenage boys. Thanks largely to these "Trekkers," *Star Trek* relaunched a decade later as a movie franchise, followed by four TV series spin-offs and possibly the most lucrative worldwide merchandising effort in television history. Live long enough, the message seemed to be, and eventually you will prosper.

APOLLO 11
Edwin "Buzz" Aldrin, July 20, 1969
COVER: BY NORMAN ADAMS, JULY 19, 1969

The TV GUIDE headline read simply: "Live—from the Moon." It was a jaw-dropping concept. Not only did the United States succeed in putting astronauts on the Moon on July 20, 1969, but it transmitted the event on television to a worldwide audience of 600 million who, gathered in their living rooms, watched the event as virtually one family. A black-and-white camera mounted near the base of *Apollo 11*'s lunar landing module recorded 38-year-old Neil Armstrong's slow climb down a ladder to the Moon's surface. We saw Armstrong reach the ground and heard him announce, "That's one small step for man, one giant leap for mankind." Fifteen minutes later, Edwin "Buzz" Aldrin joined Armstrong, who mounted the camera on a tripod so that the world could watch the most astonishing nature program ever broadcast: two guys collecting soil and rocks, setting up experiments, taking photographs and planting the American flag. "This combination of the television camera, which does not lie, and the Age of Apollo seems to me the most dramatic coupling of events in man's history," Walter Cronkite wrote in TV GUIDE the week of the landing. "It has sophisticated and educated our children to a world we thought existed only on the pulp pages of science fiction."

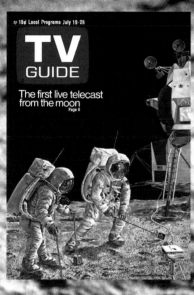

ONE SMALL STEP for MAN, ONE GIANT LEAP for MANKIND

LATE

NIGHT

Local Programs August 15-21

TV GUIDE

15¢

How One-Parent
TV Shows
Affect Your Family
—A psychologist's report
page 6

Johnny Carson

norman rockwell

THE TONIGHT SHOW STARRING JOHNNY CARSON
From below: Carson with Woody Allen; Don King; Bette Midler.
NBC, 1962–92
COVER: BY NORMAN ROCKWELL, AUGUST 15, 1970

Other shows stayed on the air longer, made more news, got higher ratings. But no television show—no television personality—was more thoroughly woven into the American conscious than *The Tonight Show* and its host of 30 years, Johnny Carson. Hearing the Carson theme song alone can instantly evoke an avalanche of pop-culture touchstones: bandleader Doc Severinsen's preposterous outfits; chortling second banana Ed McMahon and his "Heeeere's Johnny" introduction; the inimitable Carson monologue (OK, it was imitable for Rich Little); Carson in the audience playing "Stump the Band"; Carson decked out as the psychic Carnac the Magnificent; Carson warily handling exotic San Diego Zoo creatures. Carson was so utterly familiar because, in an often repeated phrase, the whole country went to bed with him every night. When he finally decided to end his remarkable run in 1992, a few months short of his 30th anniversary, TV GUIDE spoke with dozens of celebrities eager to praise the man whose show was a compulsory stop for Hollywood royalty. Mel Brooks: "Johnny is the greatest audience known to man because he listens and he *gets* it." Charlton Heston: "He is probably the best stand-up comic in America." Milton Berle: "He speaks a language that all America understands." As the magazine said at the time, one of Carson's greatest attractions was that "he frequently made failure funnier than the really funny stuff, because he accepted defeat with grace and self-deprecation. He taught America how to tell a joke—and how to get away with telling it badly. In this very important job, there is no successor to Johnny. And because all America no longer watches the same show every night, there may never be another Johnny."

LATE NIGHT 243

Allen Readies Sunday Punch For Sullivan
—See Page 17

TV GUIDE

LOCAL PROGRAM LISTINGS
WEEK OF JUNE 23-29

15¢

Steve Allen

PAAR'S STRANGE HOLD ON STAY-UP-LATE AMERICA

by Samuel Grafton

TV GUIDE

15¢

LOCAL PROGRAMS
MARCH 10-16

Jack Paar

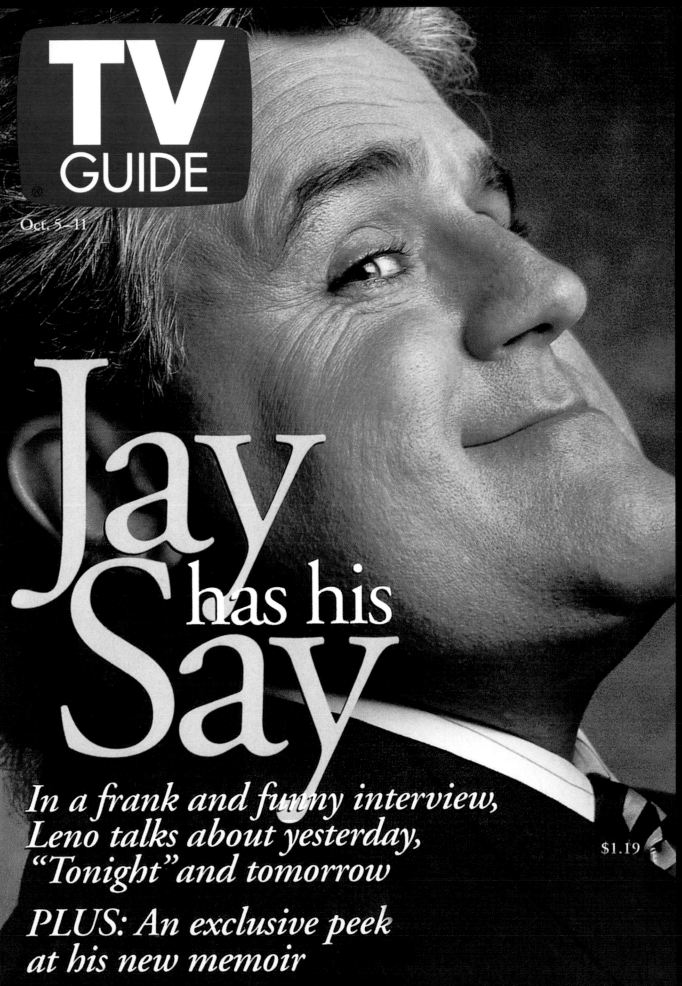

TV GUIDE

Oct. 5–11

Jay has his Say

In a frank and funny interview, Leno talks about yesterday, "Tonight" and tomorrow

PLUS: An exclusive peek at his new memoir

$1.19

THE TONIGHT SHOW
From far left: Steve Allen; Jack Paar, Hugh Downs. NBC, 1954–57 (Allen), 1957–62 (Paar) and 1992– (Jay Leno)
COVERS: BY AL HIRSCHFELD, MARCH 10, 1962. BY HOWELL CONANT, JUNE 23, 1956. BY MARK HANAUER, OCTOBER 5, 1996

When Steve Allen opened his late-night talk show on NBC in the mid-1950s, sitting at a piano and often playing his song, "This Could Be the Start of Something Big," it really *was* the start of something big: a TV institution that would still be flourishing half a century later. Johnny Carson, of course, was the *Tonight* king, but Allen, Jack Paar and Jay Leno contributed mightily to the show's legend. The innovative Allen made on-the-street remotes and audience participation reliably entertaining elements of *The Tonight Show*. (In a TV GUIDE tribute to the late Allen in 2000, comedian Jerry Stiller, a frequent guest, recalled the time the host spied someone sleeping in the back row and conducted an interview with the snoozing man. "That, to me, was classic," Stiller said.) When Paar took over in 1957, his more urbane humor still got plenty of laughs, but it was the host's mercurial emotions that made the show compelling. Paar cried if a song moved him, and spewed venom at his critics. He famously quit for a month in 1960, enraged that NBC censored a joke involving a "water closet." Paar "discovered that people like to see human beings being human. It was one of the most sensational discoveries in the history of show business," TV GUIDE said in 1962 after the host, easily bored, left *Tonight* for good. Then came Carson's phenomenal 30-year run. Though it was the very definition of a hard act to follow, genial Leno poured his heart into sustaining the franchise after landing the job in '92. Critics preferred rival David Letterman, but Leno consistently won the ratings war. "It's that old American adage," Leno told the magazine in 2002. "I'll take ambition over genius any day of the week." And for almost 50 years, Americans have taken *The Tonight Show* over the competition any night of the week.

How 'Mary Hartman' Beat the System

Page 16

TV GUIDE®

Local Programs
June 19-25
25¢

Louise Lasser as
Mary Hartman

NELSON

**MARY HARTMAN,
MARY HARTMAN**
Syndication, 1976–77
COVER: BY BILL NELSON,
JUNE 19, 1976

Over the course of 325 delicious
episodes in the mid-'70s, the
Norman Lear–produced satire
Mary Hartman, Mary Hartman
carried soap-opera sensibilities
to their logical but preposterous
conclusions. Louise Lasser
played a perpetually bewildered,
somnambulant housewife in fictional Fernwood, Ohio. Thanks to
her unquestioning acceptance of
advertising messages, Mary was
as troubled by the "waxy yellow
buildup" on her kitchen floor as
she was by her father's disap-
pearance, her daughter's kidnap-
ping or her husband's impotence.
"At its best," TV GUIDE said in
1976, "this show is the funniest
program on the air this year."

246 LATE NIGHT

THE DICK CAVETT SHOW
ABC, 1968–75
COVER: BY BERNIE FUCHS, DECEMBER 5, 1970

"I hate the fact that I ever got labeled as an intellectual," late-night talk-show host Dick Cavett told TV GUIDE in 1973, when his being tagged with a career-blunting reputation as a smarty-pants was a fait accompli (that's a "done deal" to you). He might have hated the classification, but it's hard to imagine Johnny Carson presiding, as Cavett did in 1971, over the verbal brawling between literary enemies Norman Mailer and Gore Vidal. Critics loved Cavett, relishing his witty wordplay and often startling selection of guests—Groucho Marx was as likely to turn up as John Lennon. Ultimately, though, despite ABC's repeated attempts to sell Cavett to viewers, the *I* word did indeed do him in.

SPORTSCENTER
Keith Olbermann, Dan Patrick. ESPN, 1979–

Like a stop at the water fountain after coming off the basketball court, ESPN's *SportsCenter* has been a compulsory destination for news-thirsty sports fans. The guys who made it so were Keith Olbermann and Dan Patrick, who teamed up in 1992 to host the scores-and-highlights show and promptly transformed the genre. A baseball player on a hitting tear wasn't simply on fire; in Patrick's patois, he was *"en fuego."* An injured player was listed as day-to-day, Olbermann reported, adding, "But then again, aren't we all?" The duo's dry delivery and amused asides launched a thousand imitators—many of whom later turned up as deadpan *SportsCenter* hosts themselves—but no one could beat the Dan 'n' Keith combo (though Kenny Mayne probably takes the batting doughnut for weirdly vivid home-run calls, like "I'm not sure what this pitch is, but it tastes like chicken"). Olbermann and Patrick would probably scoff at the "pioneer" label, but their knee-jerk scoffery was precisely their appeal—especially with Olbermann, whom TV GUIDE called "the patron saint of smart-ass sportscasting." That was in 2001, after he'd become a free agent and mystified fans by shuttling unhappily from one TV job to another. The still *SportsCenter*ed Patrick, however, wisely decided to stay with the home team.

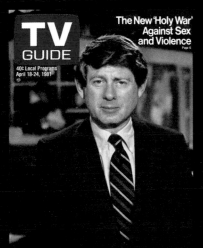

Ted Koppel of ABC News

ABC NEWS NIGHTLINE
Ted Koppel. ABC, 1980–
COVER: BY DAVID HUME KENNERLY, APRIL 18, 1981

The near-death experience of *ABC News Nightline* early in 2002, when the network aggressively courted CBS's David Letterman to take over its late-night time slot, prompted a renewed appreciation for *Nightline*'s many achievements over the course of two decades. ABC established a beachhead for late-night news in 1979 with *The Iran Crisis: America Held Hostage.* After it became clear that the standoff wasn't going to be resolved soon, the broadcast was rechristened *ABC News Nightline* in March 1980. By then, the hosting duties had been taken over by former diplomatic correspondent Ted Koppel, whose impressive showing as a substitute for anchorman Frank Reynolds (he'd taken a night off to celebrate his birthday) landed him the full-time job. Much like the *MacNeil-Lehrer Report* on PBS, *Nightline* focused on a single major news story of the day, presenting taped reports and live interviews with the principal players. The difference was the presence of Koppel. As author

David Halberstam wrote in TV GUIDE in 1985, "He is television's best interviewer, immensely skilled at keeping a show going, making it move, cutting to the heart of an issue, not letting people bore or blather on, minimizing ideology and bureaucratese." A trademark *Nightline* moment would pit two leading proponents of diametrically opposed ideas against each other, with Koppel as the serene yet impatient referee. Or as Koppel himself explained it in the magazine in '87: "Take two cables, put them together and watch the sparks fly." That describes the unprecedented debate over apartheid between South African foreign minister R.F. "Pik" Botha and Bishop Desmond Tutu in 1985, part of a series of broadcasts from South Africa that Halberstam called "the best use of television journalism in some 10 years." *Nightline*'s future may have been made uncertain by the era of the 24-hour news channel, but its contributions have never been in doubt.

DAVID LETTERMAN

Below: Letterman with Drew Barrymore. Left: Richard Simmons. Far left, bottom: with Madonna. NBC, 1982–93; CBS, 1993–

COVER: BY GREGORY HEISLER, FEBRUARY 15, 1997

Six days after September 11, 2001, David Letterman went back on the air from New York City, bewildered and visibly saddened, and explained why, at a moment like this, he was doing his show: "Mayor Giuliani encouraged us…to go back to our lives, go on living, continue trying to make New York City the place that it should be…. It's very simple. There is only one requirement for any of us, and that is to be courageous, because courage, as you might know, defines all other human behavior." It was one of the most moving statements of any delivered during that terrible time, and it was a cathartic, necessary show that reminded millions of viewers why they cherish—a word that would probably make him wince—Letterman as a familiar presence in their lives. As with a good friend, you never had to wonder what kind of mood Letterman was in. He could be cranky and miserable, but he was sweet with kids and the canine stars of "Stupid Pet Tricks," and his remote-camera chats with his mother, Dorothy, were lovely glimpses of a son's long-standing, teasing affection for his mom. It was Letterman's sensibility as an entertainer, though, that made him indispensable to his fans. On *Late Night With David Letterman* (NBC) and *Late Show With David Letterman* (CBS), he relentlessly mocked showbiz artifice, and then demonstrated his own idea of entertainment with a warped brilliance that evoked Ernie Kovacs at his best: He was the man in the Velcro suit and the fizzing Alka-Seltzer outfit, the guy who'd drop watermelons from a rooftop just to watch them pop, who'd commandeer a Taco Bell drive-through to torment customers. He played nicely with guests if they seemed to be making an effort but couldn't mask his boredom with the pretentious or preening. Critics called him mean—which left him "just crushed," Letterman told TV Guide in '97. "I don't want to be on TV and be mean. I just want to be funny." Dan Rather, a guest on that first show after the terrorist attacks of September 11, told TV Guide earlier in 2001: "Dave is always irrepressibly and unavoidably himself, and exactly what that means seems to change from night to night. In a copycat world, he is a true original."

AND THE NO. 1
SIGN SOMETHING
IS WRONG WITH YOUR
SCHOOL
LUNCH…

While growing up in Canada, I slowly became aware of the little box that had moving pictures in it. But it was the product of *that* country to the south, and I was involved in school and working in the most important medium, the one that was bound to last forever: radio. Radio, the theater of the mind, the source of employment for many Canadian actors, especially me. I put myself through college with my radio fees. But then I grew up, immigrated to America and after years of theater found myself doing stage performances in front of large boxy cameras. Now I was in live tele-

vision, putting myself through life on my television fees. The cameras, with their internal ventilation systems, sounded like cooing, warm little animals, and I thought of them as friendly, too, even with their red eyes. I was not intimidated when they would zoom in on me for a close-up—they meant no harm. After several years of live TV, my boyish visage began to show evidence of wear and tear.

And so I came of age on television. I went from shows like *Studio One*, *Playhouse 90* and *The US Steel Hour*, all coming out of New York City, to shows like *The Twilight Zone* and *Alfred Hitchcock Presents* in Los Angeles. I shuttled between coasts during those years as the industry evolved from live productions to filmed projects. I found myself doing movies of the week on location. There was more money in it because advertisers saw a novel way to reach buyers and pumped money into the emerging medium. More and more people were turning off their radio sets and not going to the movies; they were sitting at home in front of the magic square.

Steve McQueen leaped from *Wanted—Dead or Alive* to major screen stardom; that was the seminal moment when actors realized that doing a series was not a detriment to one's career, but could be used to one's advantage. So several actors made the jump from movies to television or from television to movies. TV was no longer a second-class citizen. I performed in *For the People* out of New York, one of the last of the shows to be filmed in that great city for a long time, and flew to Los Angeles when it closed, in time to do the second pilot for a show called *Star Trek*. For the next three years, we were a moderate success. And finally, it seemed, oblivion closed in.

But no, not on TV. Ten years later, *Star Trek* returned not only unscathed, but exalted. People began to look at me sideways. It went from, "Aren't you?" to "You are?" to "It's, it's…!" to "Well, I am, but hey, more than that." I had taken off the uniform and put on a tux.

And television, too, had gone to another level—the worldwide stage. It became the instrument of education and illumination. Kennedy was assassinated; wars were fought, won and lost on TV. History turned as a result of that omnipotent eye. I, along with the rest of the world, became hooked—at the expense of reading, conversation and sometimes original thought—because there in front of us lay the world, in all its glory and devastation.

But you see, TV is a mass of contradictions.

I love television. I am fascinated by looking at the screen and seeing people and events with which I could never and would never be otherwise acquainted. TV has opened my mind to philosophies, to issues, to politics and, yes, to tragedy. We are bound closer as human beings because of TV, and we are separated further as the haves and have-nots become bitterly aware of each other.

The thing that causes me as much concern and bewilderment as anything else is the sight of me aging gracelessly through the years. You've got to look at it from my perspective. I started in TV when I was practically a teenager. I'm now, by most measurements of time, an old man. And it's all happened in front of the American audience. I've watched my body go from slim adolescence to rippling manhood to (let's be kind) a middle-aged profile. I've watched my skin go from a youthful glow segueing to a flop-sweat sheen and finally to a moisturized opaqueness. I make it a point never to watch myself, whether it's something I did years ago or something I've just done.

Now, mind you, I'm also looking at a host of other people who are on the same journey. Don't you marvel at what Barbara Walters looked like when she was breaking in? Doesn't David Letterman's hairline make you curiously interested? Is Peter Falk decaying under that raincoat? And the one I really can't figure out is Regis. He looks exactly the same. Botox?

Anyway, you understand what I'm saying. Television is a chronicler of time. We see the good, the bad and the Howard Sterns move across those pixels and finally into oblivion… except for reruns.

—WILLIAM SHATNER

THE BEST OF
ACCORDING TO TV GUIDE

THE 50 GREATEST SHOWS

1. *Seinfeld*
2. *I Love Lucy*
3. *The Honeymooners*
4. *All in the Family*
5. *The Sopranos*
6. *60 Minutes*
7. *Late Show With David Letterman*
8. *The Simpsons*
9. *The Andy Griffith Show*
10. *Saturday Night Live*
11. *The Mary Tyler Moore Show*
12. *The Tonight Show Starring Johnny Carson*
13. *The Dick Van Dyke Show*
14. *Hill Street Blues*
15. *The Ed Sullivan Show*
16. *The Carol Burnett Show*
17. *Today*
18. *Cheers*
19. *thirtysomething*
20. *St. Elsewhere*
21. *Friends*
22. *ER*
23. *ABC News Nightline*
24. *Law & Order*
25. *M*A*S*H*
26. *The Twilight Zone*
27. *Sesame Street*
28. *The Cosby Show*
29. *Donahue*
30. *Your Show of Shows*
31. *The Defenders*
32. *An American Family*
33. *Playhouse 90*
34. *Frasier*
35. *Roseanne*
36. *The Fugitive*
37. *The X-Files*
38. *The Larry Sanders Show*
39. *The Rockford Files*
40. *Gunsmoke*
41. *Buffy the Vampire Slayer*
42. *Rowan and Martin's Laugh-In*
43. *Bonanza*
44. *The Bob Newhart Show*
45. *Twin Peaks*
46. *Star Trek: The Next Generation*
47. *Rocky and His Friends*
48. *Taxi*
49. *The Oprah Winfrey Show*
50. *Bewitched*

Originally published in TV GUIDE, May 4, 2002

THE 25 GREATEST MUSICAL MOMENTS

1. The Beatles on *The Ed Sullivan Show* (1964)
2. *Motown 25: Yesterday, Today, Forever* (1983)
3. Elvis Presley's TV special "comeback," *Elvis* (1968)
4. James Brown on *The T.A.M.I. Show* (1973)
5. Barbra Streisand's special *My Name Is Barbra* (1965)
6. Elvis Presley on *The Ed Sullivan Show* (1957)
7. Marvin Gaye sings the national anthem at the NBA All-Star Game (1983)
8. Julie Andrews and Carol Burnett in the special *Julie and Carol at Carnegie Hall* (1962)
9. Bette Midler sings "One for My Baby (and One More for the Road)" on Johnny Carson's final *Tonight Show* (1992)
10. Frank Sinatra in the special *Sinatra: The Main Event* (1974)
11. Leonard Bernstein sings the Beatles on *Leonard Bernstein's Young People's Concert* (1964)
12. The Notorious B.I.G. tribute on the MTV Video Music Awards (1997)
13. Frank Sinatra and Dean Martin on *The Judy Garland Show* (1962)
14. David Bowie on *Bing Crosby's Merrie Olde Christmas* (1977)
15. The Who on *The Smothers Brothers Comedy Hour* (1967)
16. Bruce Springsteen sings "Streets of Philadelphia" on the Academy Awards (1994)
17. Nirvana on *MTV Unplugged* (1993)
18. Isaac Hayes sings "Theme From *Shaft*" on the Academy Awards (1972)
19. Mary Martin in the special *Peter Pan* (1955)
20. Ricky Nelson sings "I'm Walkin'" on *The Adventures of Ozzie & Harriet* (1957)
21. *A Charlie Brown Christmas* (1965)
22. Cast sings "You've Really Got a Hold on Me" on *Roseanne* (1991)
23. The debut of *The Nat King Cole Show* (1956)
24. Ernie sings "Rubber Duckie" on *Sesame Street* (1970)
25. The special *This Is Garth Brooks, Too!* (1994)

Originally published in TV GUIDE, June 5, 1999

THE 50 GREATEST CHARACTERS

1. Louie De Palma / *Taxi*
2. Ed Norton / *The Honeymooners*
3. Lucy Ricardo / *I Love Lucy*
4. Fonzie / *Happy Days*
5. Archie Bunker / *All in the Family*
6. Mr. Spock / *Star Trek*
7. Lt. Columbo / *Columbo*
8. Emma Peel / *The Avengers*
9. Barney Fife / *The Andy Griffith Show*
10. George Costanza / *Seinfeld*
11. J.R. Ewing / *Dallas*
12. Felix Unger and Oscar Madison / *The Odd Couple*
13. Ralph Kramden / *The Honeymooners*
14. Homer Simpson / *The Simpsons*
15. Lilly Harper / *I'll Fly Away*
16. Sgt. Bilko / *The Phil Silvers Show*
17. Alex P. Keaton / *Family Ties*
18. Theo Kojak / *Kojak*
19. Maxwell Smart / *Get Smart*
20. Eddie Haskell / *Leave It to Beaver*
21. Mary Richards / *The Mary Tyler Moore Show*
22. Maynard G. Krebs / *The Many Loves of Dobie Gillis*
23. Andy Sipowicz / *NYPD Blue*
24. Paladin / *Have Gun, Will Travel*
25. Jim Rockford / *The Rockford Files*
26. Roseanne / *Roseanne*
27. Steve Urkel / *Family Matters*
28. Edina Monsoon / *Absolutely Fabulous*
29. Ted Baxter / *The Mary Tyler Moore Show*
30. Frank Pembleton / *Homicide: Life on the Street*

TELEVISION

THE 25 GREATEST COMMERCIALS

1. Apple Computer / "1984" (1984)
2. Alka-Seltzer / "Atsa spicy meatball!" (1969)
3. Volkswagen / Funeral procession (1969)
4. Volkswagen / Volkswagen driver helps out snowplow driver (1963)
5. Federal Express / "Fast-Paced World" with motormouth (1981)
6. American Tourister / Gorilla bashes luggage (1970)
7. Coca-Cola / Mean Joe Greene and young fan (1979)
8. Miller Lite / Bob Uecker brags in a bar (1975)
9. Wendy's / "Where's the beef?" (1984)
10. Life cereal / "He likes it! Hey, Mikey!" (1971)
11. Partnership for a Drug-free America / "Fried Egg": Your brain on drugs (1987)
12. Coca-Cola / "I'd Like to Teach the World to Sing" (1971)
13. California Milk Board / Who shot Alexander Hamilton: "Got Milk?" (1993)
14. Alka-Seltzer / Prison cafeteria (1970)
15. Benson & Hedges / "The Dis-advantages" (1966)
16. Keep America Beautiful / "Crying Indian" (1971)
17. Cracker Jack / Box of Cracker Jack is passed on a train (1965)
18. Nike / "Bo, you don't know diddly" (1989)
19. Energizer Batteries / Bunny keeps going...and going... (1989)
20. Lyndon B. Johnson for President / Daisy petals and nuclear countdown (1964)
21. Pepsi / Coke deliveryman sneaks a Pepsi (1996)
22. ESPN / "This Is *SportsCenter*" campaign (1995)
23. Xerox / Monk forsakes hand copying for xeroxing (1975)
24. Pepsi / Archaeologists find long-forgotten Coke can (1985)
25. Levi's / "The 501 Blues" (1984)

Originally published in TV GUIDE, July 3, 1999

THE 25 GREATEST MUSIC VIDEOS

1. "Thriller" / Michael Jackson / John Landis, director
2. "Vogue" / Madonna / David Fincher, director
3. "Smells Like Teen Spirit" / Nirvana / Samuel Bayer, director
4. "Sledgehammer" / Peter Gabriel / Stephen R. Johnson, director
5. "Walk This Way" / Run DMC and Aerosmith / Jon Small, director
6. "Sweet Child o' Mine" / Guns N' Roses / Nigel Dick, director
7. "Sabotage" / Beastie Boys / Spike Jonze, director
8. "Addicted to Love" / Robert Palmer / Terence Donovan, director
9. "California Love" / 2Pac with Dr. Dre / Hype Williams, director
10. "Express Yourself" / Madonna / David Fincher, director
11. "Hungry Like the Wolf" / Duran Duran / Russell Mulcahy, director
12. "Beat It" / Michael Jackson / Bob Giraldi, director
13. "Losing My Religion" / R.E.M. / Tarsem, director
14. "Take On Me" / A-Ha / Steve Barron, director
15. "The Rain (Supa Dupa Fly)" / Missy "Misdemeanor" Elliot / Hype Williams, director
16. "Every Breath You Take" / The Police / Kevin Godley and Lol Creme, directors
17. "Closer" / Nine Inch Nails / Mark Romanek, director
18. "Freedom" / George Michael / David Fincher, director
19. "Jeremy" / Pearl Jam / Mark Pellington, director
20. "Put Your Hands Where My Eyes Can See" / Busta Rhymes / Hype Williams, director
21. "Need You Tonight"-"Mediate" / INXS / Richard Lowenstein, director
22. "No Rain" / Blind Melon / Samuel Bayer, director
23. "Mo Money, Mo Problems" / The Notorious B.I.G. with Puff Daddy and Mase / Hype Williams, director
24. "Virtual Insanity" / Jamiroquai / Jonathan Glazer, director
25. "You Might Think" / The Cars / Jeff Stein, director

Originally published in TV GUIDE, December 4, 1999

31. Niles Crane / *Frasier*
32. Jim Ignatowski / *Taxi*
33. Diane Chambers / *Cheers*
34. Mork / *Mork & Mindy*
35. Kramer / *Seinfeld*
36. Fred Sanford / *Sanford and Son*
37. Hawk / *Spenser: For Hire*
38. Jane Hathaway / *The Beverly Hillbillies*
39. Artie / *The Larry Sanders Show*
40. Alexis Carrington / *Dynasty*
41. Dr. Mark Craig / *St. Elsewhere*
42. Bill Bittinger / *Buffalo Bill*
43. Adam / *Northern Exposure*
44. David Addison / *Moonlighting*
45. Jane Tennison / *Prime Suspect*
46. Xena / *Xena: Warrior Princess*
47. Douglas Wambaugh / *Picket Fences*
48. Miles Drentell / *thirtysomething*
49. Elliot Carlin / *The Bob Newhart Show*
50. Maurice "Buddy" Sorrell / *The Dick Van Dyke Show*

Originally published in TV GUIDE, October 16, 1999

THE 25 GREATEST GAME SHOWS

1. *The Price Is Right*
2. *Jeopardy!*
3. *G.E. College Bowl*
4. *Password*
5. *What's My Line?*
6. *$25,000 Pyramid*
7. *Who Wants to Be a Millionaire*
8. *Masquerade Party*
9. *To Tell the Truth*
10. *Match Game*
11. *The Newlywed Game*
12. *Survivor*
13. *Queen for a Day*
14. *Family Feud*
15. *Twenty One*
16. *The Gong Show*
17. *Video Village*
18. *Let's Make a Deal*
19. *The Hollywood Squares*
20. *Concentration*
21. *Truth or Consequences*
22. *The $64,000 Question*
23. *Beat the Clock*
24. *You Bet Your Life*
25. *Wheel of Fortune*

Originally published in TV GUIDE, January 27, 2001

1953–57

1953

April 3	Lucille Ball and Desiderio Alberto Arnaz IV of *I Love Lucy*
April 10	Jack Webb of *Dragnet*
April 17	"TV Ratings–Fact or Fraud?": Lucille Ball, Arthur Godfrey, Milton Berle, Imogene Coca and Sid Caesar
April 24	Ralph Edwards of *This Is Your Life*
May 1	Eve Arden of *Our Miss Brooks*
May 8	Arthur Godfrey of *Arthur Godfrey's Talent Scouts*
May 15	David Nelson and Ricky Nelson of *The Adventures of Ozzie & Harriet*
May 22	Red Buttons of *The Red Buttons Show*
May 29	Queen Elizabeth II
June 5	Dean Martin and Jerry Lewis of *The Colgate Comedy Hour*
June 12	Eddie Fisher of *Coke Time With Eddie Fisher*
June 19	Ed Sullivan of *The Ed Sullivan Show*
June 26	Dinah Shore of *The Dinah Shore Show*
July 3	Perry Como of *The Perry Como Show*
July 10	Dave Garroway and Mr. Muggs of *Today*
July 17	Lucille Ball and Desi Arnaz of *I Love Lucy*
July 24	Groucho Marx of *You Bet Your Life*
July 31	Max Liebman, Sid Caesar and Imogene Coca of *Your Show of Shows*
August 7	Ray Milland of *Meet Mr. McNutley*
August 14	Patti Page of *Scott Music Hall*
August 21	Mary Hartline and Claude Kirchner of *Super Circus*
August 28	Jayne Meadows of *I've Got a Secret* and Audrey Meadows of *The Jackie Gleason Show*
September 4	Wally Cox of *Mr. Peepers*
September 11	Joan Caulfield and Ralph Edwards of *This Is Your Life*
September 18	Fall Preview
September 25	George Reeves of *The Adventures of Superman*
October 2	Red Skelton of *The Red Skelton Show*
October 9	Bishop Fulton J. Sheen of *Life Is Worth Living*
October 16	T-Venus winners
October 23	Arthur Godfrey of *Arthur Godfrey's Talent Scouts*
October 30	Buelah Witch, Kukla and Ollie of *Kukla, Fran and Ollie*
November 6	Warren Hull of *Strike It Rich*
November 13	Jimmy Durante of *The Colgate Comedy Hour*
November 20	Dorothy McGuire and Julius LaRosa of *Arthur Godfrey's Talent Scouts*
November 27	Lugene Sanders of *The Life of Riley*
December 4	Loretta Young of *The Loretta Young Show*
December 11	Jack Webb of *Dragnet*
December 18	Bob Hope
December 25	Christmas: Perry Como, Patti Page and Eddie Fisher

1954

January 1	Bing Crosby
January 8	Joan Caulfield of *My Favorite Husband*
January 15	Martha Raye in *The Martha Raye Show*
January 22	Jayne Meadows, Henry Morgan and Joan Bennett of *I've Got a Secret*
January 29	Robert Montgomery of *Robert Montgomery Presents*
February 5	Jack Benny of *The Jack Benny Show*
February 12	Red Buttons of *The Red Buttons Show*
February 19	Ann Sothern of *Private Secretary*
February 26	Liberace of *The Liberace Show*
March 5	Frank Parker and Marion Marlowe of *Arthur Godfrey's Talent Scouts*
March 12	Maria Riva of *Studio One*
March 19	Groucho Marx of *You Bet Your Life*
March 26	Jackie Gleason of *The Jackie Gleason Show*
April 2	Eve Arden of *Our Miss Brooks*
April 9	Charlie Applewhite and Milton Berle of *The Milton Berle Show*
April 16	TV GUIDE Gold Medal Awards
April 23	Lucille Ball of *I Love Lucy*
April 30	Ben Alexander and Jack Webb of *Dragnet*
May 7	Harriet Nelson, Ricky Nelson and David Nelson of *The Adventures of Ozzie & Harriet*
May 14	Frank Sinatra in *Anything Goes*
May 21	Patricia Benoit and Wally Cox of *Mr. Peepers*
May 28	Gale Storm of *My Little Margie*
June 4	Arthur Godfrey of *Arthur Godfrey's Talent Scouts*
June 11	Ben Blue and Alan Young of *Saturday Night Revue*
June 18	Rise Stevens and Ed Sullivan of *Toast of the Town*
June 25	Bob Smith and Howdy Doody of *Howdy Doody*
July 2	Joan Davis and Jim Backus of *I Married Joan*
July 9	Arlene Francis of *What's My Line?*
July 17	Roy Rogers of *The Roy Rogers Show*
July 24	Jack Webb and Ann Robinson of *Dragnet*
July 31	William Bendix of *The Life of Riley*
August 7	Perry Como and friends of *The Perry Como Show*
August 14	Dean Martin and Jerry Lewis
August 21	Jayne Meadows and Steve Allen of *What's My Line?*
August 28	Roxanne of *Beat the Clock*
September 4	Eddie Fisher of *Coke Time With Eddie Fisher*
September 11	Betty Hutton
September 18	Liberace of *The Liberace Show*
September 25	Fall Preview
October 2	Teresa Wright and Dick Powell of *Climax*
October 9	Lucille Ball of *I Love Lucy*
October 16	Red Buttons of *The Red Buttons Show*
October 23	Walt Disney of *Disneyland*
October 30	Joan Caulfield and Barry Nelson of *My Favorite Husband*
November 6	George Burns and Gracie Allen of *The George Burns and Gracie Allen Show*
November 13	Liberace of *The Liberace Show* and Joanne Rio
November 20	Bebe Daniels and Ralph Edwards of *This Is Your Life*
November 27	Marcia Henderson and Peter Lawford of *Dear Phoebe*
December 4	George Gobel of *The George Gobel Show*
December 11	Marion Marlowe of *Arthur Godfrey and His Friends*
December 18	Imogene Coca of *The Imogene Coca Show*
December 25	Ozzie Nelson, Harriet Nelson, David Nelson and Ricky Nelson of *The Adventures of Ozzie & Harriet*

1955

January 1	Loretta Young of *The Loretta Young Show*
January 8	Arthur Godfrey of *The Arthur Godfrey Show*
January 15	Garry Moore, Bill Cullen, Jayne Meadows, Henry Morgan and Faye Emerson of *I've Got a Secret*
January 22	Ed Sullivan of *Toast of the Town*
January 29	Martha Raye of *The Martha Raye Show*
February 5	Edward R. Murrow of *Person to Person*
February 12	Dorothy Collins, Snooky Lanson, Russell Arms and Gisele MacKenzie of *Your Hit Parade*
February 19	Sid Caesar of *Caesar's Hour*
February 26	Steve Allen of *Tonight* and Judy Holliday
March 5	Liberace of *The Liberace Show*
March 12	Dinah Shore of *The Dinah Shore Show*

March 19	Art Carney of *The Honeymooners*
March 26	Gale Gordon and Eve Arden of *Our Miss Brooks*
April 2	Tony Martin of *The Tony Martin Show*
April 9	Gloria Marshall and Bob Cummings of *The Bob Cummings Show*
April 16	Garry Moore of *The Garry Moore Show*
April 23	Gale Storm of *My Little Margie*
April 30	Buddy Ebsen and Fess Parker of *Davy Crockett*
May 7	Peggy Wood and Robin Morgan of *Mama*
May 14	Perry Como of *The Perry Como Show*
May 21	Audrey Meadows and Jackie Gleason of *The Honeymooners*
May 28	Ralph Edwards of *This Is Your Life*
June 4	Eddie Fisher of *Coke Time With Eddie Fisher*
June 11	Gail Davis of *Annie Oakley*
June 18	Danny Thomas of *Make Room for Daddy*
June 25	Barbara Nichols, Sid Caesar and Cliff Norton of *Caesar Presents*
July 2	Lee Aaker and Rin Tin Tin of *The Adventures of Rin Tin Tin* and Tommy Rettig and Lassie of *Lassie*
July 9	Patti Page of *The Patti Page Show*
July 16	Julius LaRosa of *The Julius LaRosa Show*
July 23	Jack Webb and Janet Leigh of *Dragnet*
July 30	Barbara Whiting and Margaret Whiting of *Those Whiting Girls* and Lucille Ball and Desi Arnaz of *I Love Lucy*
August 6	Art Linkletter of *People Are Funny*
August 13	Roxanne and Bud Collyer of *Beat the Clock*
August 20	Hal March of *The $64,000 Question*
August 27	Groucho Marx of *You Bet Your Life*
September 3	Johnny Carson and Jody Carson of *The Johnny Carson Show*
September 10	Arthur Godfrey of *Arthur Godfrey and His Friends* and *Talent Scouts*
September 17	Milton Berle and Esther Williams of *The Milton Berle Show*
September 24	Fall Preview
October 1	Mickey Mouse, Jiminy Cricket, David Stollery and Tim Considine of *Mickey Mouse Club*
October 8	George Burns and Gracie Allen of *The George Burns and Gracie Allen Show*
October 15	Richard Boone of *Medic*
October 22	Peggy King and George Gobel of *The George Gobel Show*
October 29	Phil Silvers of *You'll Never Get Rich*
November 5	Nanette Fabray of *Your Show of Shows*
November 12	Liberace of *The Liberace Show*
November 19	Jack Benny of *Shower of Stars*
November 26	Martha Raye of *The Martha Raye Show*
December 3	Peter Lind Hayes and Mary Healy
December 10	Lucille Ball of *I Love Lucy*
December 17	Robert Montgomery of *Robert Montgomery Presents*
December 24	Christmas
December 31	Cleo of *The People's Choice*

1956

January 7	Arthur Godfrey and Goldie of *Arthur Godfrey and His Friends* and *Talent Scouts*
January 14	Loretta Young of *The Loretta Young Show*
January 21	Lawrence Welk of *The Lawrence Welk Show*
January 28	Janis Paige of *It's Always Jan*
February 4	Judy Tyler and Ed Sullivan of *The Ed Sullivan Show*
February 11	Perry Como of *The Perry Como Show*
February 18	Jimmy Durante of *The Jimmy Durante Show*
February 25	Gisele MacKenzie of *Your Hit Parade*
March 3	Lynn Dollar and Hal March of *The $64,000 Question*
March 10	Frances Rafferty and Spring Byington of *December Bride*
March 17	Maurice Evans and Lilli Palmer in *The Taming of the Shrew*
March 24	Dave Garroway of *Today*
March 31	Arlene Francis and John Daly of *What's My Line*
April 7	Jayne Meadows, Garry Moore and Faye Emerson of *I've Got a Secret*
April 14	Grace Kelly
April 21	Nanette Fabray of *Caesar's Hour*
April 28	Red Skelton of *The Red Skelton Show*
May 5	Mitzi Gaynor and George Gobel of *The George Gobel Show*
May 12	Bernadette O'Farrell and Richard Greene of *The Adventures of Robin Hood*
May 19	Phil Silvers and Elisabeth Fraser of *The Phil Silvers Show*
May 26	Alice Lon and Lawrence Welk of *The Lawrence Welk Show*
June 2	Sid Caesar and Janet Blair of *Caesar's Hour*
June 9	Patti Page of *The Patti Page Show*
June 16	Elinor Donahue, Robert Young, Lauren Chapin and Billy Gray of *Father Knows Best*
June 23	Steve Allen of *The Steve Allen Show*
June 30	Bob Cummings of *The Bob Cummings Show*
July 7	Lassie of *Lassie*
July 14	Gordon MacRae and Sheila MacRae of *The Gordon MacRae Show*
July 21	Bill Lundigan and Mary Costa of *Climax*
July 28	Gail Davis of *Annie Oakley*
August 4	Jackie Cooper and Cleo of *The People's Choice*
August 11	Democratic Convention
August 18	GOP Convention
August 25	Esther Williams
September 1	Alice Lon of *The Lawrence Welk Show*
September 8	Elvis Presley
September 15	Fall Preview
September 22	Hal March of *The $64,000 Question*
September 29	Jackie Gleason of *The Jackie Gleason Show*
October 6	Gale Storm of *The Gale Storm Show*
October 13	Harriet Nelson, Ozzie Nelson, David Nelson and Ricky Nelson of *The Adventures of Ozzie & Harriet*
October 20	Perry Como and Phyllis Goodwind of *The Perry Como Show*
October 27	Alfred Hitchcock of *Alfred Hitchcock Presents*
November 3	Edward R. Murrow of *Person to Person*
November 10	Loretta Young of *The Loretta Young Show*
November 17	Buddy Hackett of *Stanley*
November 24	Nanette Fabray in *High Button Shoes*
December 1	George Burns and Gracie Allen of *The George Burns and Gracie Allen Show*
December 8	Victor Borge
December 15	Dinah Shore of *The Dinah Shore Show*
December 22	Christmas
December 29	Jeannie Carson of *Hey, Jeannie*

1957

January 5	Arthur Godfrey of *Arthur Godfrey's Talent Scouts*
January 12	Lucille Ball of *I Love Lucy*
January 19	Jerry Lewis
January 26	Bob Hope
February 2	Jane Wyman of *Jane Wyman Theater*
February 9	Hugh O'Brian of *The Life and Legend of Wyatt Earp*
February 16	Robert Young and Jane Wyatt of *Father Knows Best*
February 23	Charles Van Doren of *Twenty One*
March 2	Dorothy Collins and Gisele MacKenzie of *Your Hit Parade*
March 9	Arthur Godfrey and Pat Boone of *The Arthur Godfrey Show*
March 16	The Emmy Awards
March 23	Tennessee Ernie Ford of *The Ford Show*
March 30	Julie Andrews in Rodgers & Hammerstein's *Cinderella*
April 6	Lawrence Welk of *The Lawrence Welk Show*
April 13	Nanette Fabray of *The Kaiser Aluminum Hour*
April 20	Loretta Young of *The Loretta Young Show*
April 27	Groucho Marx of *You Bet Your Life*
May 4	Hal March and Robert Strom of *The $64,000 Question*
May 11	James Arness of *Gunsmoke*
May 18	Esther Williams of *Lux Video Theatre*
May 25	Sid Caesar of *Caesar's Hour*
June 1	Ida Lupino and Howard Duff of *Mr. Adams and Eve*
June 8	Lassie of *Lassie*
June 15	Red Skelton of *The Red Skelton Show*
June 22	Jack Bailey of *Queen for a Day*

April 3, 1953
PHOTOGRAPHER UNKNOWN

The very first cover of TV GUIDE featured Lucy and Desi's son, Desiderio Alberto Arnaz IV. Lucille Ball timed her cesarean so that she gave birth the same night Lucy Ricardo did.

May 8, 1953
PHOTOGRAPHER UNKNOWN

Despite running away from home at 15, Arthur Godfrey became one of the most powerful men in early TV. It is estimated that at one point he was responsible for 12 percent of CBS's TV revenue.

November 13, 1953
PHOTOGRAPHER UNKNOWN

Known as "the Schnoz," beloved vaudeville veteran Jimmy Durante closed each episode of his show with the signature phrase "And good night Mrs. Calabash, wherever you are."

April 30, 1955
BY WALT DISNEY PRODS.

Davy Crockett, starring Fess Parker and Buddy Ebsen, was an early example of Disney programming and a national phenomenon. Ebsen went on to *The Beverly Hillbillies* and *Barnaby Jones*.

March 23, 1957
BY ERNEST CHIRIAKA

Tennessee Ernie Ford's folksy country charm made him a fixture on the small screen. His star was brightest during his eponymous mid-'50s show, but this comical singer also shined on *I Love Lucy* and *Hee Haw*.

April 13, 1957
BY HERB BALL

Despite a childhood stint in vaudeville, a part in *Our Gang* and time on Broadway, Nanette Fabray found her biggest success on television, including her turn as Sid Caesar's partner-in-laughs on *Your Show of Shows*.

November 22, 1958
BY GARRETT-HOWARD

Originally a minor matinee idol, Ronald Reagan developed his oratorical skills hosting several 1950s TV shows, including *General Electric Theater*. He married aspiring starlet Nancy Davis in 1952.

January 17, 1959
BY GENE TRINDL

Before he was an irreverent private detective on *The Rockford Files*, James Garner (with Jack Kelley) was an irreverent gambler in the Old West on *Maverick*.

June 29	Gale Storm of *Oh! Susanna*
July 6	John Daly, Arlene Francis, Bennett Cerf and Dorothy Kilgallen of *What's My Line?*
July 13	Gail Davis of *Annie Oakley*
July 20	Julius LaRosa of *The Julius LaRosa Show*
July 27	Garry Moore of *I've Got a Secret*
August 3	Cleo of *The People's Choice*
August 10	Ann B. Davis and Bob Cummings of *The Bob Cummings Show*
August 17	Phil Silvers of *The Phil Silvers Show*
August 24	Marjorie Lord and Danny Thomas of *The Danny Thomas Show*
August 31	Clint Walker of *Cheyenne*
September 7	Janette Davis and Arthur Godfrey of *Arthur Godfrey's Talent Scouts*
September 14	Fall Preview
September 21	Pat Boone of *The Pat Boone–Chevy Showroom*
September 28	George Burns and Gracie Allen of *The George Burns and Gracie Allen Show*
October 5	Joan Caulfield of *Sally*
October 12	"This Is the Week to Watch": Mickey Rooney, Queen Elizabeth II, Rosemary Clooney, Bing Crosby, Jane Powell and Eddie "Rochester" Anderson
October 19	Loretta Young of *The Loretta Young Show*
October 26	Peter Lawford and Phyllis Kirk of *The Thin Man*
November 2	Lucille Ball of *I Love Lucy*
November 9	James Garner of *Maverick*
November 16	Patti Page of *The Big Record*
November 25	Mary Martin in *Annie Get Your Gun*
November 30	Alfred Hitchcock of *Alfred Hitchcock Presents*
December 7	Dinah Shore of *The Dinah Shore Show*
December 14	Walt Disney, Jiminy Cricket, Mickey Mouse, Pluto, Tinkerbell and Donald Duck of *Disneyland*
December 21	Christmas
December 28	Ricky Nelson of *The Adventures of Ozzie & Harriet*

1958

January 4	Lawrence Welk of *The Lawrence Welk Show*
January 11	Gisele MacKenzie of *The Gisele MacKenzie Show*
January 18	John Payne of *The Restless Gun*
January 25	Sid Caesar and Imogene Coca of *The Sid Caesar Show*
February 1	Walter Winchell
February 8	Tab Hunter and Peggy King in *Hans Brinker*
February 15	"A Great Week"
February 22	Rosemary Clooney of *The Lux Show Starring Rosemary Clooney*
March 1	Lassie of *Lassie*
March 8	Arthur Godfrey of *Arthur Godfrey's Talent Scouts*
March 15	Amanda Blake and James Arness of *Gunsmoke*
March 22	Perry Como of *The Perry Como Show*
March 29	Tennessee Ernie Ford of *The Ford Show*
April 5	Gale Storm of *Oh! Susanna*
April 12	Hugh O'Brian of *The Life and Legend of Wyatt Earp*
April 19	Polly Bergen of *To Tell the Truth*
April 26	Guy Williams of *Zorro*
May 3	Shirley Temple of *Shirley Temple's Storybook*
May 10	Richard Boone of *Have Gun, Will Travel*
May 17	Danny Thomas, Marjorie Lord, Angela Cartwright and Sherry Jackson of *The Danny Thomas Show*
May 24	Dick Clark of *American Bandstand* and *The Dick Clark Show*
May 31	Phyllis Kirk of *The Thin Man*
June 7	Pat Boone of *The Pat Boone–Chevy Showroom*
June 14	Robert Young and Jane Wyatt of *Father Knows Best*
June 21	Ed Sullivan of *The Ed Sullivan Show*
June 28	Jerry Mathers of *Leave It to Beaver*
July 5	Bill Cullen of *The Price Is Right*
July 12	Lucille Ball of *The Lucy-Desi Comedy Hour*
July 19	Dale Robertson of *Tales of Wells Fargo*
July 26	Marvin Miller and Paula Raymond of *The Millionaire*
August 2	Walter Brennan of *The Real McCoys*
August 9	Steve Lawrence and Eydie Gorme of *Steve Allen Presents the Steve Lawrence-Eydie Gorme Show*
August 16	Robert Horton and Ward Bond of *Wagon Train*
August 23	Edie Adams and Janet Blair of *The Chevy Show*
August 30	Polly Bergen, Bud Collyer and Kitty Carlisle of *To Tell the Truth*
September 6	Arthur Godfrey of *The Arthur Godfrey Show*
September 13	Kathy Lennon, Dianne Lennon, Peggy Lennon, Janet Lennon and Lawrence Welk of *The Lawrence Welk Show*
September 20	Fall Preview
September 27	Garry Moore of *The Garry Moore Show*
October 4	Dick Clark of *American Bandstand* and *The Dick Clark Show*
October 11	Fred Astaire and Barrie Chase
October 18	Perry Como of *The Perry Como Show*
October 25	George Burns of *The George Burns Show*
November 1	Jack Paar of *The Jack Paar Show*
November 8	Loretta Young of *The Loretta Young Show*
November 15	Warner Anderson and Tom Tully of *The Lineup*
November 22	Ronald Reagan and Nancy Reagan of *General Electric Theater*
November 29	Victor Borge in *Comedy and Music*
December 6	James Arness of *Gunsmoke*
December 13	Danny Thomas of *The Danny Thomas Show*
December 20	Christmas
December 27	David Nelson and Ricky Nelson of *The Adventures of Ozzie & Harriet*

1959

January 3	Lola Albright and Craig Stevens of *Peter Gunn*
January 10	Milton Berle of *The Kraft Music Hall*
January 17	James Garner and Jack Kelly of *Maverick*
January 24	Red Skelton of *The Red Skelton Show*
January 31	George Gobel of *The George Gobel Show*
February 7	Johnny Crawford and Chuck Connors of *The Rifleman*
February 14	Alfred Hitchcock of *Alfred Hitchcock Presents*
February 21	Barbara Hale and Raymond Burr of *Perry Mason*
February 28	Richard Boone of *Have Gun, Will Travel*
March 7	Walter Brennan of *The Real McCoys*
March 14	Arthur Godfrey of *Arthur Godfrey and His Friends*
March 21	Ann Sothern of *The Ann Sothern Show*
March 28	Tennessee Ernie Ford of *The Ford Show*
April 4	Efrem Zimbalist Jr. and Roger Smith of *77 Sunset Strip*
April 11	Ward Bond of *Wagon Train*
April 18	Dinah Shore of *The Dinah Shore Show*
April 25	Dick Powell of *Dick Powell's Zane Grey Theater*
May 2	Hugh O'Brian of *The Life and Legend of Wyatt Earp*
May 9	Edd Byrnes of *77 Sunset Strip*
May 16	Loretta Young of *The Loretta Young Show*
May 23	Bob Hope in *Frances Langford Presents*
May 30	Steve McQueen of *Wanted—Dead or Alive*
June 6	Gale Storm of *The Gale Storm Show*
June 13	Pat Boone of *The Pat Boone Show*
June 20	Robert Young and Lauren Chapin of *Father Knows Best*
June 27	Lloyd Bridges of *Sea Hunt*
July 4	Jon Provost and Lassie of *Lassie*
July 11	Lola Albright and Craig Stevens of *Peter Gunn*
July 18	Janet Blair of *The Blair & Raitt Show*
July 25	John Russell of *The Lawman*
August 1	Dave Garroway of *Today*
August 8	Donna Reed of *The Donna Reed Show*
August 15	Lawrence Welk of *The Lawrence Welk Show*
August 22	Bess Myerson, Henry Morgan, Betsy Palmer and Bill Cullen of *I've Got a Secret*
August 29	Dick Clark of *American Bandstand*
September 5	James Garner and Jack Kelly of *Maverick*
September 12	Arthur Godfrey of *Arthur Godfrey and His Friends*
September 19	Fall Preview

September 26	Jackie Cooper and Abby Dalton of *Hennesey*
October 3	June Allyson of *The June Allyson Show*
October 10	Robert Taylor of *The Detectives*
October 17	Ingrid Bergman in *The Turn of the Screw*
October 24	Jay North of *Dennis the Menace*
October 31	Fred Astaire and Barrie Chase in *Astaire Time*
November 7	Jack Benny of *The Jack Benny Show*
November 14	Perry Como of *The Perry Como Show*
November 21	Clint Walker of *Cheyenne*
November 28	Art Carney of *The Honeymooners*
December 5	Gayle Polayes, Joan Chandler and Dwayne Hickman of *The Many Loves of Dobie Gillis*
December 12	Danny Thomas of *The Danny Thomas Show*
December 19	Christmas
December 26	Loretta Young of *The Loretta Young Show*

1960

January 2	Dennis Weaver, Amanda Blake, Milburn Stone and James Arness of *Gunsmoke*
January 9	Jane Wyatt and Elinor Donahue of *Father Knows Best*
January 16	Cliff Arquette of *The Charley Weaver Show*
January 23	Walter Brennan and Kathy Nolan of *The Real McCoys*
January 30	Garry Moore of *The Garry Moore Show*
February 6	Richard Boone of *Have Gun, Will Travel*
February 13	John Vivyan and Pippa Scott of *Mr. Lucky* and Lola Albright and Craig Stevens of *Peter Gunn*
February 20	Red Skelton of *The Red Skelton Show*
February 27	Robert Stack of *The Untouchables*
March 5	Jay North of *Dennis the Menace*
March 12	Chuck Connors of *The Rifleman*
March 19	Raymond Burr and Barbara Hale of *Perry Mason*
March 26	Donna Reed of *The Donna Reed Show*
April 2	Tennessee Ernie Ford of *The Tennessee Ernie Ford Show*
April 9	Efrem Zimbalist Jr. of *77 Sunset Strip*
April 16	Ann Sothern of *The Ann Sothern Show*
April 23	Hoagy Carmichael, John Smith, Bobby Crawford Jr. and Robert Fuller of *Laramie*
April 30	June Lockhart, Jon Provost and Lassie of *Lassie*
May 7	Elvis Presley and Frank Sinatra
May 14	Ernie Kovacs and Edie Adams of *Take a Good Look*
May 21	Gene Barry of *Bat Masterson*
May 28	Poncie Ponce and Connie Stevens of *Hawaiian Eye*
June 4	Darren McGavin of *Riverboat*
June 11	Noreen Corcoran, John Forsythe and Sammee Tong of *Bachelor Father*
June 18	Gardner McKay of *Adventures in Paradise*
June 25	Lorne Greene, Pernell Roberts, Dan Blocker and Michael Landon of *Bonanza*
July 2	Lawrence Welk of *The Lawrence Welk Show*
July 9	David Brinkley and Chet Huntley of *The Huntley-Brinkley Report*
July 16	Lucille Ball
July 23	John Daly of *What's My Line?*
July 30	Mike Connors and Ruta Lee of *Tightrope*
August 6	Esther Williams
August 13	Nick Adams of *The Rebel*
August 20	Betsy Palmer
August 27	Roger Smith, Efrem Zimbalist Jr., Edd Byrnes and Richard Long of *77 Sunset Strip*
September 3	Arlene Francis of *What's My Line?*
September 10	Dick Clark of *American Bandstand*
September 17	June Allyson and Dick Powell of *The DuPont Show With June Allyson*
September 24	Fall Preview
October 1	Dinah Shore of *The Dinah Shore Chevy Show*
October 8	Arthur Godfrey of *Candid Camera*
October 15	Marion Lorne and Carol Burnett of *The Garry Moore Show*
October 22	Debbie Reynolds
October 29	Danny Kaye
November 5	Loretta Young of *The Loretta Young Show*
November 12	Fred MacMurray and Tramp of *My Three Sons*
November 19	Ward Bond of *Wagon Train*
November 26	Abby Dalton, Jackie Cooper, Roscoe Karns and Henry Kulky of *Hennesey*
December 3	Shirley Temple of *The Shirley Temple Show*
December 10	Amanda Blake and James Arness of *Gunsmoke*
December 17	Sebastian Cabot, Anthony George and Doug McClure of *Checkmate*
December 24	Christmas
December 31	Dorothy Provine of *The Roaring Twenties*

1961

January 7	Richard Boone of *Have Gun, Will Travel*
January 14	Perry Como of *The Perry Como Show*
January 21	Barbara Stanwyck of *The Barbara Stanwyck Show*
January 28	Andy Griffith and Ronny Howard of *The Andy Griffith Show*
February 4	Eric Fleming and Clint Eastwood of *Rawhide*
February 11	Lola Albright and Craig Stevens of *Peter Gunn*
February 18	Nanette Fabray of *Westinghouse Playhouse*
February 25	Dorothy Collins, Allen Funt and Arthur Godfrey of *Candid Camera*
March 4	Raymond Burr of *Perry Mason*
March 11	Robert Stack of *The Untouchables*
March 18	Marjorie Lord of *The Danny Thomas Show*
March 25	Alfred Hitchcock of *Alfred Hitchcock Presents*
April 1	Roger Smith of *77 Sunset Strip*
April 8	Lori Martin and King of *National Velvet*
April 15	Mitch Miller of *Sing Along With Mitch*
April 22	Garry Moore of *The Garry Moore Show*
April 29	Rod Taylor of *Hong Kong*
May 6	Donna Reed of *The Donna Reed Show*
May 13	Lorne Greene of *Bonanza*
May 20	Walter Brennan and Richard Crenna of *The Real McCoys*
May 27	Ronald Reagan and Dorothy Malone of *General Electric Theater*
June 3	Paul Burke and Horace McMahon of *Naked City*
June 10	Nanette Fabray and Efrem Zimbalist Jr.
June 17	Lawrence Welk of *The Lawrence Welk Show*
June 24	John McIntire and Robert Horton of *Wagon Train*
July 1	The Flintstones of *The Flintstones*
July 8	Harry Morgan and Cara Williams of *Pete and Gladys*
July 15	Gardner McKay of *Adventures in Paradise*
July 22	Martin Milner and George Maharis of *Route 66*
July 29	Bob Keeshan of *Captain Kangaroo*
August 5	Fred MacMurray, William Frawley and Stanley Livingston of *My Three Sons*
August 12	"The World of Soap Opera"
August 19	Troy Donahue of *Surfside 6*
August 26	Hugh Downs of *The Jack Paar Show*
September 2	Dwayne Hickman and Bob Denver of *The Many Loves of Dobie Gillis*
September 9	Sebastian Cabot, Anthony George and Doug McClure of *Checkmate*
September 16	Fall Preview
September 23	Mitch Miller of *Sing Along With Mitch*
September 30	Carol Burnett of *The Garry Moore Show*
October 7	Walter Cronkite of *CBS Reports* and Dwight D. Eisenhower
October 14	Red Skelton of *The Red Skelton Show*
October 21	Joe E. Ross and Fred Gwynne of *Car 54, Where Are You?*
October 28	"This Is the Week to Watch": Ernie Kovacs, Bob Hope in *The World of Bob Hope*, Joan Crawford in *The Ziegfeld Touch* and Sir Laurence Olivier in *The Power and the Glory*
November 4	Dorothy Provine of *The Roaring Twenties*
November 11	Robert Stack of *The Untouchables* and Mrs. Robert Stack
November 18	Garry Moore, Durward Kirby and Marion Lorne of *The Garry Moore Show*
November 25	Amanda Blake and James Arness of *Gunsmoke*
December 2	Joey Bishop of *The Joey Bishop Show*
December 9	Dick Van Dyke and Mary Tyler Moore of *The Dick Van Dyke Show*
December 16	Raymond Massey and Richard Chamberlain of *Dr. Kildare*

June 27, 1959
BY RUSS HALFORD

One of the most popular shows of the '50s, *Seahunt* starred, almost exclusively, Lloyd Bridges, patriarch of the Bridges family—though son Beau made several appearances as a boy.

June 18, 1960
BY SHERMAN WEISBURD

James Michener created *Adventures in Paradise* and then dropped out. Viewers, though, stuck around for three seasons to watch the South Seas adventures of hunky Gardner McKay.

October 15, 1960
BY CURT GÜNTHER

Carol Burnett's first of 16 appearances on TV GUIDE's cover came thanks to her star-making role on *The Garry Moore Show*. Also shown is Marion Lorne, who went on to play Aunt Clara on *Bewitched*.

September 23, 1961
BY PHILIPPE HALSMAN

Even after rock and roll had taken hold, *Sing Along With Mitch* (Mitch Miller, that is) made it OK to love the old standards. With the help of the lyrics flashing on the TV screen, anyone could be a star in their own living room.

September 29, 1962
BY PHILIPPE HALSMAN

Lucille Ball holds the distinction of gracing more covers of TV GUIDE than any other individual: 34, as of the magazine's 50th anniversary. It's a record she'll most likely keep.

January 12, 1963
BY RUSS HALFORD

Before Arnold Palmer, golfers were known for being cool and quiet. With his passion and charisma, this telegenic pro has been called the perfect figure to usher in golf's television era.

June 22, 1963
BY PHILIPPE HALSMAN

One of the original "reality" shows, Candid Camera filmed unsuspecting folks set up in odd and crazy pranks. Allen Funt (center) hosted various incarnations since its 1948 debut.

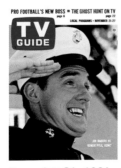

November 21, 1964
BY GENE TRINDL

The Andy Griffith Show spun off two popular comedies: Mayberry R.F.D. and Gomer Pyle, U.S.M.C., with Jim Nabors as the dim but lovable bumpkin gone military.

June 4 — Andy Griffith of The Andy Griffith Show
June 11 — Tina Louise, Alan Hale Jr. and Bob Denver of Gilligan's Island
June 18 — Elizabeth Montgomery, Agnes Moorehead and Tabitha of Bewitched
June 25 — William Smith, Peter Brown, Philip Carey and Neville Brand of Laredo
July 2 — Walter Cronkite of CBS Evening News
July 9 — Brian Kelly and Flipper of Flipper
July 16 — Fred MacMurray and William Demarest of My Three Sons
July 23 — Efrem Zimbalist Jr. and Stephen Brooks of The F.B.I.
July 30 — Johnny Carson of The Tonight Show
August 6 — Marshall Thompson and Clarence of Daktari
August 13 — Melody Patterson and Larry Storch of F Troop
August 20 — Red Skelton of The Red Skelton Show
August 27 — Barbara Feldon, Don Adams and K-13 of Get Smart
September 3 — Eva Gabor of Green Acres
September 10 — Fall Preview
September 17 — "1967 TV Set Buyers' Guide": Joey Heatherton
September 24 — Barbara Eden of I Dream of Jeannie
October 1 — "The Vietnam War: Is TV Giving Us the Picture?"
October 8 — Jim Nabors of Gomer Pyle, U.S.M.C.
October 15 — Peter Deuel and Judy Carne of Love on a Rooftop
October 22 — Lucille Ball of The Lucy Show
October 29 — Van Williams and Bruce Lee of The Green Hornet
November 5 — Robert Vaughn and David McCallum of The Man From U.N.C.L.E.
November 12 — Marlo Thomas of That Girl
November 19 — Bob Crane and Robert Clary of Hogan's Heroes
November 26 — Ron Ely of Tarzan
December 3 — Lawrence Casey, Chris George and Justin Tarr of The Rat Patrol
December 10 — James Arness of Gunsmoke
December 17 — Michael Callan and Patricia Harty of Occasional Wife
December 24 — Christmas
December 31 — Stefanie Powers of The Girl From U.N.C.L.E.

1967
January 7 — Ben Gazzara of Run for Your Life
January 14 — Art Carney of The Jackie Gleason Show
January 21 — Diana Rigg and Patrick Macnee of The Avengers
January 28 — Mickey Dolenz, Peter Tork, Mike Nesmith and Davy Jones of The Monkees
February 4 — Dale Robertson of The Iron Horse
February 11 — Steven Hill, Barbara Bain and Martin Landau of Mission: Impossible
February 18 — Dean Martin of The Dean Martin Show
February 25 — Phyllis Diller of The Pruitts of Southampton
March 4 — William Shatner and Leonard Nimoy of Star Trek
March 11 — Dorothy Malone of Peyton Place
March 18 — Jackie Gleason of The Jackie Gleason Show
March 25 — Robert Culp and Bill Cosby of I Spy
April 1 — Cheryl Miller and Judy of Daktari
April 8 — Dick Van Dyke
April 15 — "The Starlet, 1967": Karen Jensen and Jeff Scott
April 22 — Anissa Jones, Sebastian Cabot and Brian Keith of Family Affair
April 29 — Lawrence Welk of The Lawrence Welk Show
May 6 — Harry Morgan and Jack Webb of Dragnet '67
May 13 — Elizabeth Montgomery of Bewitched
May 20 — Andy Griffith and Aneta Corsaut of The Andy Griffith Show
May 27 — Ken Berry, Forrest Tucker and Larry Storch of F Troop
June 3 — Dennis Cole and Howard Duff of Felony Squad
June 10 — Dick and Tom Smothers of The Smothers Brothers Comedy Hour
June 17 — Ed Sullivan of The Ed Sullivan Show
June 24 — Barbara Feldon and Don Adams of Get Smart
July 1 — Chet Huntley and David Brinkley of The Huntley-Brinkley Report
July 8 — Efrem Zimbalist Jr. of The F.B.I. and J. Edgar Hoover
July 15 — Lucille Ball of The Lucy Show
July 22 — Michael Landon, Dan Blocker and Lorne Greene of Bonanza
July 29 — Justin Tarr, Gary Raymond, Lawrence Casey and Chris George of The Rat Patrol
August 5 — Hugh Downs and Barbara Walters of Today
August 12 — Mike Douglas of The Mike Douglas Show
August 19 — Barry Morse and David Janssen of The Fugitive
August 26 — Jim Nabors of Gomer Pyle, U.S.M.C.
September 2 — Eddie Albert and Eva Gabor of Green Acres
September 9 — Fall Preview
September 16 — Raymond Burr of Ironside
September 23 — Mickey Dolenz, Peter Tork, Mike Nesmith and Davy Jones of The Monkees
September 30 — Sally Field of The Flying Nun
October 7 — Richard Benjamin, Jack Cassidy and Paula Prentiss of He & She
October 14 — Johnny Carson of The Tonight Show
October 21 — Mia Farrow in Johnny Belinda
October 28 — "Who Killed Hollywood Society?"
November 4 — Stuart Whitman of Cimarron Strip
November 11 — Yvette Mimieux
November 18 — William Shatner and Leonard Nimoy of Star Trek
November 25 — Christopher Carey, Cesare Danova, Rudy Solari, Brendon Boone and Ron Harper of Garrison's Gorillas
December 2 — Danny Thomas of The Danny Thomas Hour and Marlo Thomas of That Girl
December 9 — Kaye Ballard and Eve Arden of The Mothers-in-Law
December 16 — Sebastian Cabot of Family Affair
December 23 — Christmas
December 30 — Carol Burnett of The Carol Burnett Show

1968
January 6 — Robert Conrad of The Wild Wild West
January 13 — Bob Hope
January 20 — Leif Erickson, Linda Cristal and Cameron Mitchell of The High Chaparral
January 27 — Elizabeth Montgomery of Bewitched
February 3 — Ben Gazzara in Run for Your Life
February 10 — Dick and Tom Smothers of The Smothers Brothers Comedy Hour
February 17 — Efrem Zimbalist Jr. and William Reynolds of The F.B.I.
February 24 — Joey Bishop of The Joey Bishop Show
March 2 — David Canary and Lorne Greene of Bonanza
March 9 — Jackie Gleason of The Jackie Gleason Show
March 16 — Sally Field and Alejandro Rey of The Flying Nun
March 23 — Bill Cosby and Robert Culp of I Spy
March 30 — Lucille Ball of The Lucy Show
April 6 — Barbara Anderson and Raymond Burr of Ironside
April 13 — Carl Betz of Judd, for the Defense
April 20 — Barbara Feldon of Get Smart
April 27 — Leslie Uggams
May 4 — Greg Morris, Peter Graves, Barbara Bain and Martin Landau of Mission: Impossible
May 11 — Fess Parker, Darby Hinton and Patricia Blair of Daniel Boone
May 18 — Mike Connors of Mannix
May 25 — Diana Hyland of Peyton Place
June 1 — Ed Sullivan of The Ed Sullivan Show
June 8 — "Salvador Dali's View of Television": Hugh Downs and Johnny Carson
June 15 — Linda Cristal and Leif Erickson of The High Chaparral
June 22 — Toni Helfer
June 29 — Robert Wagner of It Takes a Thief
July 6 — Barbara Eden of I Dream of Jeannie
July 13 — "The Wondrous Andy Griffith TV Machine": Jim Nabors, Griffith and Don Knotts
July 20 — Barbara Stanwyck, Richard Long and Linda Evans of The Big Valley
July 27 — Joey Heatherton and Frank Sinatra Jr. of Dean Martin Presents the Golddiggers
August 3 — David Brinkley, Chet Huntley, Walter Cronkite and Howard K. Smith
August 10 — Dennis Weaver, Ben, Clint Howard and Beth Brickell of Gentle Ben
August 17 — Milburn Stone, James Arness and Amanda Blake of Gunsmoke
August 24 — DeForest Kelley, William Shatner and Leonard Nimoy of Star Trek
August 31 — Johnny Carson of The Tonight Show
September 7 — Anissa Jones, Johnnie Whitaker, Kathy Garver and Sebastian Cabot of Family Affair
September 14 — Fall Preview: Darren McGavin, Doris Day and Tommie Smith

September 21 — Dan Rowan and Dick Martin of Rowan and Martin's Laugh-In
September 28 — Dean Martin of The Dean Martin Show
October 5 — Fred MacMurray, Tina Cole and Don Grady of My Three Sons
October 12 — The Olympics
October 19 — Jim Nabors
October 26 — Hope Lange of The Ghost and Mrs. Muir
November 2 — Peggy Lipton, Clarence Williams III and Michael Cole of The Mod Squad
November 9 — Barbara Feldon of Get Smart
November 16 — Bob Denver and Herb Edelman of The Good Guys
November 23 — Frank Sinatra
November 30 — Ann-Margret
December 7 — E.J. Peaker and Robert Morse of That's Life
December 14 — Diahann Carroll of Julia
December 21 — Christmas
December 28 — Doris Day of The Doris Day Show

1969
January 4 — David Soul, Bridget Hanley, Bobby Sherman and Robert Brown of Here Come the Brides
January 11 — Bob Hope
January 18 — Darren McGavin in The Outsider
January 25 — Deanna Lund and Gary Conway of Land of the Giants
February 1 — Cameron Mitchell, Henry Darrow, Mark Slade and Leif Erickson of The High Chaparral
February 8 — Peter Lupus, Greg Morris, Peter Graves, Barbara Bain and Martin Landau of Mission: Impossible
February 15 — Raymond Burr of Ironside
February 22 — James Stacey, Wayne Maunder and Andrew Duggan of Lancer
March 1 — Lucille Ball, Desi Arnaz Jr. and Lucie Arnaz of Here's Lucy
March 8 — Ruth Buzzi, Jo Anne Worley, Goldie Hawn, Arte Johnson, Chelsea Brown, Judy Carne and Henry Gibson of Rowan and Martin's Laugh-In
March 15 — Buddy Foster and Ken Berry of Mayberry R.F.D.
March 22 — Elizabeth Montgomery of Bewitched
March 29 — Tony Franciosa, Gene Barry and Robert Stack of The Name of the Game
April 5 — Tom and Dick Smothers of The Smothers Brothers Comedy Hour
April 12 — Dick Van Dyke and Mary Tyler Moore
April 19 — Lawrence Welk of The Lawrence Welk Show
April 26 — Jack Paar
May 3 — Madeleine Sherwood and Sally Field of The Flying Nun
May 10 — "The Raging Controversy Over TV's Role in Space Shots"
May 17 — Marlo Thomas of That Girl
May 24 — Hugh Downs, Barbara Walters, Joe Garagiola and Frank Blair of Today
May 31 — Anissa Jones, Sebastian Cabot and Johnnie Whitaker of Family Affair
June 7 — "The Hollywood Dancer": Debbie Macomber
June 14 — Glen Campbell of The Glen Campbell Goodtime Hour
June 21 — Jackie Gleason of The Jackie Gleason Show
June 28 — Marc Copage and Diahann Carroll of Julia
July 5 — Kent McCord and Martin Milner of Adam 12
July 12 — Peggy Lipton, Clarence Williams III and Michael Cole of The Mod Squad
July 19 — "The First Live Telecast From the Moon"
July 26 — June Lockhart, Edgar Buchanan, Lori Saunders, Meredith MacRae and Linda Kaye of Petticoat Junction
August 2 — Andrew Duggan of Lancer
August 9 — "Will Soaring Costs Knock Sports Off TV?"
August 16 — Merv Griffin of The Merv Griffin Show
August 23 — Linda Cristal and Leif Erickson of The High Chaparral
August 30 — Johnny Cash of The Johnny Cash Show
September 6 — Eddie Albert and Eva Gabor of Green Acres
September 13 — Fall Preview
September 20 — Jim Nabors of The Jim Nabors Show
September 27 — Robert Young and James Brolin of Marcus Welby, M.D.
October 4 — Bill Cosby of I Spy
October 11 — "What Is TV Doing to Them [children]?"
October 18 — Peter Lupus, Greg Morris, Leonard Nimoy and Peter Graves of Mission: Impossible
October 25 — Joan Hotchkis, William Windom and Lisa Gerritsen of My World and Welcome to It
November 1 — Denise Nicholas, Michael Constantine and Lloyd Haynes of Room 222
November 8 — Andy Williams of The Andy Williams Show
November 15 — Dan Dailey and Julie Sommars of The Governor & J.J.
November 22 — Barbara Eden of I Dream of Jeannie
November 29 — Michael Landon, Lorne Greene, Dan Blocker and David Canary of Bonanza
December 6 — Doris Day of The Doris Day Show
December 13 — Michael Parks of Then Came Bronson
December 20 — Christmas
December 27 — "Remember 1969?": Richard Nixon, Spiro Agnew, Dick and Tom Smothers, astronauts and New York Mets

1970
January 3 — "Here Come the '70s: How They Will Change the Way You Live"
January 10 — Fred MacMurray and Beverly Garland of My Three Sons
January 17 — Don Mitchell, Barbara Anderson, Don Galloway and Raymond Burr of Ironside
January 24 — Tom Jones of This Is Tom Jones
January 31 — Debbie Reynolds of The Debbie Reynolds Show
February 7 — Elizabeth Montgomery and Dick Sargent of Bewitched
February 14 — Linda Harrison, Laraine Stephens and Karen Jensen of Bracken's World
February 21 — James Daly and Chad Everett of Medical Center
February 28 — Clarence Williams III, Michael Cole and Peggy Lipton of The Mod Squad
March 7 — Gordie Tapp, Louis Jones, Jeannine Riley, Diana Scott, David Akeman, Lulu Roman, Buck Owens, Roy Clark and Cathy Baker of Hee Haw
March 14 — Diahann Carroll of Julia
March 21 — Jackie Gleason of The Jackie Gleason Show
March 28 — Dan Rowan and Dick Martin of Rowan and Martin's Laugh-In
April 4 — Florence Henderson, Robert Reed, Maureen McCormick, Ann B. Davis, Mike Lookinland, Barry Williams, Eve Plumb, Susan Olsen and Christopher Knight of The Brady Bunch
April 11 — Carol Burnett of The Carol Burnett Show
April 18 — Burl Ives, James Farentino and Joseph Campanella of The Bold Ones
April 25 — Raquel Welch and John Wayne in Raquel!
May 2 — Glen Campbell of The Glen Campbell Goodtime Hour
May 9 — David Frost of The David Frost Show
May 16 — Vice President Spiro T. Agnew
May 23 — Mike Wallace, Tricia Nixon and Harry Reasoner
May 30 — Julie Sommars of The Governor & J.J.
June 6 — Robert Young of Marcus Welby, M.D.
June 13 — Johnny Cash of The Johnny Cash Show
June 20 — John Forsythe, Joyce Menges, Susan Neher and Melanie Fullerton of To Rome With Love
June 27 — Liza Minnelli
July 4 — Miyoshi Umeki, Brandon Cruz and Bill Bixby of The Courtship of Eddie's Father
July 11 — Raymond Bailey, Donna Douglas, Max Baer Jr., Irene Ryan and Buddy Ebsen of The Beverly Hillbillies
July 18 — Jackie Chidsey, Michelle della Fave, Paula Cinko, Pauline Antony, Tara Leigh, Wanda Bailey, Rosetta Cox, Patricia Mickey, Micki McGlone and Susan Lund of Dean Martin Presents the Golddiggers
July 25 — Buddy Foster, George Lindsey, Jack Dodson, Arlene Golonka, Paul Hartman and Ken Berry of Mayberry R.F.D.
August 1 — Chet Huntley of The Huntley-Brinkley Report
August 8 — Ted Bessell and Marlo Thomas of That Girl
August 15 — Johnny Carson of The Tonight Show
August 22 — James Arness, Amanda Blake, Milburn Stone and Ken Curtis of Gunsmoke
August 29 — Eddie Albert of Green Acres
September 5 — Richard Burton and Elizabeth Taylor with Lucille Ball of Here's Lucy
September 12 — Fall Preview
September 19 — Mary Tyler Moore of The Mary Tyler Moore Show
September 26 — Lloyd Haynes, Denise Nicholas, Karen Valentine and Michael Constantine of Room 222

March 5, 1966
BY ANDY WARHOL

Get Smart's entire existence depended on the pop-culture phenomenon of 007, James Bond. Who better to put a pop stamp of approval on Barbara Feldon's Agent 99 than Andy Warhol?

October 29, 1966
BY IVAN NAGY

Once a '40s radio program, *The Green Hornet*, starring Van Williams, was produced by the same team behind *Batman*. It also gave the world an early look at future martial-arts legend Bruce Lee.

January 21, 1967
BY TERRY O'NEILL

A secret-agent import from the United Kingdom, *The Avengers* starred Patrick Macnee with trademark derby and cane. The first year, actress Honor Blackman was by his side; then Diana Rigg stepped into the catsuit.

January 28, 1967
BY GENE TRINDL

Pre-MTV, the Monkees were a fabricated boy band in the mold of the Beatles whose show featured a lot of fast edits, surreal imagery and slapstick humor. The kids bought it.

June 8, 1968
ILLUSTRATION BY SALVADOR DALI,
PHOTOGRAPHS BY PHILIPPE HALSMAN

The late '60s were a crazy time, so why not a cover from a crazy surrealist? Dali's "Today, Tonight and Tomorrow" featured Johnny Carson and Hugh Downs on thumbnail TV screens.

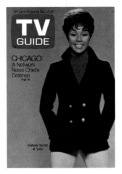

December 14, 1968
BY PRIGENT

While not a bad comedy, *Julia* is best known for being the first show to star an African-American woman, Diahann Carroll, in a lead role where she wasn't hired help. The public accepted the integrated show with no problem.

August 7, 1971
BY SHELDON SECUNDA

As the World Turns premiered in 1956 and has been a springboard for some major talent. Just a few of the headline names include Julianne Moore, Meg Ryan, Marisa Tomei and Lauryn Hill.

October 30, 1971
BY RAPHAEL

On the short-lived comedy *The Good Life*, Larry Hagman and Donna Mills played a husband and wife working as butler and cook. Seven years later, he was *Dallas*'s mogul, J.R. Ewing, and she was his sister-in-law on *Knots Landing*.

July 15, 1972
BY GENE TRINDL

One widow and five kids equaled TV's most famous family band, *The Partridge Family*. The show spawned a few hit singles and made David Cassidy a pinup for a generation.

June 16, 1973
BY AL HIRSCHFELD

In *Maude*, Beatrice Arthur gave TV one of its strongest female figures. Even by today's standards, the comedy's subjects of abortion, alcoholism and facelifts were daring. So were the knee-length sweater-vests.

September 15, 1973
BY LEROY NEIMAN

The colorful and famed sports illustrator LeRoy Neiman painted a tribute to the Super Bowl in which the Miami Dolphins eventually beat the Washington Redskins, 14-7.

March 1, 1975
BY AL HIRSCHFELD

"Loooking goood!" Freddie Prinze (right) was a Latino sex symbol, but the *Chico and the Man* star was really named Frederick Pruetzel (Hungarian dad, Puerto Rican mom). Prinze was for "Prince of Comedy."

May 10, 1975
BY BERNARD FUCHS

If one athlete held the spotlight for the whole decade of the '70s, it was Muhammad Ali. Famous bouts with Joe Frazier, George Foreman and Leon Spinks had everyone watching.

June 26, 1976
BY TONY ESPARZA

Third on the all-time list, Mary Tyler Moore has graced 24 TV GUIDE covers. Her first TV appearance, though, was as the Hotpoint Appliance elf on a commercial during *Ozzie & Harriet*.

October 23, 1976
BY PETER KREDENSER

Based on the Martin Scorsese feature film *Alice Doesn't Live Here Anymore*, Linda Lavin's working-class comedy *Alice* ran for nine seasons and was guilty for the catchphrase "Kiss my grits."

September 10, 1977
ILLUSTRATOR UNKNOWN

Don't let the quiet illustration of a few trees fool you—this is actually the cover of the best-selling issue in TV GUIDE's history. Obviously, it's what's on the inside that counts.

January 14, 1978
BY CHARLES ADDAMS

It was only right that master of the dark Charles Addams commemorate the Super Bowl's first nighttime game. With 102 million viewers, it was the largest audience for a sporting event to date.

July 21, 1979
BY PETE TURNER

The '70s had its share of silly comedies, and *B.J. and the Bear* was one of them. Greg Evigan (Danny in the original production of *Grease*) was a trucker teamed with a chimpanzee. Hilarious high jinks ensued.

June 21, 1980
BY RICHARD AMSEL

Inspired by the *Thin Man* films of the '30s, *Hart to Hart* showed Robert Wagner and Stefanie Powers outsmart the criminal world in high style. As their manservant, Max, said, "When they met, it was 'moider.'"

July 12, 1980
BY JOHN THOMPSON

Not since *The Beverly Hillbillies* did a family of country folk capture attention like this. *The Dukes of Hazzard* even entered the vernacular with "Daisy Dukes," a term for short-shorts of the denim variety.

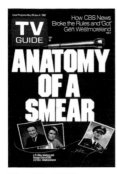

May 29, 1982
BY RICHARD NEWTON

CBS found itself on the defensive when Gen. William C. Westmoreland sued for libel over the documentary *The Uncounted Enemy: A Vietnam Deception.* After 18 weeks of testimony, the suit was settled out of court.

March 19, 1983
BY ROBERT PHILLIPS

Nancy Reagan took time out from her first-lady duties to guest-star in an episode of *Diff'rent Strokes.* In a very special antidrug episode, Arnold (Gary Coleman) learned to "Just say no."

August 10, 1985
BY BOB PEAK

The '80s will be remembered as the decade that gave birth to music videos and Madonna, icon of the new genre. In a world that goes through its pop stars quickly, she has endured.

January 4, 1986
BY PETER KREDENSER

Next to the Fall Preview issue, this was the top-selling TV GUIDE of '86. Connie Sellecca and the future Mr. Barbra Streisand, James Brolin, hosted rotating guests—including Liberace!—on *Hotel.*

February 17 — Michael Tucker and Jill Eikenberry of *L.A. Law*; and Patricia Wettig and Ken Olin of *thirtysomething*
February 17 — Michael St. Gerard in *Elvis* and Elvis Presley
February 24 — Brian Kerwin, Joe Morton, Julie Fulton, Richard Jenkins, Barry Bostwick, Karen Allen and Keone Young in *Challenger*
March 3 — "Parents' Guide to Children's Television": Fred Savage of *The Wonder Years*, Muppet Babies, Babar, Winnie the Pooh, Fred Rogers of *Mister Rogers' Neighborhood* and Pee-wee Herman of *Pee-wee's Playhouse*
March 10 — Larry Drake, Susan Ruttan, Corbin Bernsen, Alan Rachins, Jimmy Smits, Richard Dysart, Michele Greene, Michael Tucker, Susan Dey, Blair Underwood, Harry Hamlin and Jill Eikenberry of *L.A. Law*
March 17 — Bart Simpson, Lisa Simpson, Maggie Simpson, Marge Simpson and Homer Simpson of *The Simpsons*
March 24 — The Oscars: Billy Crystal
March 31 — Bob Saget of *America's Funniest Home Videos*
April 7 — Spring Preview: Valerie Bertinelli of *Sydney*; Michael Woods, Lloyd Bridges and Helen Slater of *Capital News*; and Carol Burnett of *Carol & Company*
April 14 — "America's Top TV Critics Tell What's In, What's Out"
April 21 — Arnold Schwarzenegger of *Tales From the Crypt*
April 28 — Sweeps Preview: Robin Williams, Whoopi Goldberg and Billy Crystal in *Comic Relief '90*; Flying Continental in the Kentucky Derby; Greg Kean, Casey Sander, Bo Foxworth, Andrew Myler and Bruce Greenwood in *Summer Dreams: The Story of the Beach Boys*; and Ariel in *The Little Mermaid*
May 5 — Oprah Winfrey in *Brewster Place*
May 12 — Barbara Cameron, Kirk Cameron and Joanna Kerns of *Growing Pains*
May 19 — Carol Burnett of *Carol & Company*
May 26 — "TV Goes to the Movies": Madonna in *Dick Tracy*; Michael J. Fox and Christopher Lloyd in the *Back to the Future* trilogy; and James Woods and Melanie Griffith in *Women and Men*
June 2 — "Summer Shape-Up Special": Steve Bond of *Santa Barbara* and Barbara Crampton of *The Young and the Restless*
June 9 — "America's New Love Affair With Cartoons": Bart Simpson, the Teenage Mutant Ninja Turtles and the Little Mermaid
June 16 — Dana Delaney of *China Beach*
June 23 — Arsenio Hall of *The Arsenio Hall Show*
June 30 — Summer Preview: Jose Canseco; Carey Lowell and Timothy Dalton in *Licence to Kill*; and Isabella Rossellini and John Lithgow in *The Last Elephant*
July 7 — "The Best and the Worst": Suzanne Pleshette and Bob Newhart of *Newhart*; Energizer Bunny; Sherilyn Fenn and Kyle MacLachlan of *Twin Peaks*; Andrew "Dice" Clay; Erika Eleniak, Shawn Weatherly and David Hasselhoff of *Baywatch*; Lynn Redgrave and Jackie Mason of *Chicken Soup*; and Sam Donaldson and Diane Sawyer of *PrimeTime Live*
July 14 — Sinbad, Dawnn Lewis, Jasmine Guy and Kadeem Hardison of *A Different World*
July 21 — "TV's Top Teen Superstars": Malcolm-Jamal Warner of *The Cosby Show*, David Faustino of *Married...With Children*, Neil Patrick Harris of *Doogie Howser, M.D.* and Alyssa Milano of *Who's the Boss?*
July 28 — "Guide to Home Video's High Flying New Season": Peter Pan
August 4 — "Dressed to Thrill": Candice Bergen of *Murphy Brown*, Nicollette Sheridan of *Knots Landing* and Kirstie Alley of *Cheers*
August 11 — "TV, Sports and Money": Joe Montana, Michael Jordan and Bo Jackson
August 18 — Annie Potts, Delta Burke, Dixie Carter and Jean Smart of *Designing Women*
August 25 — "Is One of These Women the Most Beautiful on TV?": Nicollette Sheridan, Dana Delany and Jaclyn Smith
September 1 — "Why Women Now Rule Rock": Janet Jackson, Paula Abdul and Madonna
September 8 — Sheryl Lee, Lara Flynn Boyle and Peggy Lipton of *Twin Peaks*
September 15 — Fall Preview
September 22 — Fall Preview II: Bart Simpson of *The Simpsons* and Bill Cosby of *The Cosby Show*
September 29 — Fall Preview III: Lenny Clarke of *Lenny*, Will Smith of *The Fresh Prince of Bel Air* and Laila Robbins of *Gabriel's Fire*
October 6 — Fall Preview IV: "What's Best...and What's Waiting in the Wings"
October 13 — "A High School Report Card on the New Teen Shows": Corin Nemec of *Parker Lewis Can't Lose*, Will Smith of *The Fresh Prince of Bel Air* and Charlie Schlatter of *Ferris Bueller*
October 20 — "The Best and Worst Dressed on TV": Marge Simpson of *The Simpsons*, Oprah Winfrey of *The Oprah Winfrey Show* and Delta Burke of *Designing Women*
October 27 — "Why We Go Batty for Horror on TV": Ari Lehman in *Friday the 13th*, the Crypt Keeper of *Tales from the Crypt*, Ben Cross of *Dark Shadows* and Robert Englund of *Freddy's Nightmares*
November 3 — Woody Harrelson, Ted Danson, Roger Rees, Kirstie Alley, George Wendt, Kelsey Grammer, Bebe Neuwirth, Rhea Perlman and John Ratzenberger of *Cheers*
November 10 — Susan Lucci of *All My Children*
November 17 — Bert and Ernie of *Sesame Street*, Miss Piggy and Kermit the Frog of *The Muppets* and Jim Henson
November 24 — Linda Evans
December 1 — Holiday Preview: Jasmine Guy, Patti LaBelle and Kadeem Hardison of *A Different World*; the Grinch in *How the Grinch Stole Christmas*; Dolly Parton in *Home for Christmas*; and Chevy Chase in *National Lampoon's Christmas Vacation*
December 8 — David Coulier, Ashley Olsen and Mary-Kate Olsen of *Full House*
December 15 — Dixie Carter of *Designing Women*
December 22 — "How Hollywood Brings Our Comic-Book Heroes to Life": Warren Beatty in *Dick Tracy*, Michael Keaton in *Batman* and Jon Wesley Shipp of *The Flash*
December 29 — Charles Kimbrough, Candice Bergen, Joe Regalbuto, Robert Pastorelli, Faith Ford, Grant Shaud and Pat Corley of *Murphy Brown*

1991
January 5 — Jane Pauley of *Real Life*
January 12 — Farrah Fawcett and Ryan O'Neal of *Good Sports*
January 19 — Mike Wallace, Morley Safer, Harry Reasoner and Ed Bradley of *60 Minutes*
January 26 — Cybill Shepherd in *Which Way Home*
February 2 — Sweeps Preview: Julia Roberts in a Barbara Walters special, M.C. Hammer at the Grammys and Gary Cole in *Son of the Morning Star*
February 9 — Lucille Ball and Desi Arnaz
February 16 — "Watching the War: How TV Has Stirred Our Patriotism, Pride, Anger and Fear"
February 23 — Roseanne Barr of *Roseanne*; "TV's War Stars": Christiane Amanpour, Arthur Kent and Peter Arnett; and Fred Rogers
March 2 — "Parents' Guide to Children's Television": Jaleel White of *Family Matters*, Captain Planet, Bart Simpson, Big Bird, the Teenage Mutant Ninja Turtles and Tiny Toons
March 9 — Dreyfuss of *Empty Nest*
March 16 — "Cartoons Grow Up": Barbara Walters with the Teenage Mutant Ninja Turtles
March 23 — The Oscars: Whoopi Goldberg, Julia Roberts and Kevin Costner
March 30 — Cheryl Ladd in *Changes*
April 6 — Bo Jackson, Nolan Ryan, Roger Clemens and Jose Canseco
April 13 — Delta Burke of *Designing Women*
April 20 — Burt Reynolds, Marilu Henner and Caroline Rhymer of *Evening Shade*
April 27 — Sweeps Preview: Earl Sinclair of *Dinosaurs*, Magic Johnson and Patrick Bergin in *Robin Hood*
May 4 — Larry Hagman of *Dallas*
May 11 — Jimmy Smits, Harry Hamlin, Susan Dey, John Spencer, Cecil Hoffmann and Amanda Donohoe of *L.A. Law*
May 18 — Robin Thomas, Candice Bergen and Jay Thomas of *Murphy Brown*
May 25 — Summer Movie Preview: Arnold Schwarzenegger, *101 Dalmatians* and Julia Roberts
June 1 — Jasmine Guy of *A Different World*
June 8 — Michael Landon
June 15 — "The Best 50 Videos to Watch Over and Over Again": Ray Bolger, Jack Haley, Judy Garland and Bert Lahr in *The Wizard of Oz*; Julie Andrews in *Mary Poppins*; Dustin Hoffman and Jessica Lange in *Tootsie*; Humphrey Bogart and Ingrid Bergman in *Casablanca*; and R2-D2 and C-3PO in *Star Wars*
June 22 — Gerald McRaney of *Major Dad* and Delta Burke of *Designing Women*
June 29 — "The Battle for Carson's Crown": Arsenio Hall of *The Arsenio Hall Show*, Johnny Carson of *The Tonight Show*, David Letterman of *Late Night With David Letterman* and Jay Leno
July 6 — "The Best and the Worst": Baby Sinclair of *Dinosaurs*, Abraham Lincoln,

July 13 — Katie Couric of *Today*, Frances Fisher and Maurice Benard in *Lucy and Desi: Before the Laughter* and Roseanne Barr of *Roseanne*
July 13 — Michael Landon
July 20 — Michael Landon
July 27 — "The 2,000th Issue of TV GUIDE"
August 3 — Madonna
August 10 — "TV's Most Beautiful Women": Jaclyn Smith, Candice Bergen and Vanna White
August 17 — "Viewers' Guide to Home Video's Hottest Season": Kevin Costner and Macaulay Culkin
August 24 — Shannen Doherty of *Beverly Hills, 90210*
August 31 — Patrick Stewart of *Star Trek: The Next Generation* and William Shatner of *Star Trek*
September 7 — Janine Turner of *Northern Exposure*
September 14 — Fall Preview
September 21 — Julia Duffy and Jan Hooks of *Designing Women*
September 28 — "Parents' Guide to the New Kids' Shows": Wilma and Waldo of *Where's Waldo?*, Duck Dawking of *Duck Dawking*, Hammerman of *Hammerman*, Doug and Porkchop of *Doug* and Macaulay Culkin
October 5 — "The Best and Worst Dressed on TV": Sharon Gless and Arsenio Hall
October 12 — Jacqueline Kennedy Onassis
October 19 — Linda Evans and Joan Collins in *Dynasty: The Reunion*
October 26 — Joan Rivers
November 2 — Michael Jackson
November 9 — "Is Network News Crumbling?": Tom Brokaw of *NBC Nightly News*, Peter Jennings of *World News Tonight* and Dan Rather of *The CBS Evening News*
November 16 — Valerie Bertinelli in *In a Child's Name*
November 23 — Madonna
November 30 — Naomi Judd and Wynonna Judd
December 7 — Holiday Preview: Babar; Winnie the Pooh; Opus; Bob Hope; Richard Thomas and Katharine Isobel; and Andy Rooney, Mickey Mouse and Goofy
December 14 — Luke Perry and Jason Priestley of *Beverly Hills, 90210*
December 21 — John Corbett of *Northern Exposure*
December 28 — John Goodman of *Roseanne*

1992
January 4 — Roseanne Arnold of *Roseanne*
January 11 — Jane Fonda in *Fonda on Fonda*
January 18 — Dreyfuss of *Empty Nest*
January 25 — Super Bowl
February 1 — Jessica Lange in *O Pioneers!*
February 8 — The Olympics
February 15 — Regis Philbin and Kathie Lee Gifford of *Live With Regis and Kathie Lee*
February 22 — "Fake News: A Special Report"
February 29 — Corey Carrier of *The Young Indiana Jones Chronicles*
March 7 — Macaulay Culkin
March 14 — Jane Pauley of *Dateline NBC*
March 21 — Magic Johnson
March 28 — The Oscars: The Beast of *Beauty and the Beast*
April 4 — Ronn Moss and Katherine Kelly Lang of *The Bold and the Beautiful*
April 11 — "S.O.S.: Save Our Shows"
April 18 — Patricia Richardson and Tim Allen of *Home Improvement*
April 25 — Burt Reynolds of *Evening Shade*
May 2 — Woody Harrelson and Jackie Swanson of *Cheers*
May 9 — Johnny Carson of *The Tonight Show*
May 16 — Oprah Winfrey of *The Oprah Winfrey Show*
May 23 — Jerry Seinfeld of *Seinfeld*
May 30 — Dan Lauria, Alley Mills, Jason Hervey and Fred Savage of *The Wonder Years*
June 6 — Grant Show of *Melrose Place*
June 13 — Bob Saget of *Full House*
June 20 — "The Year's Best and Worst": Ross Perot, Burt Reynolds and Michael Jeter of *Evening Shade*, Candice Bergen of *Murphy Brown*, Bette Midler and Johnny Carson of *The Tonight Show* and Anita Hill
June 27 — Phil Donahue of *Donahue*
July 4 — Delta Burke of *Delta*
July 11 — Luke Perry and Shannen Doherty of *Beverly Hills, 90210*
July 18 — "TV's Top Turn-Ons": Patrick Stewart of *Star Trek: The Next Generation* and Cindy Crawford
July 25 — The Olympics: Kim Zmeskal
August 1 — Dana Carvey and David Letterman
August 8 — Princess Diana and Prince Charles
August 15 — "America Zaps! The All-Powerful Remote Control": Whoopi Goldberg, Roseanne Arnold, Homer Simpson, Ted Koppel and Michele Pfeiffer
August 22 — "Is TV Violence Battering Our Kids?"
August 29 — Roseanne Arnold of *Roseanne*
September 5 — Joan Lunden of *Good Morning America*
September 12 — Fall Preview
September 19 — Candice Bergen of *Murphy Brown*
September 26 — The Country Music Awards: Billy Ray Cyrus and Reba McEntire
October 3 — Bob Newhart of *Bob*
October 10 — "Would You Give Up $1,000,000 to Give Up TV Forever?"
October 17 — "TV's Best Dressed": Leeza Gibbons of *Entertainment Tonight* and Jay Leno of *The Tonight Show*
October 24 — Goofy and Max of *Goof Troop*
October 31 — Sweeps Preview: Julia Roberts, Peter Falk, Jaclyn Smith and E.T.
November 7 — Frank Sinatra and Philip Casnoff in *Sinatra*
November 14 — Michael Jackson
November 21 — Diane Sawyer of *PrimeTime Live*
November 28 — John Ritter and Markie Post of *Hearts Afire*
December 5 — John Stamos, Blake Tuomy-Wilhoit and Dylan Tuomy-Wilhoit of *Full House*
December 12 — Katey Sagal of *Married...With Children*
December 19 — Tiny Toon Adventures
December 26 — "Year in Cheers and Jeers": Angela Lansbury of *Murder, She Wrote*, Ted Danson of *Cheers*, Michael Jordan and Madonna

1993
January 2 — Avery Brooks of *Star Trek: Deep Space Nine* and Patrick Stewart of *Star Trek: The Next Generation*
January 9 — Bill Clinton and Hillary Clinton
January 16 — "How to Be a Funny President": Dana Carvey and Phil Hartman
January 23 — Will Smith of *The Fresh Prince of Bel Air*
January 30 — Craig T. Nelson of *Coach*
February 6 — Katie Couric of *Today*
February 13 — The Grammys: Billy Ray Cyrus
February 20 — Jane Seymour of *Dr. Quinn, Medicine Woman*
February 27 — "Parents' Guide to Kids' TV": Jane Pauley and Barney of *Barney & Friends*
March 6 — Regis Philbin of *Live With Regis and Kathie Lee*
March 13 — Mary Tyler Moore
March 20 — "Soaps' Sexiest Stars": Antonio Sabato Jr. of *General Hospital* and Hunter Tylo of *The Bold and the Beautiful*
March 27 — The Oscars: Billy Crystal
April 3 — Heather Locklear of *Melrose Place*
April 10 — Ted Danson and Shelley Long of *Cheers*
April 17 — "40th Anniversary Issue"
April 24 — Patricia Richardson and Tim Allen of *Home Improvement*
May 1 — Michele Lee, Joan Van Ark, Nicollette Sheridan and Donna Mills of *Knots Landing*
May 8 — Arsenio Hall of *The Arsenio Hall Show*
May 15 — Kirstie Alley, Ted Danson, Woody Harrelson, Rhea Perlman, Kelsey Grammer, John Ratzenberger and George Wendt of *Cheers*
May 22 — Linda Ellerbee
May 29 — Richard Simmons
June 5 — Connie Chung of *Eye to Eye With Connie Chung*
June 12 — Joey Lawrence of *Blossom*
June 19 — A Martinez of *L.A. Law* and Cody Martinez
June 26 — "Supermodels Take on TV": Cindy Crawford, Lauren Hutton, Naomi Campbell and Beverly Johnson
July 3 — Vanna White of *Wheel of Fortune*

August 1, 1987
BY BERNARD BOUDREAU

The No. 1 soap opera for 12 consecutive
years, *The Young and the Restless*,
opens with the haunting piano
melody "Nadia's Theme"—originally
from the movie *Bless the Beasts and
the Children*.

March 31, 1990
BY TONY COSTA

America's Funniest Home Videos
featured real-life submissions from
viewers who didn't mind showing the
world how thick-skulled or clumsy
they could be.

March 16, 1991
BY STEVE FENN

One of TV GUIDE's more surreal covers
featured Barbara Walters with the
Teenage Mutant Ninja Turtles. During
the interview, she made all but
Michelangelo cry.

July 13, 1991
BY NBC/GLOBE PHOTOS

Michael Landon is the No. 2 champ for
most TV GUIDE covers ever (26). No
wonder—he starred in three of TV's most
beloved shows: *Bonanza*, *Little House
on the Prairie* and *Highway to Heaven*.

July 11, 1992
BY JEFF KATZ

Aaron Spelling's *Beverly Hills, 90210*, a high school soap opera full of romance, betrayal and Clearasil, made stars out of Luke Perry and Shannen Doherty.

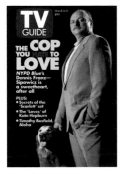

March 5, 1994
BY TIMOTHY WHITE

It could have been called "blue" because of all the skin and swearing, but viewers tuned in to *NYPD Blue* for its quality. The show switched leading men four times, but Dennis Franz stood tall as the irascible cop's cop, Andy Sipowicz.

February 11, 1995
BY DAVIS FACTOR

The multigenerational shenanigans of *Dallas* were replaced in the '90s with fare like *Melrose Place*, filled with pretty, if un-emotive, faces. Heather Locklear's, however, was worth watching.

March 15, 1997
BY JOHN E. BARRETT (©1997 CTW, ©JIM HENSON PRODUCTIONS, INC.)

Sesame Street boasted a neighborhood full of famous characters, but in the '90s, it introduced a giggly, red-furred young muppet named Elmo whom everyone wanted to tickle.

March 7, 1998
BY FERGUS GREER

Dawson's Creek brought more fresh-faced kids (such as James Van Der Beek) with continuing problems, but this time the teens had snappier dialogue and were more self-aware than their adult prime-time peers.

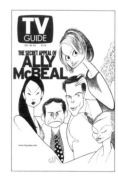

December 18, 1999
BY AL HIRSCHFELD

This love-it or hate-it "dramedy" *Ally McBeal* made ample use of musical numbers, stunt casting and digital dancing babies. The neurotic Ally seemed to spend more time on the couch than in her law office.

February 12, 2000
BY CHALLENGE RODDIE

Ellen may have opened the closet door, but *Will & Grace* came out dancing. Appealing leads, a madcap supporting cast and sharp scripts made everyone a little gayer–happier, that is.

July 22, 2000
BY DAVID BURNETT

This drama about a U.S. president (Martin Sheen) and his staff was a hit from the start. *The West Wing* also set a new record for most Emmys won by a series in a single season (nine).

January 13, 2001
BY NBC/GLOBE PHOTOS

With the reissue of a classic Presley documentary, *That's the Way It Is*, and by adorning the cover of the year's best-selling issue, Elvis proved he was still the King in 2001.

December 8, 2001
BY ALEX ROSS

As seen in *Smallville*, Superman's 21st-century incarnation (Tom Welling) didn't wear the traditional tights. Instead, Clark Kent's salad days were portrayed in a contemporary hybrid of teen-angst soap opera and sci-fi spectacle.

December 22, 2001
BY JAMIE WYETH

With terrorist attacks against the United States, the fall of 2001 saw much heartache and patriotism. TV GUIDE ended the year with a five-cover issue—this one by Jamie Wyeth—featuring the American flag by different artists.

February 23, 2002
BY KATE GARNER

The cop genre took its darkest turn yet with *CSI*, a smart and graphic depiction of criminal forensics starring William Petersen and Marg Helgenberger. Viewers might have winced, but they didn't change the channel.

PHOTOGRAPHY CREDITS

Pages 12-13, WARNER BROS. CARTOONS (both): "What's Opera, Doc?", Looney Tunes characters, names and all related indicia are trademarks of Warner Bros. © 2002; Page 17, LASSIE: Zinn Arthur; Page 20, MARY TYLER MOORE: MTM; Page 21, MARY TYLER MOORE (top left): CBS Photo Archive; Page 23, BOB NEWHART: CBS Photo Archive; Page 25, AMERICAN BANDSTAND (top): ABC Photography Archives; (bottom): Curt Gunther; Page 26, LORETTA YOUNG: Elmer W. Holloway/NBC; Page 27, JACK BENNY: George E. Joseph; Pages 28-29, YOUR SHOW OF SHOWS: NBC; Page 30, FANTASY ISLAND: ABC Photography Archives; LOVE BOAT (both): Jim McHugh; Page 31, SATURDAY NIGHT LIVE (top left and bottom left): NBC; (top right): Al Levine/NBC; (bottom right and bottom center): Edie Baskin Studios; Page 33, SATURDAY NIGHT LIVE: Edie Baskin Studios; Page 35, NFL: Walter Iooss Jr./SI; Page 36, NASCAR (top): AP/Wide World; (bottom): Robert Laberge/Getty Images; Page 37, WIDE WORLD OF SPORTS: ABC Photography Archives; Page 42, SIMPSONS: TM and © 20th Century Fox Film Corp. All rights reserved, Page 44, BULLWINKLE SHOW: TM & © Ward Productions Inc.; Page 46, MASTERPIECE THEATRE (left): Eric Roth for WGBH Boston; (right): BBC Picture Archives; Page 47, MASTERPIECE THEATRE (left): BBC Picture Archives; (right): Granada; Page 49, GUNSMOKE (both): Zinn Arthur; Page 50, BONANZA: NBC; Page 51, DINAH SHORE: NBC; Pages 52-53, ED SULLIVAN (all): CBS Photo Archive; Page 54-55, SOPRANOS (both): Photographs from "The Sopranos®" courtesy of HBO®; Page 58, TODAY: NBC; Page 59, TODAY (top): Sarah Friedman/Corbis Outline; (middle right): NBC/Media Village; (bottom): Lisa Berg/NBC News Today; Page 61, MISTER ROGERS: Family Communication TV; Page 63, PRICE IS RIGHT (top): ABC Photography Archives; (bottom): CBS Photo Archive; Page 64, JEOPARDY!: Jeopardy! Productions, Inc./Steve Crise; Page 68, FRENCH CHEF: A La Carte Communications; Page 69, MARTHA STEWART: Victoria Pearson/Martha Stewart Living Omnimedia; Page 70, GONG SHOW: Gene Trindl; Page 71, TABLOID TV: Todd Buchanan/Newsmakers; Page 72, OPRAH WINFREY (top): © 1996 Harpo Productions, Inc./George Burns; (bottom): © 1997 Harpo Productions, Inc./George Burns; Page 73, OPRAH WINFREY: © 2000 Harpo Productions, Inc./George Burns; Page 76, MTV: C. Taylor Crothers; Page 77, MICKEY MOUSE CLUB: Walt Disney Television/ABC Photography Archive; Page 79, AFTERSCHOOL SPECIALS: ABC Photography Archive; Page 80, GENERAL HOSPITAL: Erik Hein/ABC Photography Archive; Page 81, PRINCE CHARLES AND LADY DIANA: Wally McNamee/Corbis; Page 82, ALL MY CHILDREN: ABC Photography Archive; Page 84, JOHN F. KENNEDY: Bob Jackson/Library of Congress; Page 85, JOHN F. KENNEDY (top): Library of Congress; (bottom): Cecil Stoughton/Library of Congress; Page 86, O.J. SIMPSON: 1994 Branimir Kvartuc/ZUMA Press; Page 87, CHALLENGER: Corbis; Page 88, SEPTEMBER 11: AP/Wide World; Page 92, EDWARD R. MURROW (both): CBS Photo Archive; Page 93, WALTER CRONKITE (both): CBS Photo Archive; Page 94, CNN/GULF WAR: AP/Wide World; Page 97, KENNEDY-NIXON (bottom): Corbis; (top left and right): Bettmann/Corbis; Page 102, LUCILLE BALL: John Engstead/MPTV; Page 103, LUCILLE BALL (all): CBS Photo Archive; Page 104, HAPPY DAYS: Carl Furuta; Page 107, BRADY BUNCH: Gene Trindl; Page 108, SURVIVOR: Monty Brinton/CBS Photo Archive; Page 109, GILLIGAN'S ISLAND: Gene Stein; Page 110, TWENTY ONE: NBC; Page 113, WHO WANTS TO BE A MILLIONAIRE: Maria Melin/ABC Photography Archive; Page 114, ADDAMS FAMILY: ABC Photography Archive; BRADY BUNCH: Bud Gray/MPTV; FAMILY TIES: Ken Whitmore/MPTV; COSBY SHOW: Mario Casilli/MPTV; Page 115, LEAVE IT TO BEAVER: 1991 Universal Studios Inc.; BEVERLY HILLBILLIES: CBS Photo Archive; SIMPSONS: TM & © 20th Century Fox Film Corp. All rights reserved; Page 118, FLINTSTONES: Hanna Barbera; Page 119, EVERYBODY LOVES RAYMOND: Darryl Tooley; Page 123, PERRY MASON: Gene Trindl; Page 124, FUGITIVE: ABC Photography Archive; Page 126, DRAGNET: NBC; Page 130, WALTONS: Albert Watson; Page 131, LITTLE HOUSE ON THE PRAIRIE: NBC; Page 132, BRIAN'S SONG (both): ABC Photography Archive; Page 133, PLAYHOUSE 90: CBS Photo Archive; Page 135, BRIDESHEAD REVISITED: Granada; Page 136,

HALLMARK HALL OF FAME: Bob Greene/CBS Photo Archive; Pages 136-137, ROOTS: ABC Photography Archives; Page 140, ELVIS: NBC; Page 142, CHARLIE'S ANGELS: ABC Photography Archive; Page 143, BAYWATCH: All American TV; Page 144, DALLAS: Warner Bros.; Page 145, DYNASTY: ABC Photography Archive; Page 147, TWIN PEAKS: ABC Photography Archive; Page 148, BEWITCHED: ABC Photography Archive; Page 149, BUFFY THE VAMPIRE SLAYER: Warner Bros.; Page 150, TWILIGHT ZONE (left): Julian Wasser/Getty Images; Page 153, STAR TREK/NEXT GENERATION: Paramount; Page 154, LONE RANGER, ADVENTURES OF RIN TIN TIN, LANCELOT LINK and BARETTA: ABC Photography Archive; FLIPPER: NBC; Page 155, PEOPLE'S CHOICE: NBC; MY THREE SONS: Long Photography, Inc.; JETSONS: Hanna Barbera; DAKTARI: Gunther/MPTV; GENTLE BEN: Allan Gould; CROCODILE HUNTER: Discovery; Page 156, AMERICAN FAMILY: Courtesy Thirteen/WNET New York; Page 157, OSBOURNES: Stewart Volland; Page 159, ADDAMS FAMILY: ABC Photography Archive; Page 162, ODD COUPLE: ABC Photography Archive; Page 163, BEAVIS AND BUTT-HEAD: Used with permission by MTV: Music Television; Page 164, SOUTH PARK: Comedy Central; Page 166, CANNON: Marv Newton/MPTV; Page 167, STARSKY AND HUTCH: ABC Photography Archive; MACGYVER: ABC Photography Archive; QUINCY: Gene Trindl/MPTV; POLICE SQUAD: ABC Photography Archive; WISEGUY: CBS Photo Archive; POIROT: LWT; PRIME SUSPECT: John Timbers Studio London; Page 171, SONNY AND CHER: CBS Photo Archive; Page 172, ERNIE KOVACS: CBS Photo Archive; Page 174, LAUGH-IN (top): Ed Thrasher/MPTV; (middle and bottom): Douglas Jones/Look Magazine Collection, Library of Congress; Page 175, IN LIVING COLOR (top left and bottom right): Nicola Goode/20th Century Fox Film Corp.; (top right and bottom left): 20th Century Fox Film Corp.; Page 176, MILTON BERLE: NBC; Page 177, CAROL BURNETT: Ken Whitmore/MPTV; Page 180, ROLLER DERBY: ABC Photography Archive; Page 181, MONDAY NIGHT FOOTBALL: Ben Weaver; Page 183, WRESTLING: Globe Photos; Page 184, A-TEAM: Gene Trindl/MPTV; Page 187, ADVENTURES OF SUPERMAN: ABC Photography Archive; Page 188, NBA: Fernando Medina/NBAE/Getty Images; Page 189, MAJOR LEAGUE BASEBALL: AP/Wide World; Page 190, HILL STREET BLUES: Paramount; Page 192, LAW & ORDER: Al Levine/MPTV, Page 193, ER: Warner Bros.; Page 194, ST. ELSEWHERE: Gene Trindl/MPTV; Page 195, M*A*S*H: 20th Century Fox Film Corp.; Page 202, PATTY DUKE: ABC Photography Archive; Page 203, MY SO-CALLED LIFE: ABC Photography Archive; Page 204, CHEERS: Paramount; Page 205, FRIENDS: Dann Feld/Warner Bros.; Page 208, 77 SUNSET STRIP: ABC Photography Archive; CAR 54, WHERE ARE YOU?: NBC; ADAM-12: NBC; SCOOBY-DOO: ABC Photography Archive; PARTRIDGE FAMILY: ABC Photography Archive; Page 209, GIDGET: ABC Photography Archive; DUKES OF HAZZARD: CBS Photo Archive; Page 211, BARNEY MILLER: ABC Photography Archive; Page 212, LARRY SANDERS: Darryl Estrine; Page 213, FRASIER: Paramount; Page 215, BOB HOPE: Jack Albin; Page 217, MARRIED...WITH CHILDREN: Tony Costa; Page 221, THIRTY-SOMETHING: ABC Photography Archive; Page 223, COPS: Brian Davis/20th Century Fox Film Corp.; Page 225, COLUMBO: ABC Photography Archives; Page 231, ROSEANNE: ABC Photography Archive; Page 232, HONEYMOONERS (left): Arthur Rothstein/Look Magazine Collection, Library of Congress; (top right and bottom right): CBS Photo Archive; Page 233, HONEYMOONERS: Lester Glassner/CBS Photo Archive; Page 234, SEX AND THE CITY: Photograph from "Sex and the City®" courtesy of HBO®; Page 235, SEINFELD: Gino Mifsud/Castle Rock; Page 238, STAR TREK: Paramount; Page 239, APOLLO 11: NASA; Page 242, TONIGHT SHOW/JOHNNY CARSON: NBC; Page 243, TONIGHT SHOW/JOHNNY CARSON (top left, top right and bottom right): NBC; (bottom left): Gene Arias/NBC; Page 244, TONIGHT SHOW/STEVE ALLEN: NBC; TONIGHT SHOW/JACK PAAR: NBC; Page 247, DICK CAVETT: Christopher Little; Page 248, NIGHTLINE: ABC Photography Archive; Page 249, SPORTSCENTER: Danny Clinch; Page 250, DAVID LETTERMAN (middle left): R.M. Lewis Jr./NBC; (top right and bottom right): Alan Singer/CBS Photo Archive; (bottom left): Patrick Pagnano/CBS Photo Archive; Page 251, DAVID LETTERMAN: Alan Singer/CBS Photo Archive; Page 252, AFTERWORD: Paramount

THE FOLLOWING IMAGES APPEAR COURTESY OF:

Bonanza Ventures: Page 50, BONANZA

Everett Collection: Page 18, ALL IN THE FAMILY; Page 23, BOB NEWHART; Page 52, ED SULLIVAN (bottom left); Page 103, LUCILLE BALL (top); Page 126, DRAGNET; Page 140, ELVIS; Page 142, CHARLIE'S ANGELS; Page 143, BAYWATCH; Page 145, DYNASTY; Page 150, TWILIGHT ZONE (right); Page 151, TWILIGHT ZONE (right); Page 165, LEAVE IT TO BEAVER; Page 166, KOJAK; Page 211, BARNEY MILLER; Page 214, PEANUTS; Page 230, DICK VAN DYKE; Page 231, ROSEANNE

Foto Fantasies: Page 21, MARY TYLER MOORE (top left); Page 31, SATURDAY NIGHT LIVE (top left); Page 33, SATURDAY NIGHT LIVE; Page 133, PLAYHOUSE 90; Page 151, TWILIGHT ZONE (middle); Page 173, MONTY PYTHON'S FLYING CIRCUS; Page 208, CAR 54, WHERE ARE YOU?; LOST IN SPACE; ADAM-12; Page 209, CHIPS; Page 213, FRASIER; Page 252, STAR TREK

Getty Images: Page 124, FUGITIVE

Globe Photos: Pages 28-29, YOUR SHOW OF SHOWS; Page 59, TODAY (middle left); Page 114, ADDAMS FAMILY; Page 115, GOOD TIMES

Kobal Collection: Page 30, FANTASY ISLAND; Page 62, ROMPER ROOM; Page 106, ANDY GRIFFITH; Page 125, PRISONER; Page 132, BRIAN'S SONG (top); Page 166, I SPY; IRONSIDE; Page 182, RAWHIDE; Page 224, HAWAII FIVE-O; Page 226, MAGNUM, P.I.; Page 238, STAR TREK

Library of American Broadcasting, University of Maryland: Page 151, TWILIGHT ZONE (left); Page 202, PATTY DUKE

Movie Still Archives: Page 116, MAKE ROOM FOR DADDY; Page 244, TONIGHT SHOW/JACK PAAR

MPTV: Page 115, ROSEANNE; Page 121, SANFORD AND SON; Page 131, LITTLE HOUSE ON THE PRAIRIE; Pages 136-137, ROOTS; Page 158, ADVENTURES OF OZZIE & HARRIET; Page 166, MAN FROM U.N.C.L.E.; Page 186, BATMAN (top); Page 210, TAXI

Neal Peters Collection: Page 9, INTRODUCTION; Page 15, PEE-WEE'S PLAYHOUSE; Page 21, MARY TYLER MOORE (bottom); Page 31, SATURDAY NIGHT LIVE (bottom right and bottom center); Page 110, TWENTY ONE; Page 114, FATHER KNOWS BEST; Page 115, ALL IN THE FAMILY; Page 141, MY NAME IS BARBRA; Page 144, DALLAS; Page 152, XENA; Page 160, SMOTHERS BROTHERS; Page 186, BATMAN (bottom); Page 233, HONEYMOONERS (top right)

Personality Photos: Page 52, ED SULLIVAN (top right); Page 167, STARSKY AND HUTCH; Page 176, MILTON BERLE; Page 232, HONEYMOONERS (top right and bottom right); Page 243, TONIGHT SHOW/JOHNNY CARSON (top right)

Photofest: Page 16, DENNIS THE MENACE; Page 47, MASTERPIECE THEATRE (right); Page 48, HAVE GUN, WILL TRAVEL; Page 92, EDWARD R. MURROW (bottom); Page 108, SURVIVOR; Page 112, $64,000 QUESTION; Page 118, FLINTSTONES; Page 148, BEWITCHED; Page 154, FLIPPER; Page 155, MAD ABOUT YOU; Page 167, WISEGUY; POLICE SQUAD; Page 190, HILL STREET BLUES; Page 208, BATMAN; PARTRIDGE FAMILY; Page 209, MY MOTHER THE CAR; MURDER, SHE WROTE; Page 221, THIRTYSOME-THING; Page 223, COPS; Page 251, DAVID LETTERMAN

ScreenScenes: Page 20, MARY TYLER MOORE; Page 31, SATURDAY NIGHT LIVE (top right); Page 63, PRICE IS RIGHT (bottom); Page 153, STAR TREK/NEXT GENERATION

TV Guide: Page 40, ALFRED HITCHCOCK PRESENTS; Page 114, ADVENTURES OF OZZIE & HARRIET; Page 168, ARTHUR GODFREY; Page 170, GEORGE BURNS AND GRACIE ALLEN; Page 216, FAMILY TIES

THIS BOOK WAS PRODUCED BY
MELCHER MEDIA, INC.
55 VANDAM STREET, NEW YORK, NY 10013

PUBLISHER
Charles Melcher

EDITOR-IN-CHIEF
Duncan Bock

ASSOCIATE PUBLISHER
Jessica Marshall

PROJECT EDITOR
April P. Bernard

DESIGN
Helicopter

PHOTOGRAPHY EDITOR
Gwen Smith

TV GUIDE SENIOR EDITOR
Beth Arky

EDITOR-AT-LARGE
David S. Cashion

TEXT EDITOR
Tim Moss

DIRECTOR OF PRODUCTION
Carolyn Clark

EDITORIAL ASSISTANTS
Andrew Ackermann,
Anne Gardiner and Max Levine

MELCHER MEDIA WOULD LIKE TO THANK
Jenny Frost, Kristin Kiser and Steve Ross at Crown; Helene Curley,
Michael Fell, Jay Gissen, Hazel Hammond, Amanda Kelley, Lori Bishop Murphy,
Steven Reddicliffe and Nancy Schwartz at TV GUIDE; Gerana Barbosa,
Mike Blaxill, Laura Ciechanowski, Kevin Ford, David Georgi, Sue Hostetler,
Bruce Kluger; Marcy Lovitch, John Meils, Allison Murray, Anne Newgarden,
Amy Pastan, Lia Ronnen, Brooke Showell, Patti Wilson, Megan Worman
and Giulia Zarr.

TV GUIDE WOULD LIKE TO THANK
Max Alexander, Diane Clehane, Hilary de Vries, Frank DeCaro, Robin Honig, Ted Johnson,
Shawna Malcom, Mark Nollinger, Joe Rhodes, Ileane Rudolph, Janet Weeks and Tim Williams.

ABOUT THE CONTRIBUTORS
MARK LASSWELL is a writer and editor who lives in New York City. His articles have
appeared in publications including *New York* magazine, the *Wall Street Journal*
and TV GUIDE, where he is a frequent contributor.

HELICOPTER is partners Ethan Trask and Joshua Liberson,
a design studio based in New York City.

MELCHER MEDIA is an award-winning book producer, based in New York City.

Look for the new TV GUIDE compact disc,
TV GUIDE's 50 Greatest TV Themes.
From *I Love Lucy* to *Cheers* to *Friends,*
this is a celebration of the top TV
theme songs from each of the last 50 years.
AVAILABLE EVERYWHERE FROM TVT RECORDS

OR ONLINE AT SHOP.TVGUIDE.COM.